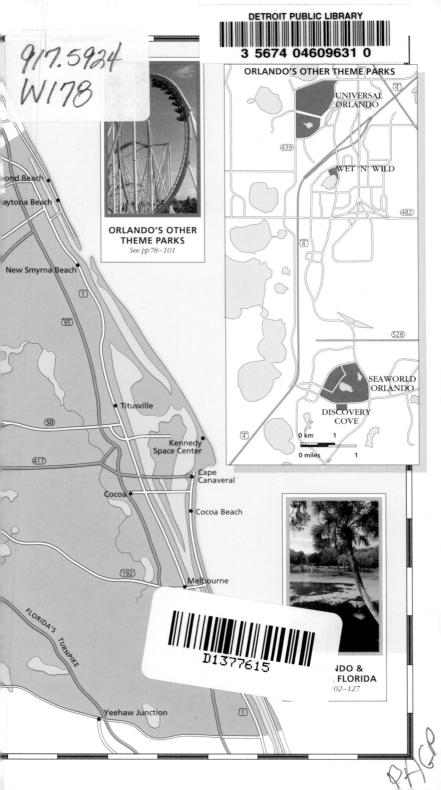

ond Beach
aytona Beach

New Smyrna Beach

ORLANDO'S OTHER
THEME PARKS
See pp78–101

Titusville

Kennedy
Space Center

Cocoa

Cape
Canaveral

Cocoa Beach

Melbourne

FLORIDA'S TURNPIKE

Yeehaw Junction

ORLANDO'S OTHER THEME PARKS

UNIVERSAL
ORLANDO

WET 'N' WILD

SEAWORLD
ORLANDO

DISCOVERY
COVE

0 km   1

0 miles   1

NDO &
FLORIDA
02–127

D1377615

EYEWITNESS TRAVEL

WALT DISNEY WORLD® RESORT & ORLANDO

EYEWITNESS TRAVEL

WALT DISNEY WORLD®
RESORT & ORLANDO

DK

LONDON, NEW YORK, MELBOURNE, MUNICH AND DELHI
www.dk.com

MANAGING EDITOR Aruna Ghose
ART EDITOR Benu Joshi
SENIOR EDITOR Rimli Borooah
EDITOR Shahnaaz Bakshi
DESIGNER Kavita Saha
PICTURE RESEARCHER Taiyaba Khatoon
CARTOGRAPHER Suresh Kumar
DTP COORDINATOR Shailesh Sharma
DTP DESIGNER Vinod Harish

MAIN CONTRIBUTORS
Phyllis and Arvin Steinberg, Joseph Hayes, Charles Martin

CONSULTANT
Richard Grula

Reproduced by Colourscan (Singapore)
Printed and bound in China by L. Rex Printing Co. Ltd

First American Edition 2005
07 08 09 10 9 8 7 6 5 4 3 2 1

Published in the United States by
DK Publishing, Inc., 375 Hudson Street,
New York, New York 10014

Reprinted with revisions 2006, 2007

Published in Great Britain by Dorling Kindersley Limited.

A CATALOGING IN PUBLICATION RECORD IS AVAILABLE FROM THE
LIBRARY OF CONGRESS.

ISSN 1542 1554
ISBN 978-0-75662-437-8

This book makes reference to various trademarks,
marks, and registered marks owned by the Disney
Company and Disney Enterprises, Inc.

Front cover main image:
Cinderella Castle during the fireworks spectacular "Wishes" at
Magic Kingdom, Walt Disney World Resort®, Orlando

◁ Spectacular fireworks above Cinderella's Castle at Magic Kingdom®, Walt Disney World® Resort

A ride at Universal Orlando's
Islands of Adventure *(see pp96–7)*

CONTENTS

INTRODUCING WALT DISNEY WORLD® RESORT & ORLANDO

Dolphins performing at a show
at SeaWorld *(see pp82–5)*

Primeval Whirl®, at Disney's Animal Kingdom® *(see pp64–7)*

Highway patrol insignia

A boardwalk trail at Blue Spring
State Park *(see p114)*

Space shuttle launch pad
(see pp22–3)

INTRODUCING WALT DISNEY WORLD® RESORT & ORLANDO

O.129—A. C. L. Railway Station, Orlando, Fla.
"The City Beautiful"

FOUR GREAT DAYS IN ORLANDO

Orlando's family-oriented selection of attractions includes a world-famous concentration of theme parks with enough larger-than-life personalities and adrenaline-pumping thrills to dazzle even the most jaded imagination. Assuming Mickey Mouse and Co. represent just one part of your Orlando visit, with some forethought you can easily accommodate the region's other

Ponce de Leon lighthouse

highlights. The following four itineraries guide you to the area's best, whether you are traveling with young children or in a group of adults, with an eye towards the Space Coast or looking to go no further than Disney's Main Street, USA®. Key sights have page references so you can check for more details. Price guides include the estimated cost of travel, food, and admission charges.

The façade of the impressive Mission: SPACE at Epcot®

BEST OF DISNEY

- **Go international at Epcot®**
- **Ride the rails on Big Thunder Mountain**
- **Enjoy Main Street's lights and delights**

FAMILY OF 4 allow at least $425

Morning

Try to arrive at **Epcot®** *(see pp42–53)* an hour before the official opening time. Pick up a Fastpass for Test Track *(see p46)* if you are with young children, or Mission: SPACE *(see pp44–5)* for older children. While waiting for your allocated Fastpass time, explore Innoventions East *(see p43)* for some high-tech video gaming. After the rides, stroll around World Showcase *(see pp50–3)*. Either find a pavilion that is of particular interest to your group, or join the line for Spaceship Earth *(see p43)*.

Afternoon

Take the monorail to the **Magic Kingdom®** *(see pp34–41)* and hop aboard the steam train at Main Street, USA® *(see p36)* which takes 20 minutes to skirt the perimeter of the park. Disembark at Fantasyland® *(see pp38–9)* for classic child-friendly attractions such as Dumbo the Flying Elephant and "it's a small world" or, for older children, at Frontierland® *(see p37)* for Big Thunder Mountain Railroad and the exhilarating Splash Mountain®. For the latter two, secure Fastpasses before sitting down to affordably priced sandwiches and salads at Pecos Bill's. After the rides, head to Adventureland® *(see pp36–7)* and get a Fastpass for Pirates of the Caribbean, one of the park's best original

rides. Alternatively, take a leisurely Jungle Cruise with a highly entertaining boatman. Once the thrills are over, stroll back to Main Street, USA® to witness the dazzling late-afternoon parade.

ORLANDO FOR ADULTS

- **World-famous golf courses**
- **Priceless pre-Columbian art**
- **Picnic in idyllic Lake Eola Park**

TWO ADULTS allow at least $200; $600 for golf/basketball itinerary

Morning

Weather permitting, golf enthusiasts can shoot a round of nine at one of Central Orlando's award-winning courses. **Falcon's Fire Golf Club** *(see p176–7)* offers top-quality rental equipment as well as online tee-time booking. Alternatively, aesthetically

Falcon's Fire, one of Orlando's premier golf courses

Dueling Dragons®, popular with coaster addicts at the Islands of Adventure

inclined visitors will enjoy the pre-Columbian, Mesoamerican, and Impressionist collections at the **Orlando Museum of Art** (see p107).

Afternoon
Golfers might wish to return to their hotels to freshen up. They and museum visitors should then head south to **Thornton Park** (see p108) to carry out lunch from one of the more casual establishments located in this charming neighborhood, such as **Dexters** (see p151). Browse the antique shops here before heading to nearby **Lake Eola Park** (see p108). After picnicking amid quaint footbridges and gorgeous palmetto trees, take a trip around the lake in a fairytale-perfect, swan-shaped paddleboat built for two.

Evening
Even for sold-out games, the box office of the **TD Waterhouse Center** (see p179) often releases Orlando Magic basketball tickets on gameday; call ahead to confirm. Alternatively, gastronomes and non-sports fans can head to **Downtown Disney®** (see pp74–5) for a casual feast of regional seafood delights at popular **Fulton's Crab House** (see p148), followed by a stroll among the Marketplace shops and later, dancing at a Pleasure Island night club.

SLIDES & RIDES

- **Splash at Wet 'n' Wild®**
- **Hollywood thrills at Universal Studios Florida®**
- **Shopping and people-watching on CityWalk®**

FAMILY OF 4 allow at least $400

Morning
Head to **Wet 'n' Wild®** (see pp100–101), where there are numerous attractions for young children as well as for older thrill-seekers. Grab lunch at one of the many concessions in the area.

Afternoon
Given the wildly different experiences offered by **Universal Studios Florida®** (see pp89– 93) and **Islands of Adventure** (see pp96–7), choose the one that best suits your needs. At Universal, families should head to Shrek 4-D™ (see p89), one of the top attractions, and then to Woody Woodpecker's Kid Zone (see p92) to experience ET Adventure®. Bigger kids will be more interested in the revolutionary roller coasters at the Islands of Adventure – particularly those of Marvel Super Hero Island® (see p96). Rides at The Lost Continent® (see p97) are suitable for all ages, and make a smooth transition to an evening of winding down on **Universal CityWalk®** (see pp98–9).

COASTAL FLORIDA

- **Stroll and swim the Space Coast**
- **Blast off at Kennedy Space Center**
- **Get acquainted with Shamu at SeaWorld®**

TWO ADULTS allow at least $200

Morning
Equipped with swimsuits, sunblock, snacks, and water bottles, head to Florida's beautiful Space Coast, approximately a 45-minute trip from the resorts. Tour the emblematic **Ponce de Leon Inlet Lighthouse** (see p117) and its surrounding trail network. The waves here are reliably gentle if you want to swim, but riptides occur so do not venture far from shore.

Afternoon
Spend the early part of the afternoon at **Kennedy Space Center** (see pp126–7) and visit the Astronaut Hall of Fame. Take lunch in the cafeteria before setting out for **SeaWorld® Orlando** (see pp82–5). Enjoy the surprising acrobatics of killer whales at The Shamu Adventure®, the faithful replications of Caribbean habitats at Key West at SeaWorld®, and the popular Manatee Rescue show. Journey to Atlantis® and the ridiculously fast Kraken® ride will satisfy even the most discriminating adrenaline addict.

A trainer perfoming stunts at the Shamu Adventure® show

Putting Central Florida on the Map

At the approximate geographic center of Florida, the Greater Orlando area covers around 2,850 sq miles (7,380 sq km). Flanked by beaches, peppered with lakes, and blessed with exceptional weather, the area's 1.8 million residents play host to over 46 million visitors a year. Walt Disney World® Resort and the region's other theme parks are the top attractions for the majority of vacationers. A sizeable number also visit the surrounding Central Florida area – including the beaches on the east, Ocala National Forest to the north, and the Kennedy Space Center on the Space Coast, named for its heavy concentration of space and defense industries.

The state seal of Florida

Fireworks in Walt Disney World® Resort's Magic Kingdom®

0 km   50

0 miles   50

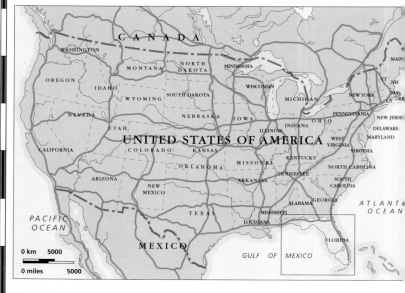

0 km   5000

0 miles   5000

◁ Fun and frolic in the waters and sands of Discovery Cove

GEORGIA

Fernandina Beach
Amelia Island

1
23

A1A

301

7

41

JACKSONVILLE

Jacksonville Beach

ive Oak
51

Lake
City

Olustee

10

1

21

16

Mandarin

A1A

ST AUGUSTINE

100

nhatchee
oss
ty
349

301

Cross
Creek

GAINESVILLE

Palatka

95

Marineland

ATLANTIC
OCEAN

See inside front cover

Micanopy

19
24

OCALA
NATIONAL

1

17

Ormond Beach
DAYTONA BEACH

ar Key

19
98

OCALA

FOREST

Lake
George

92

4

Ponce Inlet
New Smyrna
Beach

Silver
Springs

40

DeLand

Crystal River

75

27

Homosassa
Springs

98

Mount
Dora

Weeki Wachee

50

Clermont

Sanford

441

95

Titusville

Tarpon Springs

19

52

Dade City

WALT
DISNEY
WORLD

ORLANDO

Kennedy
Space Center
Cape Canaveral

Dunedin
CLEARWATER

TAMPA

Lakeland

4

98

Kissimmee

Cocoa
Cocoa Beach

Winter Haven

MELBOURNE

ETERSBURG

Tampa
Bay

Gibsonton

41

7

Bartow

Lake
Wales

60

A1A

etersburg Beach

Sebastian Inlet

17

Sebring

441

Yeehaw
Junction

Sebastian

Vero Beach

Anna Maria

Bradenton

70

Fort Pierce

SARASOTA

Myakka

75

Arcadia

27

441

70

Hutchinson Island

Venice

41

Port
Charlotte

78

Okeechobee

95

Stuart

1

Jupiter Island

Boca Grande

771

75

29

Lake
Okeechobee

Pahokee

Jupiter
WEST PALM BEACH

Cayo Costa

Caloosahatchee

FORT
MYERS

Clewiston

441

Palm Beach
Lake Worth

Captiva Island

867

Belle
Glade

27

A1A

Delray Beach

Sanibel Island

Immokalee

BOCA RATON

GULF

Bonita
Springs

FORT LAUDERDALE

OF

41

29

Naples

ALLIGATOR ALLEY

75

Davie

Dania
Hollywood

MEXICO

Ochopee

THE EVERGLADES

41

MIAMI

Marco Island

Everglades
City

Ten Thousand Islands

Biscayne
Bay

BISCAYNE
NATIONAL
PARK

Homestead

Florida
City

9336

1

Flamingo

Florida Bay

Key Largo

Tavernier

Islamorada

1

FLORIDA KEYS

Big Pine Key

Dry
Tortugas

KEY
WEST

Marathon
Bahia Honda

St Lucie

St Lucie
Canal

FLORIDA'S TPK

FLORIDA'S TURNPIKE

KEY

International airport

Cruise terminal

Amtrak train station

Expressway

Major highway

Secondary route

Rail line

A PORTRAIT OF CENTRAL FLORIDA

*S*un-drenched beaches with aquamarine waters and the never-ending amusement offered by its theme parks make Central Florida the ultimate family vacation destination. Adding to the mix are scenic nature preserves, unique cultural and historic attractions, fantastic shopping, and evening entertainment options.

In the last 50 years, Orlando and Central Florida have witnessed a spurt of development unmatched by any other region of the state. The initial fillip to this primarily agricultural community was provided by the increased employment opportunities associated with the space program at Cape Canaveral.

Juan Ponce de Leon

Then Walt Disney World arrived on the scene, opening its first theme park – Magic Kingdom – in 1971. The rest, as they say, is history.

HISTORY

The first Europeans to set foot on the Florida peninsula were Spanish explorers who sighted land between Cape Canaveral and the Matanzas Inlet in 1513. On April 2, 1513, Ponce de Leon claimed the territory for King Phillip of Spain and named it La Florida – the Place of Flowers. Spain, France, and England ruled the region in turns. The 20-year British rule, from 1763 to 1783, is notable for the growth of a flourishing plantation economy: the Daytona Beach area, for instance, successfully produced cotton, sugarcane, rice, and indigo. In 1821, Florida was finally ceded to the United States by Spain. The plantation system soon entered the Industrial Revolution, with the application of steam power to sugar and rum processing: the first steam-operated mill was at the Dummett Plantation in Ormond Beach.

A 16th-century map of Florida and the Gulf of Mexico

◁ **A lifeguard sits on duty at Daytona Beach, one of the country's most popular beaches**

Attempts by the Americans to remove the Seminole Indians, who had settled in the area in the 17th century, continued for decades. Central Florida's plantation economy suffered major losses when the Seminole Indians destroyed many plantations and sugar mills during the seven-year Second Seminole War, which ended in 1842. Orlando was born during this period, developing around an Army post, Fort Gatlin.

Oranges, Central Florida's juiciest crop

With ample land available for grazing, Central Florida fostered a thriving cattle industry. By the early 1860s, cattle and cotton were the mainstays of the region's economy. The Civil War, however, sounded the death knell of the cotton industry by taking away much of its workforce. Then came a hurricane in 1871, which wiped out the whole crop. Farmers turned to citrus, which was easier to grow than cotton. The region's citrus industry grew by leaps and bounds, helped along by developments such as the extension of the South Florida Railroad into Central Florida in 1880. Freezing weather in 1894–95 hit Central Florida's citrus

industry very hard, but it recovered and continued on course to make the region one of the world's leading producers of citrus fruit.

During the hard freezes, an innovative citrus grower, John B. Steinmentz, converted his citrus packing house into a skating rink, built a bathhouse and picnic area, and created a toboggan slide that led into a spring. Thus was set up the region's first entertainment complex, a precursor of things to come.

With the advent of electricity in 1900, telephones in 1901, and the first cars in 1903, Central Florida entered the 20th century. The Orlando Municipal Airport opened in 1928. A major turning point was in 1955, when the NASA space program was launched at Cape Canaveral near Orlando. The Glenn L. Martin Company set up a missile factory south of the city in 1956, and became the area's largest employer before Walt Disney arrived.

The success of Disney's Magic Kingdom led to a proliferation of theme parks. SeaWorld Orlando opened in 1973, while Walt Disney World continued to expand with the setting up of Epcot, Disney-MGM Studios, and Animal Kingdom. In 1977, Wet 'n Wild, the world's first water park, opened with a splash. In 1990, Universal Orlando entered the arena with Universal Studios Florida, followed a few years later by Universal CityWalk and Islands of Adventure. Discovery Cove opened in 2000. This wealth of entertainment options has earned Orlando the title of "Theme Park Capital of the World," and has firmly entrenched it as one of the world's topmost vacation spots.

BEYOND THE THEME PARKS
Central Florida's tourist appeal is not limited to its theme parks. The great outdoors beckons along the East Coast and the forests and waterways of the interior. Pristine beaches, lush state and county parks, and natural sanctuaries are all within easy reach of the highways and at times run parallel to

A dizzying thrill ride at SeaWorld® Orlando

A Disney Cruise Line® ship at a gleaming terminal in Port Canaveral

them, making driving in the area an enjoyable experience. Another way to enjoy the region's natural beauty is to board a seaplane from Orlando: rides and tours take passengers from the water to the air for amazing sightings of alligators, eagles, deer, and other wildlife in their natural habitat.

Outdoor activities are available in plenty, from biking, hiking, and golfing to swimming, angling, boating, and most other watersports. Additionally, outstanding professional sports bring tourists to the region in droves. The cruise industry is also flourishing, with Port Canaveral, the world's second largest multi-day cruise port, just 45 minutes east of Orlando. Thousands of visitors take the Disney Cruise Line ships and other luxury cruises from this port to destinations around the world.

Along the Space Coast is the Kennedy Space Center, home to NASA. Opened to the public in 1996, it now attracts more than 2 million visitors each year to see shuttles launched into space and to explore its workings and technology.

Farther north up the Space Coast is Daytona Beach, synonymous with car racing. From 1903 to 1935, all of the world's land speed records were set here. Stock cars began racing at Ormond Beach in 1936, and the first Daytona 200 motorcycle race took place there the following year. In 1959 Daytona International Speedway opened, and racing on the beach was abandoned. The speedway hosts numerous sports car, motorcycle, and go-karting races, attracting racing aficionados from all over the world.

Apart from the big theme parks, Central Florida offers countless smaller entertainment venues, ranging from the old-fashioned to the ultra-glitzy. Trendy nightspots, dinner shows, rodeos, fine dining, and a surfeit of shopping options add to the Orlando area's charm. There is plenty of cultural activity as well, with art and history museums dotting the area, and a highly active theater, opera, ballet, film, and live concert scene.

A Florida Film Festival poster

Central Florida's weather plays no small role in the region's appeal. Many people think of the area as a place where the sun always shines and the temperatures are warm, but this is not always so and there are days and

Shuttle launch at Kennedy Space Center

Glittering high-rises reflected in the placid waters of Lake Eola in Downtown Orlando

evenings in December, January, and February when it can get extremely cold. However, this in no way detracts from Central Florida's status as a year-round destination.

ECONOMY & TOURISM

For most of its history, the main source of revenue of the region – and the entire state – has been agriculture. Improved communications and transportation have kept the citrus and cattle industries buoyant. The area along the Kissimmee River is Florida's principal cattle ranching country, and the town of Kissimmee is known as the state's "Cow Capital." The region has contributed hugely to making Florida second only to Kentucky in the raising of beef cattle in the Southeastern states. Central Florida also continues to be the state's major supplier of citrus fruits; here, fruit trees stretch as far as the eye can see. The high-tech

Tourists riding a trail at a resort in Orlando

industry has also become a significant factor in the region's economy.

However, it is tourism that is now the mainstay of the economy of Central Florida. Theme parks dominate the region's tourism industry, but Orlando has also emerged as one of the country's leaders in the meetings and conventions industry. The city's Orange County Convention Center is one of the country's largest. The broader Orlando area has more than 110,000 hotel rooms, testifying to the huge numbers of visitors drawn by its many entertainment and business opportunities. Today, tourism is the largest employer in Metropolitan Orlando, accounting for around 27 percent of the jobs.

PEOPLE & CULTURE

The state "where everyone is from somewhere else," Florida has always been a mix of cultures and nationalities. The Seminole Indians, who arrived in the 17th century, now live mostly on reservations. The best candidates for the title of "true Floridian" are probably the Cracker farmers, whose ancestors settled in Central Florida and its environs in the 1800s; their name comes perhaps from the cracking of their cattle whips or the cracking of corn to make grits. However, visitors rarely encounter a Cracker in Orlando or the nearby heavily populated areas.

North Americans have poured into Florida since World War II; the 20th most populous state in the US in 1950, Florida is now ranked fourth. The largest single group to move south has been the retirees, for whom Florida's climate and leisurely lifestyle hold great appeal after a life of hard work. They take full advantage of Central Florida's abundance of recreational and cultural opportunities. Many seniors can be seen playing a round of golf, fishing, or browsing around the state-of-the-art shopping malls. An increasing number of new arrivals are young people who see Central Florida as a land of opportunity because of its booming tourism industry. They find it easy to get jobs as tour guides, hotel staff, theme park workers, and numerous other posts related to the thriving tourist-oriented economy.

From 1959 on, there has also been massive immigration from Latin America. There are many Mexican farm-workers as well as a large Cuban population in Florida. Many businesses in Central Florida hire employees who speak Spanish in addition to English because of the numerous residents and vacationers from Latin American countries. This ethnic diversity is celebrated in the local food, which features genuine re-creations of Caribbean and other ethnic dishes. Several exciting and innovative dishes have also originated in the region as a result of the craze for cross-cultural cuisine.

The diversity of Central Florida's people is also celebrated in many festivals held throughout the year, such as the Native American Festival in November in Silver Springs, the Epcot International Food and Wine Festival in October and November, and the Kissimmee Bluegrass Festival in March. Another significant cultural event is held in Eatonville, the oldest incorporated African-American community in the US. This festival is named for its native daughter Zora Neale Hurston (1891–1960), a well-known novelist, folklorist, and anthropologist.

Relaxed and laidback are the words that best describe the people of Central Florida. It is also the area's dress code: rarely will visitors come across a place that requires them to wear a jacket and a tie. People are often seen in the fanciest of restaurants in blue jeans and tennis shoes. Central Florida is a place where tourists can ask a native for directions, and get a friendly smile and an answer, no matter how complicated the question. Folk here are rarely in a rush to get anywhere. They came to Central Florida to escape the harsh winters in the north and elsewhere. They are here to relax and have fun, and they are quite proficient at it.

Zora Neale Hurston, leading writer of her time

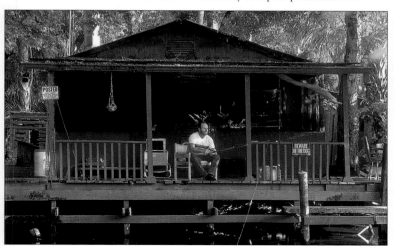

A cabin owner fishes from his front porch at the Wekiva River Corridor near Orlando

Theme Parks

The attractions at Walt Disney World, Universal Orlando, SeaWorld, Discovery Cove, and Wet 'n' Wild give a whole new meaning to the word "fun." There is something for everyone, young and old, at these amazing theme parks. On offer are the high-voltage excitement of rides – including roller coasters as well as simulator and flume rides – the thrill of animal encounters and Space Age attractions, the magic of fairy-tales and the movies, the visual extravaganza of parades and fireworks, and much more, with one theme park usually specializing, or scoring over the others, in a particular area.

Fireworks
Dazzling displays against the superb setting of Cinderella's Castle make the fireworks at Magic Kingdom difficult to beat.

Kid's rides at their best are to be found at Magic Kingdom's Fantasyland. Most of them are based on classic Disney films.

Parades
Magic Kingdom has the biggest and best parades, along Main Street, in the afternoons and evenings. Spectacular affairs, they feature grandiose floats, with colorfully clad Disney characters and special effects.

Science attractions at Epcot's Future World win hands-down. One of the most popular is the simulated adventure Mission: SPACE, designed with the help of professional astronauts.

Magic Kingdom® Park
(See pp34–41)

Bay Lake

Lake Tibet

Lake Mabel

Lake She

WALT DISNEY WORLD® RESORT

WINTER GARDEN-VINELAND ROAD

WORLD DRIVE

EPCOT CENTER DRIVE

Epcot®
(See pp42–53)

Downtown Disney®
(See pp74–

Typhoon Lagoon
(See p71)

Disney's Animal Kingdom®
(See pp64–7)

Disney-MGM Studios
(See pp54–63)

Blizzard Beach
(See p70)

Disney's Wide World of Sports®
(See p178)

(424)

(4)

Wildlife
Real and mythical animals crowd the best theme park in which to view wildlife, Animal Kingdom. Glimpse hippos, giraffes, and zebras on a jeep ride through a re-created African landscape on Kilimanjaro Safaris.

Sports
With facilities for more than 30 sports – including baseball, basketball, tennis, and much more – Disney's Wide World of Sports overshadows all other sports venues at theme parks.

Thrill Rides
Universal Orlando reigns supreme in thrill rides, using amazing special effects. One of the best rides is the new Revenge of the Mummy – The Ride, a high-speed indoor roller coaster that takes guests into an ancient Egypt of curses and horrifying creatures; the set is a masterpiece of design and the effects are mind-blowing.

'ERSAL
ANDO **Universal Studios Florida®** Ⓐ
(See pp89–93)

lands of dventure
See pp96–7) ⟨439⟩

Universal CityWalk®
(See pp98–9)

Wet 'n' Wild
(See pp100–101) ⟨482⟩

TURKEY LAKE ROAD

Big Sand Lake

BEE LINE EXPRESSWAY ⟨528⟩

SeaWorld Orlando®
(See pp82–5)

Discovery Cove
(See pp86–7)

Ⓐ

INTERNATIONAL DRIVE

0 km   1
0 miles   1

Water Rides
Wet 'n' Wild takes the honors as the water park with the best rides – though suitable only for older children and adults. Its big-thrill water rides include the Flyer, a six-story toboggan ride with plenty of exciting watery curves.

LOCATOR MAP

  Area covered

Sealife
SeaWorld is the park for those who want close encounters with sea creatures. See incredible live shows with highly trained dolphins, whales, sea otters, penguins, and more.

Wildlife & Natural Habitats

Central Florida's great variety of habitats and wildlife is due to the meeting of temperate and subtropical climates in many areas, complemented by its humidity, sandy soils, low elevation, and proximity to the water. An amazing diversity of habitats is found within several wildlife preserves, such as Merritt Island National Wildlife Refuge, and numerous state and county parks. Native flora in Central Florida ranges from longleaf and slash pines to various palms and cypress trees, while the region is home to more than 4,000 species of wildlife – from alligators and loggerhead sea turtles to brown pelicans and red-bellied woodpeckers.

Oranges
This introduced plant has thrived in Central Florida. The state's citrus industry supplies the bulk of the nation's crop.

SCRUBS & SANDHILLS

Called "Florida's Ancient Islands," the ridges of Central Florida were formed along the backbone of peninsular Florida millions of years ago when ocean levels were much higher than they are today. The sandy, porous soils of the ridges are home to two types of high and dry plant communities – scrubs and sandhills. Several species of plants and animals unique to Central Florida are found in this habitat.

PINE FLATWOODS

Pine flatwoods are the most common plant community in Central Florida. Dominated by an overstory of pines, the subcanopy of flatwoods is comprised mainly of saw palmetto shrubs, but there may be 50 to 75 different plant species per acre. Pine flatwoods are often interspersed with swamps and other habitats, and thrive when periodically swept by fire. The plants and animals here have adapted to survive the difficult conditions.

Scrub oaks are generally less than 10 ft (3 m) in height. These hardy plants produce plentiful acorns for the region's fauna.

The bobcat has a distinctive short tail with a dark tip, facial ruff, and spotted coat, and hunts by both day and night.

The gopher tortoise, *the only type found in Florida, has a large, thick shell and heavily scaled legs.*

Palmetto *is one of the most wide-spread plants in Florida. The saw palmetto variety is harvested and used for medicinal purposes.*

PROTECTING THE SEA TURTLE

At Marine Science Center, Ponce Inlet

From May through October, the East Coast beaches of Central Florida are host to three species of sea turtles – green, loggerhead, and leatherback turtles. These magnificent animals emerge from the surf at night to lay their eggs in nests, dug into the dry sand, then return to the sea. Two months later, about 100 baby turtles emerge from each of these nests and crawl to the ocean. To protect these gentle creatures, beach driving, parking, and lighting on beachfront properties are regulated. Avoid walking or cycling in places posted as nesting areas, and never disturb the protective screening over turtle nests.

Loggerhead turtle hatchlings heading to sea

FRESHWATER MARSHES & SWAMPS

Freshwater marshes and swamps are usually inundated with water throughout or during a portion of the year. Such wetlands once comprised about 50 percent of the land area in Central Florida. Freshwater swamps are dominated by cypress or bay trees, while marshes tend to be open, vegetated mostly by rushes and sedges. They are rich in bird life, such as varieties of herons, storks, and warblers.

RIVERS

The floodplain – the low land along either bank that is periodically flooded – of a Central Florida river contains forests of water-tolerant trees or low marshes. Some rivers "bubble up" from natural free-flowing springs while others start slowly as small streams. As rivers make their way toward the sea, they form brackish estuaries that support saltwater fish and wildlife.

Pitcher plants *grow in acidic, saturated soil. The species found in Central Florida is called Sarracenia minor, and has gracefully curved yellow flowers.*

Bald cypress, *one of the largest trees in North America, is a long-lived wetland species, known for its "knees" – projections from its submerged roots – and buttressed trunk.*

The great blue heron *is gray-blue, and has a white head with a black stripe above the eye. This big, long-legged, yellow-billed wader usually holds its neck in an "S" curve.*

The bald eagle, *an endangered species found by the ocean, lakes, and rivers, has a distinctive white head and tail and a dark brown body. Its wings span 7 ft (2 m).*

The Space Shuttle

Shuttle mission insignia

The Space Coast's Kennedy Space Center is NASA's launch headquarters and the home of the space shuttle program. The program was begun in the late 1970s, by which time the cost of sending astronauts into space had become too much for the American space budget; hundreds of millions of dollars were spent lifting the Apollo missions into space, with little more than a scorched command module ever returning to earth. It was time to develop a reusable spacecraft made for years of service, whose main cost after production would lie in maintenance. The answer was the space shuttle – *Columbia* was launched into space on April 12, 1981.

When in orbit, *the shuttle's cargo doors are opened. The Hubble telescope was one of its payloads.*

The flight deck *of the shuttle is extremely complex – even more so than the shuttle itself, which is built along the lines of an aircraft. You can get some idea of how the shuttle is navigated at the Launch Status Center (see p127).*

Tracks enable the tower to be moved away before liftoff.

The Crawlerway *is a double pathway, 100 ft (30 m) wide. It has been specially designed to withstand the weight of the shuttle as it is taken to the launch pad by gigantic crawlers. The rock surface overlies a layer of asphalt and a 7-ft (2-m) bed of crushed stone.*

The Crawler backs away once the shuttle is in place.

SHUTTLE CYCLE

The Space Shuttle has three principal elements: the main orbiter spacecraft (with its three engines), an external tank of liquid hydrogen and oxygen fuel, and two solid-fuel booster rockets, which provide the extra thrust needed for liftoff. Like earlier rockets, the shuttle reaches orbit in stages.

1. Prelaunch
The external tank and rocket boosters are fitted to the orbiter in the Vehicle Assembly Building. Then it is moved to the launch pad.

2. Launch
After a final check, the shuttle blasts off, using its own three engines and its two booster rockets.

The service tower gives access for fueling and cargo installation.

The access arm is a corridor through which the astronauts board the shuttle.

Orbiter

Solid Rocket Booster

The flame trench channels the burning gases away from the vehicle.

Vent for spent gases   **Steel pedestals**

SHUTTLE LAUNCH
The launch pad is made of 2 million cu ft (56,000 cu m) of reinforced concrete, supported by six steel pedestals. The flame trench is flooded with cooling water when the engines ignite, producing an immense cloud of steam.

THE SHUTTLE LAUNCHES
Since the shuttle's maiden voyage in 1981, there have been many missions shared between the *Columbia*, *Challenger*, *Discovery*, *Atlantis*, and *Endeavour* vehicles. The program was severely crippled when *Challenger* exploded shortly after liftoff in 1986, and again when *Columbia* disintegrated on re-entry in 2003. Regular launches will be held again when the safety of the other shuttles is assured. You need a ticket to view the launches at the Space Center. Free viewing sites are available on US 1 at Titusville and A1A at Cocoa Beach and Cape Canaveral.

Shuttle clearing the launch tower

For landing *back on Earth, the shuttle re-enters the atmosphere and begins to glide with its engines off. It heads toward the Space Center and proceeds to land on the runway at an incredible speed of 220 mph (360 km/h).*

PLAN OF THE LAUNCH PAD

Hydrogen tank

Oxygen tank

Water tower

Service tower

Launch pad

Crawlerway

3. Separation
Two minutes later, the boosters separate and are parachuted back to earth. At eight minutes, the external tank detaches.

4. Orbital Operations
Using its own engines, the shuttle maneuvers itself into orbit and begins its operations. The mission may last between 7 and 18 days, flying at an altitude of 115–690 miles (185–1,110 km).

5. Re-entry
The shuttle re-enters the atmosphere backward, using its engines to decelerate. It turns nose-first as it descends into the stratosphere and uses parachutes to stop.

CENTRAL FLORIDA THROUGH THE YEAR

Livestock show, Central Florida Fair

One of Central Florida's biggest attractions is its year-round mild weather. The region's climate has long been its top drawing card for tourists and residents. The average annual temperature is a comfortable 72.4°F (22.4°C) and the average rainfall is 50 in (1,270 mm), keeping the area green with flowering plants and trees year-round. The busiest time in the Orlando area is from November to December, when tourists come in huge numbers to enjoy the mild winters. Summer can be somewhat hot, but Orlando's theme parks still attract families with kids on school vacations, with some hotels offering special summer rates for families, including free transportation to the theme parks. Whatever time of year you visit, you will encounter an entertaining festival of some kind. For a complete schedule of festivals, contact the local tourist offices.

Motorcyclists show off their bikes during Bike Week, Daytona Beach

SPRING

Starting in late February, students from all over the US head for Florida's coastal resorts, such as the Daytona Beach area, for spring break. For six weeks these areas are bursting, putting pressure on accommodation. Major League Baseball's "spring training" camps are also a big attraction in Central Florida.

MARCH

Orlando Bike Week *(first weekend)*. Harley enthusiasts throughout the globe eagerly anticipate this annual event, headquartered at the Orlando Historic Factory dealership.
Bike Week *(first weekend)*, Daytona Beach. A huge and popular motorcycle event brimming with shows, concerts, and exhibits.

Kissimmee Bluegrass Festival *(first weekend)*. Features music styles ranging from bluegrass and Creole to Texas swing.
Central Florida Fair *(early Mar)*, Orlando. This large fair features more than 90 rides and exhibits.
SeaWorld, Bud & BBQ Fest *(early Mar)*, Orlando. Two weekends of fun, food, and racing at this park-wide event.
Annual Winter Park Sidewalk Arts Festival *(mid-Mar)*, Orlando. The most prestigious outdoor fine arts festival in Southeastern USA, this features three days of art, food, music, children's activities, and jazz.
Antique Boat Festival *(late Mar)*, Mount Dora. Display of more than 150 classic and historic boats.

Annual Downtown Antique Fair *(late Mar)*, Mount Dora. Treasures on display in downtown streets.
Florida Film Festival *(late Mar)*, Orlando. Ranked among the best film festivals in the world, this features more than 100 films, documentaries, and shorts from around the globe.
Orlando-UCF Shakespeare Festival *(Mar–May)*, Lake Eola Park. Outdoor productions at Walt Disney Amphitheater *(see p107)*.

APRIL

Spring Fiesta in the Park *(Apr)*, Orlando. Booths full of regional arts and crafts line the shores of Lake Eola.
Epcot Flower & Garden Festival *(Apr–Jun)*. Epcot blooms with elaborate gardens and topiary displays. You can attend gardening workshops.
Kissimmee Jazz Fest *(early Apr)*. This jazz concert held at the Kissimmee Lakefront includes entertainment from local high school performers to top jazz artists, as well as crafts and good food.
Maitland Arts & Fine Crafts Festival *(mid-Apr)*. The juried arts and fine crafts show highlights original artwork by the finest craftsmen in Southeast USA.

FLORIDA FILM FESTIVAL

Florida Film Festival logo

Boats on display at the Antique Boat Festival, Mount Dora

Annual Taste of Winter Park *(mid-Apr)*. Sample cuisine from local restaurants.
Black College Reunion *(mid-Apr)*, Daytona Beach. Thousands of students and alumni of black colleges and universities come together for this reunion.
Festival of Exotic Cars *(mid-Apr)*, Mount Dora. More than 150 rare and exotic cars can be seen on the downtown streets.
Festival of Music & Literature *(mid-Apr)*. Mount Dora. Outstanding artistic programs in music, literature, and other genres.
Indian River Festival *(mid-Apr)*, Titusville. Live music, carnival rides, food, arts, crafts, and antiques are some of the highlights here.
Cracker Day *(late Apr)*, DeLand (near Daytona Beach). Celebration of Florida heritage with games for the entire family. Features a cattleman's barbecue.

MAY

Viva La Musica *(mid-May)*, SeaWorld Orlando. Two spicy weekend fiestas of Latino music, dance, culture, and great food.
Orlando International Fringe Festival *(mid-May)*. The 10-day festival of theatrical performances showcases original works; premiere performances; and first-class improvizational comedy, musicals, drama, mime, and dance in 500 shows by performers from around the world.

SUMMER

Many families head to Orlando for the summer season and for good reason. The hotel rates are discounted for families and the theme parks stay open for a longer period, giving tourists more time to enjoy the attractions. The big summer holiday is of course Independence Day on July 4, which is celebrated with fireworks, parades, and picnics.

JUNE

Suncoast Gun & Knife Show *(mid-Jun)*, DeLand. Features a large collection of antique firearms and supplies, hunting rifles, collectibles, and more, at the Volusia County Fairgrounds.
Fiesta San Juan en Wet 'n' Wild *(late Jun)*. Wet 'n' Wild celebrates Latin culture in this fiesta of dancing, music, competitions, Latin food, and local Latin entertainment.

JULY

Lake Eola Picnic in the Park *(early Jul)*, Orlando. Celebrate the Fourth of July at this Downtown Orlando tradition with games and entertainment. Fireworks wrap up the show at 9pm.
Pepsi 400 *(early Jul)*, Daytona Beach. NASCAR racing on Daytona International Speedway during the Independence weekend. Other activities include concerts and beach parties.
Christmas in July Craft Fair *(mid-Jul)*, Lakeland. Shop from local vendors for beautiful handmade gifts for family and friends.
Florida International Festival *(mid-Jul)*, Daytona Beach. This multi-day event features performances by ensembles such as the London Symphony Orchestra.

AUGUST

Ocala Shrine Club Rodeo *(mid-Aug)*. Cow-roping, steer-riding, and more, are on offer at this action-packed annual attraction, held at the Livestock Pavilion.
Ocala Sturgis Rally & Bike Show *(mid-Aug)*. Field events are open to spectators.
International Food Festival *(mid-Aug)*, Auburndale (near Lakeland). On offer at "A Taste of Auburndale" are delicacies from local restaurants and lots of entertainment options.

A contest at Fiesta San Juan en Wet 'n' Wild

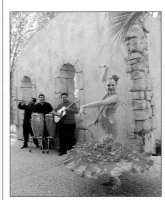

Flamenco dancer at the Viva La Musica, SeaWorld® Orlando

FALL

The theme parks are less crowded in the fall and the temperatures are cooler, making this an ideal time to visit Central Florida. Halloween is the big fall holiday in Orlando, with several theme parks offering special celebrations. Thanksgiving is the other major holiday. Fall is the best time for bird-watching and visiting the region's wildlife preserves.

SEPTEMBER

Viva La Musica *(mid-Sep)*, SeaWorld Orlando. A celebration of Hispanic food and culture during Hispanic Heritage Month. Live performances by hot Latino bands.
Lake Mirror Classic Auto Festival *(mid-Sep)*, Lakeland. All types of classic automobiles on display.

CLIMATE OF ORLANDO

°F/°C			
	91/33		
83/28		85/29	
	73/23		71/22
59/15		66/19	
			49/9

10 hrs	10 hrs	10 hrs	9 hrs
1.8 in	7.2 in	2.4 in	2.3 in
month	Apr	Jul	Oct	Jan

OCTOBER

Epcot International Food & Wine Festival *(Oct–Nov)*. The temptation to dine your way around World Showcase is intensified by cooking demonstrations, samples of exotic dishes, and international wines and desserts.
Bicycle Festival *(second weekend)*. Mount Dora. Attracting 1,500 cyclists, this is Florida's oldest and largest bicycling event.
Biketoberfest *(third weekend)*, Daytona Beach. International motorcycle show, demonstrations, and concerts.
Craft Fair *(fourth weekend)*, Mount Dora. More than 350 craftspeople and 250,000 visitors come from all over the nation for this fair.

NOVEMBER

Fall Fiesta in the Park *(first weekend)*, Downtown Orlando. Enjoy 550 booths full of regional arts and crafts along Lake Eola. One of the top five outdoor arts and crafts shows in Florida.
Plant & Garden Fair *(first weekend)*, Mount Dora. More than 10,000 rare and exotic plants and accessories displayed at the lakefront at Simpson's in Mount Dora.
Halifax Art Festival *(early Nov)*, Daytona Beach. This annual festival features the works of more than 250 artists, plus live entertainment.
Native American Festival *(early Nov)*, Silver Springs. A celebration of Native American culture, arts, crafts, and entertainment.
Annual Orlando Beer Festival *(mid-Nov)*. An impressive assortment of beers at this festival, sponsored by Universal CityWalk. Enjoy ales, lagers, pilsners, stouts, and barley wines.
ABC Super Soap Weekend *(mid-Nov)*, Disney MGM Studios. In the world's biggest soap fan event,

actors from the ABC daytime soap operas such as *Port Charles* and *General Hospital* visit the studios, affording autograph and photo opportunities.
Festival of the Masters *(mid-Nov)*, Downtown Disney. More than 200 artists participate in this three-day festival of the fine arts. Music and food round out the activities.
Annual Championship Ocala Scottish Games & Irish Fest *(mid-Nov)*. Grand parade, games, food, and entertainment.
Birding & Wildlife Festival *(mid-Nov)*, Titusville. This festival features birding trips, wildlife seminars, workshops, an art competition, and paddling adventures.
Daytona Turkey Run *(late Nov)*. Car show and swap meet on the Thanksgiving weekend at the Daytona International Speedway.
Birthplace of Speed Celebration *(late Nov)*, Ormond Beach. Gaslight parade of antique cars, as well as a car show.
Light Up Mount Dora *(Nov 28)*. Close to two million sparkling lights switch on in celebration of the holiday season. Festivities include singing in the community choir, ballet, and other entertainment, at Donnelly Park.

PUBLIC HOLIDAYS

New Year (Jan 1)
Martin Luther King Day (3rd Mon, Jan)
Presidents' Day (3rd Mon, Feb)
Memorial Day (last Mon, May)
Independence Day (Jul 4)
Labor Day (1st Mon, Sep)
Columbus Day (2nd Mon, Oct)
Election Day (1st Tue, Nov)
Halloween (Oct 31)
Veterans Day (Nov 11)
Thanksgiving (4th Thu, Nov)
Christmas Day (Dec 25)

Zora Neale Hurston Festival of Arts & Humanities, Orlando

WINTER

The crowds multiply in winter as the flood of "snowbirds" from the north intensifies. The celebrities arrive too, some to relax, others to perform during the region's busiest entertainment season. The parks are all aglow with Christmas lights and festivities – there are special Christmas parades and parties. Magic Kingdom is at its most colorful.

DECEMBER

Mickey's Very Merry Christmas Party *(all month)*, Magic Kingdom. Evening of seasonal fun complete with snow and enchanting parades with a Christmas theme.
Festival of Trees *(early Dec)*, Ocala. Decorated trees and lovely wreaths are displayed at the Appleton Museum of Art, along with crafts and decorations created by local artisans, which are for sale.
Festival of Lights *(mid-Dec)*, Silver Springs. Follow millions of sparkling lights through a maze of illuminated gardens, twinkling topiaries, and dozens of holiday scenes. A holiday buffet is on offer.

JANUARY

Renninger's Antique Extravaganza *(third weekend, Jan, Feb & Nov)*, Mount Dora. An antique lover's dream, this event held at Renninger's Twin Markets has more than 1,500 dealers selling their wares.
Zora Neale Hurston Festival of Arts & Humanities *(late Jan)*, Orlando. This festival at Eatonville highlights the life and works of America's most celebrated collectors and interpreters of Southern rural African-American culture.

Features art exhibits, theatrical performances, and educational programs.

FEBRUARY

Mount Dora Arts Festival *(first weekend)*. Celebrated on the streets of Mount Dora since 1977, this festival showcases the works of more than 300 juried artists. Artists compete for awards in painting, printmaking, photography, jewelry, sculpture, and a variety of other categories. Live entertainment, children's activities, and food are also part of the festivities.
Speedweeks *(first three weeks)* Daytona. Daytona International Speedway becomes the World Center of Racing during three weeks in February. Action kicks off with the Rolex 24 Hours at Daytona, followed by events leading up to the Daytona 500.
ArtsFest *(mid-Feb)*, Orlando. Showcases Central Florida's best in arts and culture, with more than 50 planned events, which range from symphony and ballet performances to art exhibits and lessons in Central Florida's history.
Mardi Gras at Universal Orlando *(mid-Feb–mid-Mar)*. Music and pageantry, colorful costumes, parades, food, and high-energy excitement at this annual Mardi Gras celebration at Universal.

Daytona 500 race at Daytona International Speedway, during Speedweeks

Moss-covered oaks in Lake Kissimmee State Park ▷

WALT DISNEY WORLD® RESORT & CENTRAL FLORIDA AREA BY AREA

WALT DISNEY WORLD® RESORT 30–77

ORLANDO'S OTHER THEME PARKS 78–101

ORLANDO & CENTRAL FLORIDA 102–127

WALT DISNEY WORLD® RESORT

T*he largest entertainment complex on earth, Walt Disney World® Resort sprawls across 47 sq miles (121 sq km), encompassing four theme parks renowned for their imaginative and state-of-the-art attractions. Two water parks, a sports complex, a cruise ship line, and a range of hotels, restaurants, nightclubs, golf courses, and shops combine to make it the complete vacation experience.*

Unless you're a cynic, Walt Disney World will amaze you. Peerless in its creativity and attention to detail, the resort offers a respite from the real world and takes you on a trip into a realm of fantasy and wonder.

Disney's first theme park, Magic Kingdom, opened in 1971. Consisting of seven "Lands," it remains one of the most popular theme parks of all time. In 1982, the ever-evolving Disney set up the 300-acre (120-ha) Epcot, an international and futuristic showplace, which focuses on discoveries and scientific achievements, and also provides an insight into the cultures of 11 nations across the world.

Disney-MGM Studios followed in 1989. The smallest of the four parks, it celebrates films and television in its shows and rides. Disney's Animal Kingdom, the newest park, covers 500 acres (200 ha) of jungles and savanna featuring exotic creatures, safaris, and trails. Then there are the water parks, Typhoon Lagoon and Blizzard Beach, with their ingenious landscaping and some thoroughly enjoyable rides. Downtown Disney amalgamates nightclubs, shows, restaurants, and shops into a vibrant entertainment area that pulsates at night.

The possibilities at Disney seem endless. Its cruise line offers two luxury ships with various amenities and cruise options. A sports lover's paradise, the resort boasts the massive Disney's Wide World of Sports complex, 18-hole and mini golf courses, and activities such as hiking, horseback riding, tennis, watersports, and race car driving. Accommodation options are equally varied, with several resorts and a camping ground.

The Primeval Whirl®, a thrilling ride at Disney's Animal Kingdom®, Walt Disney World® Resort

◁ **Cinderella's Castle, a fairy-tale fantasy in full bloom at Magic Kingdom®**

Exploring Walt Disney World® Resort

Let your imagination take flight at this world-class entertainment center, where there is something for everyone, regardless of their age. Plan to spend at least a day in each of Disney's "big four" – Magic Kingdom, Epcot, Disney-MGM Studios, and Disney's Animal Kingdom. Don't miss a chance to cool off at the two water parks – Blizzard Beach and Typhoon Lagoon. Or you might choose to let off steam at Disney's Wide World of Sports complex; golf courses; hiking and riding trails; and pools and lakes for swimming, boating, waterskiing and much more. With 31 resorts on the premises, you can go back to your hotel to rest before returning to one of the parks for the fireworks finale or checking out a show at Downtown Disney.

Magic Kingdom®
Seven Lands of fantasy and adventure encircle the stunningly beautiful Cinderella's Castle.

SIGHTS AT A GLANCE

Blizzard Beach ❺
Disney-MGM Studios ❸
Disney's Animal Kingdom® ❹
Downtown Disney® ❽
Epcot® ❷
Fort Wilderness Resort & Campground ❼
Magic Kingdom® ❶
Typhoon Lagoon ❻

0 meters   500
0 yards   500

MAGIC KINGDOM® ❶

Ticket and Transportation Center

DISNEY'S ANIMAL KINGDOM® ❹

TAMPA

Blizzard Beach

Winter Summerland

IRLO BRONSON MEMORIAL HIGHWAY

(192)

Disney's Animal Kingdom®
Experience the thrill of the wild through encounters with animals, as well as the pure fun of African safaris, river rafting, treks, and some enjoyable rides.

KEY

🅿 Parking
⛽ Gas station
⛳ Golf course
— Monorail
═ Interstate highway
═ Major highway
═ Secondary route

Blizzard Beach
Thrilling rides and exhilarating water slides are on offer at this cleverly designed and delightful 66-acre (27-ha) water theme park.

Epcot®
Travel across continents, blast into space on a rocket to Mars, embark on an underwater adventure, and take a peek into the future with remarkable discoveries and inventions.

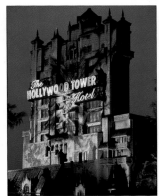

Disney-MGM Studios
There's no business like show business at the Disney-MGM Studios, where guests of all ages are immersed in the glitz, glamor, and magic of Hollywood.

SEE ALSO
- **Where to Stay** pp138–40
- **Where to Eat** pp148–50

GETTING AROUND
An extensive, efficient transportation system handles an average of 200,000 guests each day. The transportation hub of Walt Disney World is the Ticket and Transportation Center (TTC). Monorails, ferryboats, and motorcoach shuttle services operate daily. Additionally, hotels outside the resort area offer free shuttle services to the parks. For further details, see page 76.

ORLANDO

Downtown Disney®   Exit 27

536   Exit 26B

Typhoon Lagoon

Orlando International Airport

DISNEY-MGM STUDIOS

ey's Wide of Sports®   Exit 25B

← KISSIMMEE

Magic Kingdom Resort Area
Epcot Resort Area
Disney-MGM Studios
Disney's Animal Kingdom Resort Area
Downtown Disney Resort Area

Downtown Disney®
Themed celebrity restaurants, nightclubs, shows, and the largest outlet for Disney merchandise – all this and much more are on offer at this exciting entertainment and shopping complex.

Magic Kingdom® ❶

As Disney's quintessential theme park, Magic Kingdom makes a popular reappearance in similar form in California, Japan, and France. Cartoon characters and nostalgic visions of how the world, and particularly America, once was and how it might be again fill its relentlessly cheerful 107 acres (43 ha). The park is made up of seven Lands evoking a particular theme or era, such as the Wild West, Colonial America, and the future. Symptomatic of the park's effervescence are elaborate parades, entertaining musical street performers, and three-dimensional Disney characters.

TACKLING THE PARK

Unless you are a guest at one of the Disney hotels, plan your visit at midweek or toward the end of the week as the park is busiest on weekends and early in the week. If you are staying at a Disney resort, you are in luck. As their guest, you will have access to early entry privileges on two days a week –

Thursday and Sunday. Take this excellent opportunity and reach the entrance turnstiles an hour and a half before the official opening time. This will allow an extra 90 minutes of precious time to enjoy Fantasyland and Tomorrowland before the rest of the park opens.

Upon arrival at the park, you will receive a leaflet listing the Lands and rides as

well as the timings for the shows and parades. A notice board at the top of Main Street also offers this information and, additionally, gives a list of waiting times at various attractions. Getting around the park is relatively easy as the Lands emanate from the central hub, in front of Cinderella's Castle.

The most popular attractions are situated at opposite ends of the park, a considerable distance apart. As a result, you will probably end up walking more than you might expect. However, there are also other, more novel forms of transport. Main Street has a series of vehicles which, in keeping with the Disney storytelling ideal, serve to tell the story of transport from the horse-drawn tram to the motor car. A steam train makes a 20-minute circuit of the park, stopping at Main Street, Frontierland, and Mickey's Toontown Fair.

EATING & DRINKING

The park offers a wide selection of fast foods and an equally vast range of quick service places to choose from. For a reasonable meal, try the Liberty Tree Tavern.

Visitors on Main Street, USA® with Cinderella's Castle in the background

If you would like a quieter dining experience, the Crystal Palace is a good option. Cinderella's Royal Table, located within the castle itself, gives you a taste of royalty with its stately and regal ambience. Their specialty is prime ribs and, overall, the food is agreeable. The frequent appearances by Disney characters keep the kids entertained and makes for a magical meal. However, it is a good idea to make advance reservations in order to ensure a table at this popular eatery.

If you're looking for sandwiches, Aunt Polly's on Tom Sawyer Island is one of the best places to head for. However, this is the only fare on offer here.

WALT DISNEY'S VISION

Walt Disney (1901–66), the father of Mickey Mouse, was a pioneer in the field of animation. Watching his children at play in a squalid amusement park, Disney was struck by his ultimate inspiration – to build a place that was clean and filled with various attractions that parents and kids could enjoy together. He envisioned a theme park revolving around five Lands: Main Street, a setting plucked from late-19th/early 20th-century America; Adventureland, imbued with the mystery of exotic locales; Frontierland, a homage to the pioneers; Fantasyland, a place of whimsy inspired by the song "When You Wish Upon A Star;" and Tomorrowland, with a futuristic theme fit for the emerging Space Age. Disney picked a 160-acre (65-ha) site in Anaheim, California, and oversaw every aspect of the planning and construction of Disneyland. When Magic Kingdom opened its gates in 1955 and 28,000 people stormed in, tears reportedly streamed down Walt Disney's cheeks – his great dream had finally become a reality. Today, the Disney empire stretches across the globe, with theme parks in Paris and Tokyo. Orlando's Walt Disney World® Resort opened on October 21, 1971.

1 DAY ITINERARY

If you really want to cover the Magic Kingdom in one day, be warned, it's a daunting task because of the distances involved. This is specially true in the summer.

1. After leaving the turnstiles, head immediately for the central hub. If the entire park is open, turn right and head for **Space Mountain**. There might be ropes across areas at the hub. If so, wait at the rope entrance to Tomorrowland and head for Space Mountain when the rope drops. This is an exciting ride for those looking for thrills. Alternatively, if you'd prefer a tamer start, make a beeline for **Buzz Lightyear's Space Ranger Spin**.
2. After Space Mountain, choose between the **Tomorrowland Indy Speedway** and the **Tomorrowland Arcade**. If you have preschoolers, you should head for Fantasyland through Tomorrowland (keep the speedway on your right and turn left at the Mad Tea Party) and ride **The Many Adventures of Winnie the Pooh**.
3. After Winnie, turn left and head across Dumbo the Flying Elephant toward **Peter Pan's Flight** and enjoy the ride.
4. Exit left, head to Liberty Square and visit **The Haunted Mansion** on the right.
5. On leaving Haunted Mansion, turn to the right and continue to **Splash Mountain**. If the waiting period is more than half an hour, it might be a good idea at this point to get a Fastpass for this ride. Turn right from here and cross to the **Big Thunder Mountain Railroad**.
6. Take the exit from Big Thunder and cross the bridge bearing right to **Pirates of the Caribbean**. Take the ride.
7. Now you can return to ride the Splash Mountain.
8. After Splash Mountain, backtrack to the **Jungle Cruise**. If the time slot is right, ride, otherwise see the **Enchanted Tiki Room**.
9. Obtain a Fastpass for **Mickey's PhilharMagic** and grab a light lunch.
10. By the time lunch is over, you should be due to see Mickey's PhilharMagic.
11. Afterward, take preschoolers to Mickey's Toontown. If you have older children with you, take them to the rest of Fantasyland: **it's a small world**, **Peter Pan's Flight**, **Snow White's Scary Adventures**, **Dumbo the Flying Elephant**, **Ariel's Grotto**, or the **Mad Tea Party**.
12. Cross the central hub to Tomorrowland and obtain a Fastpass ticket for **Buzz Lightyear**.
13. Visit the **The Timekeeper** and **Stitch's Great Escape!**, and choose between **Astro Orbiter** and **Walt Disney's Carousel of Progress**.
14. Return to ride Buzz Lightyear.
15. Cross the central hub to Frontierland, and find a comfortable, vantage spot to enjoy the full splendor of the **afternoon parade**.
16. Following the parade, you have a chance to take one last relaxing ride before dinner. Choose between the **Jungle Cruise** in Adventureland or climb aboard the **Liberty Square Riverboat**.
17. Following dinner, don't miss the **SpectroMagic Parade**. If the park is closing early, view the parade from the Town Square. If it's open late, it's a good idea to see the parade from Main Street on the Tomorrowland side so that, when the parade has passed, you can return to the attractions in Tomorrowland, Mickey's Toontown Fair, and Fantasyland to catch any rides you missed (or ride particular favorites again).
18. Finally, enjoy dinner at the California Grill (see p150) and watch the fireworks in comfort from the restaurant's wall of windows overlooking Magic Kingdom.

TOP 10 ATTRACTIONS

① **SPLASH MOUNTAIN®**

② **BIG THUNDER MOUNTAIN RAILROAD**

③ **BUZZ LIGHTYEAR'S SPACE RANGER SPIN**

④ **IT'S A SMALL WORLD**

⑤ **PIRATES OF THE CARIBBEAN**

⑥ **SPACE MOUNTAIN®**

⑦ **THE MAGIC CARPETS OF ALADDIN**

⑧ **THE HAUNTED MANSION**

⑨ **PETER PAN'S FLIGHT**

⑩ **THE MANY ADVENTURES OF WINNIE THE POOH**

MAIN STREET, USA®

On entering Main Street, take a step into Disney's fantasy of a small-town Victorian America that never was. As you walk down Main Street, you pass beneath the Main Street Station. From here, you can catch the train for a ride around the park. The trains run every ten minutes. Beneath the station are lockers where, for a small fee, you can store valuables and bags.

As you enter the Town Square, **City Hall** lies to your left. This is a good place to visit first if you are looking for information regarding the shows being performed and any special events that might be taking place during your stay. The **Town Square Exposition Hall** lies to the right as you enter the square. You can pick up film rolls and other camera supplies here, but the main shops are, as you would expect, along Main Street.

Main Street itself is a magnificent melange of color, shapes and music, all in astonishing detail. At night, the entire street

assumes a magical ambience as thousands of glittering lights bring a resplendent glow to the spotlessly clean sidewalk. It's also an excellent place to see the popular **SpectroMagic Parade** *(see p39)*, a shimmering fantasy of music, live action and illuminated floats.

ADVENTURELAND®

Lush foliage, evocative drumbeats, and Colonial buildings combine to conjure up vivid images of Africa and the Caribbean. Reached via a wooden bridge from the central hub, Adventureland is an exciting and entertaining fusion of the exotic and the tropical.

One of the first attractions you come across in this Land, the **Swiss Family Treehouse** is a great way to start your tour of this area of the park. The large, man-made replica of the elaborate treehouse described in the beloved 19th-century children's tale is magnificent to behold. Replete with little details and small signs, the tree is reminiscent of the ingenuity and Christian values of the fictional castaways. Climbing the tree provides you with a splendid overhead view of this section of the park. The exhibit also offers a refreshingly shady and breezy educational tour that is certain to capture the interest of pre-teen kids.

Guests enjoying The Magic Carpets of Aladdin ride, Adventureland®

The **Jungle Cruise** boat ride takes its guests around a variety of animatronically designed settings of deepest Africa, India, and South America. A much sought-after ride, it owes a huge part of its popularity to the immense entertainment value of the "boatman" whose often wacky and infectious humor never fails to amuse.

The recently much improved **Enchanted Tiki Room** is an amusing and cleverly animated attraction. It is also a pleasant way to spend 20 minutes or so if you want to get out of the heat. Featuring characters from *Aladdin* and *The Lion King*, it is certainly worth a visit, just to see the walls change shape.

The **Pirates of the Caribbean** is an extremely entertaining and remarkably

The Jungle Cruise, a journey into deep forests with a zany boatsman

detailed voyage. This thrilling journey takes you on a seemingly realistic cruise through crumbling, underground prisons, past fighting galleons of the 16th century, and through scenes of debauchery and mayhem. The colorful characters and loving detail have ensured that it remains one of the best of the original rides. Following the runaway success of the film version, this ride has recently been given a facelift and now may be too scary for young children. Although it has been said that it is not as good as the version presented in Disneyland Paris, the Audio-Animatronic® effects are well done and the ride is a favorite with park visitors.

In another popular ride, **The Magic Carpets of Aladdin**, four-passenger carpets circle around a giant replica of a genie's bottle; the carpets move at the "command" of the riders, while whimsical camels "spit" at the airborne guests.

At the exit, you will find one of the most interesting stores in the park. An excellent selection of essential Disney accessories and memorabilia is available for purchase here.

The careening Big Thunder Mountain Railroad ride

FRONTIERLAND®

Set in a Hollywood-inspired Wild West, this Land abounds with raised walkways and trading posts. The **Frontierland Shootin' Arcade** is reminiscent of both the Wild West and of country fairs gone by. The **Country Bear Jamboree**, on the other hand, provides a completely animatronic musical animal show, much liked by youngsters, and a welcome respite on a hot summer's day.

A stunningly conceived and superbly executed journey through America's Wild West on an out-of-control mine train, **Big Thunder Mountain Railroad** remains one of the park's enduring attractions. In roller coaster terms, it's a relatively gentle experience, although the rear cars provide a wilder ride than the front. It acquires long lines of people from early in the day, so this is a ride to be enjoyed sooner, rather than later.

Opposite Big Thunder Mountain is the landing stage from where a raft can be taken to **Tom Sawyer Island**. Complete with a fort, swinging bridges, waterfalls, and tunnels, this is a child's dream adventure playground.

An outstanding attraction which threatens to get you a lot wetter than it actually does is **Splash Mountain®**. This is the epitome of what Disney does best, with a seamless integration of music, special effects, and beautifully crafted creatures. This, combined with a multitude of small drops prior to the big one, makes it one of the finest flume rides in the world. Guaranteed to make you want to repeat the adventure, the ride soon develops long queues that remain until closing. Fast-passes for Big Thunder Mountain Railroad and Splash Mountain are highly recommended.

Plunging down on the thrilling Splash Mountain® ride

LIBERTY SQUARE

The smallest of all the Lands, Liberty Square is set in post-Colonial America and hosts three attractions: the **Liberty Square Riverboat**, **The Hall of Presidents**, and **The Haunted Mansion**. The Liberty Square Riverboat is a relaxing trip back in time to the days of the new frontier, the Louisiana Purchase, and the birth of the Southern culture. The ride is usually not very crowded and is a great way to beat the summer heat.

Another interesting option is a visit to the never-crowded Hall of Presidents. This is an impressive animatronic show that features the recorded voice of the current president joining in on readings by the great presidents from the past. The animatronic portion is preceded by a multimedia film showcasing the trials and tribulations of the early days of the United States. The film takes an unusually honest and candid look at slavery and ends on a stirringly patriotic note.

The first ride constructed at Walt Disney World, The Haunted Mansion still holds its own as one of the best. While the scare factor has ebbed noticeably over the years, the clever introduction, ingenious ghost-projection, and attention to detail throughout the ride still warrant admiration. The

Cinderella's Golden Carrousel, against the backdrop of the Castle

ride's ability to take in large groups of people nearly continuously ensures that even long lines – now rare – move quickly. Very young children may still be frightened by some of the sudden "gotchas," but most others will find this more wonderfully amusing than frightfully scary.

FANTASYLAND®

Dominated by the soaring spires of Cinderella's Castle, this Land forms the core of the Magic Kingdom. The delightfully designed attractions inspire feelings of amazement and enchantment in even the most cynical.

TOP TIPS

• A little known shortcut from Mickey's Toontown Fair to Tomorrowland is just to the right of the train station.
• The benches in Mickey's Toontown Fair opposite Mickey's house provide a good vantage point from which to watch the fireworks.
• The Tomorrowland Arcade (see p40) can be a useful place to "park" easily bored youngsters while you take toddlers to savor the delights of Mickey's Toontown Fair or take in some of the quieter shows.

A relaxing ride on the Liberty Square Riverboat

SHOWS & PARADES

Don't miss checking out at least one of these amazing events. The shows – Mickey's PhilharMagic, a wonderful 3-D film experience, and The Enchanted Tiki Room – are superb in their own right but the parades are unique. Floats of towering proportions, surrounded by a multitude of actors and dancers, travel on a set route between Frontierland and Town Square on Main Street. There is always an afternoon parade and, during the peak holiday season, the SpectroMagic Parade takes place twice in the evenings, usually at 8:30pm and 10:30pm. The evening also features the Wishes™ Nighttime Spectacular, a brilliant choreography of fireworks and music.

This Land is usually the first destination for kids as their favorite storybook characters come to life here. **Dumbo the Flying Elephant** proves a compelling draw for young children whilst **Cinderella's Golden Carrousel**, a genuine 1917 restoration, seems to entice both old and young onto its gallopers. **Snow White's Scary Adventures**, which recounts the fairy-tale, is a basic tracked ride and may be slightly frightening for very young children. **Peter Pan's Flight**, however, is deservedly popular, combining the feeling of flying with the delight of perfectly matched music and movement. Opposite this is **it's a small world**, a waterborne journey through a series of animated tableaux.

Situated at the entrance to Cinderella's castle is the newest attraction, **Cinderellabration**, a musical stage show featuring Cinderella's enchanting princess coronation pageant.

The Many Adventures of Winnie the Pooh incorporates the latest in ride vehicle technology, lighting, and multi-channel sound effects. A popular attraction, it is worthy of its Fastpass status.

Inspired by the Mad Hatter and the March Hare's nonsensical "unbirthday" party in *Alice in Wonderland*, the **Mad Tea Party** ride has guests sitting in teacups that go right and left in circular motions. This musical ride is a must for young children.

The 3-D film, **Mickey's PhilharMagic,** embodies the high standards associated with Disney, though it might be overwhelming for young children. The newest of the 3-D films shown around the Disney parks, it may also be the most perfected. It features a strong plotline – Donald Duck getting into trouble after appropriating Mickey's Sorcerer's Hat during a warm-up for an enchanted symphony. This sends the hapless duck spiraling through several of Disney's most popular animated musicals, trying to undo his mischief. The music is magnificent, the addition of 3-D to beloved scenes from Disney's stable of hits is incredible, and the sensory enhancement at certain times is used very well and often for comic effect.

Ariel's Grotto hosts the "interactive fountain" and greeting area. Here, small children can play in an aquatic environment, meet the Little Mermaid herself, and get totally soaked.

Pooh's Playful Spot is a "splendiferous" playground from Winnie the Pooh, where children can bounce like Tigger and play like Roo.

MICKEY'S TOONTOWN FAIR®

This land appeals mainly to younger children. Here, Mickey's and Minnie's houses await, with the opportunity to be photographed with Mickey himself. Both houses are walk-through attractions but Mickey's is actually a queuing area for the Judge's Tent where you can meet Mickey Mouse "in the flesh."

Toontown Hall of Fame Tent provides an alternative character encounter, but the lines for its three entrances can move very slowly.

The Barnstormer at Goofy's Wiseacre Farm is the only "thrill" ride as such, but hardly lives up to its name.

Donald's Boat, a playground and fountain, offers further opportunities for the very young to have a whale of a time getting wet.

Walt Disney World® Railroad is a real steam train with stops that include Mickey's Toontown Fair.

Whirling round in teacups on the Mad Tea Party ride

The futuristic building that houses the Space Mountain® ride

TOMORROWLAND®

Based on a futuristic theme, Tomorrowland has undergone numerous reformations in Disney's attempts to revitalize the Land. Management continues to routinely close, replace, or add rides in its efforts to find the right mix. The seriously terrifying ExtraTERRORestrial Alien Encounter, for example, was finally judged – after complaints – to be too scary for Disney and is now closed. This has been replaced by **Stitch's Great Escape!**, in the fall of 2004. Inspired by the film *Lilo and Stitch*, the ride showcases the mayhem caused by the mischievous Stitch's adventures in outer space.

There is plenty more to enjoy here. **Space Mountain®** is a fast ride through tight bends and sharp drops in the dark against projections of asteroids and the like. The impression of traveling through space is excellent, but the ride, though wilder than Big Thunder Mountain (*see p37*), may seem somewhat tame for seasoned thrillseekers.

Next door to Space Mountain is the **Tomorrowland Arcade**, an enormous showcase of video games and various high-tech demonstrations.

Handling large crowds with ease, **Walt Disney's Carousel of Progress** is a sit-down attraction where the auditorium rotates around a central stage. It examines the transformations in domestic life through the times and, although rather quaint, is a firm favorite, particularly late in the evening.

A 360-degree Circle-Vision trip through time, **The Timekeeper** has proved to be a very popular show. A standing attraction, it draws large crowds and takes 1,000 people a showing. It is also a wonderful place to escape the afternoon heat.

Visitors can soar high on silvery rockets on the **Astro Orbiter** ride, which affords an excellent view of Tomorrowland. The **Tomorrowland Transit Authority** is a serene, quiet, and interesting 10-minute ride, which affords some of the best views of the park and an opportunity to relax after a lot of walking. Almost never busy, it travels through Space Mountain and offers glimpses inside several other attractions as well.

One of this Land's recent innovations is **Buzz Lightyear's Space Ranger Spin**. An extremely fast loader, it's one of the park's best rides. This highly addictive journey through comic books sets you in a two-seater car, fitted with laser cannons and electronic scoreboards. A control allows you to rotate the car rapidly for a better aim. Shooting at all the targets with a red laser beam causes bangs, crashes, and rapid increases in your scores. It's one of the few rides that kids have to tear their parents away from. Located on the border of Mickey's Toontown Fair is the new **Tomorrowland® Indy**

Guests fly high in the sky during a ride on the Astro Orbiter

The peaceful Tomorrowland Transit Authority ride

SHOPPING

There are shops everywhere in the Magic Kingdom and they sell just about every type of clothing, confectionery – except chewing gum! – and badged merchandise imaginable. All Lands have their own shops selling items based on the theme of the Land and on the nearest ride. Much piratical memorabilia can be purchased near Pirates of the Caribbean, for instance. Do your shopping on your way out so that you don't have to carry your purchases around with you all day.

Speedway, a large, safe course where kids and adults 4.3 ft (1.3 m) and taller can drive their own race cars around a twisting track – smaller children must have an adult drive with them. Nowhere near as difficult, or as thrilling as Epcot's Test Track *(see p46)*, the ride is more in line with family-oriented go-kart race courses.

RIDES & SHOWS CHECKLIST

This chart is designed to help you plan what to visit in the Magic Kingdom. The rides and shows are listed alphabetically within each Land.

		WAITING TIME	HEIGHT/AGE RESTRICTION	BUSIEST TIME TO RIDE	FASTPASS	LOADING SPEED	MAY CAUSE MOTION SICKNESS	OVERALL RATING
ADVENTURELAND®								
R	JUNGLE CRUISE	○		11am–5pm	➡	❷		▼
R	THE MAGIC CARPETS OF ALADDIN	○	3 yrs +	9am–7pm			✓	▼
R	PIRATES OF THE CARIBBEAN	○		10am–5pm		❷		◆
S	THE ENCHANTED TIKI ROOM	◗		noon–4pm		❷		▼
FRONTIERLAND®								
R	BIG THUNDER MOUNTAIN RAILROAD	●	3 ft 4 in	9am–7pm	➡		✓	★
R	SPLASH MOUNTAIN®	○	3 ft 4 in	9am–7pm	➡			★
S	COUNTRY BEAR JAMBOREE	○		10am–7pm		❶		▼
LIBERTY SQUARE								
R	THE HAUNTED MANSION	◗		noon–7pm		❶		◆
R	LIBERTY SQUARE RIVERBOAT	◗				❶		▼
S	THE HALL OF PRESIDENTS	○				❶		▼
FANTASYLAND®								
R	DUMBO THE FLYING ELEPHANT	○		10am–4pm		❷		▼
R	IT'S A SMALL WORLD	○		9am–7pm		❷		★
R	MAD TEA PARTY	○		10am–6pm		❶	✓	▼
R	THE MANY ADVENTURES OF WINNIE THE POOH	○		10am–5pm	➡	❷		◆
R	PETER PAN'S FLIGHT	○		10am–5pm	➡	❷		★
R	SNOW WHITE'S SCARY ADVENTURES	○		10am–5pm		❷		◆
S	MICKEY'S PHILHARMAGIC	○		10am–6pm	➡	❶		★
S	CINDERELLABRATION	○		10am–7pm				◆
MICKEY'S TOONTOWN FAIR®							✓	
R	THE BARNSTORMER AT GOOFY'S WISEACRE FARM	○		10am–6pm		❶		◆
TOMORROWLAND®								
R	ASTRO ORBITER	○			➡			▼
R	BUZZ LIGHTYEAR'S SPACE RANGER SPIN	○	3 ft 8 in	10am–7pm	➡		✓	◆
R	SPACE MOUNTAIN®	○		9am–7pm	➡	❸		◆
R	STICH'S GREAT ESCAPE!	○	4 ft 4 in	10am–6pm				◆
R	TOMORROWLAND® INDY SPEEDWAY	○		10am–7pm		❸		◆
R	TOMORROWLAND TRANSIT AUTHORITY	○				❷		◆
R	WALT DISNEY'S CAROUSEL OF PROGRESS	○				❷		◆
S	THE TIMEKEEPER	○				❷		▼

Key: Ride – R Show – S; Waiting Time Short – ○ Average – ◗ Long – ●; Loading Speed Fast – ❶ Leisurely – ❷ Slow – ❸; Overall Rating Good – ▼ Excellent – ◆ Outstanding – ★

Epcot® ❷

Epcot, an acronym for the Experimental Prototype Community of Tomorrow, was Walt Disney's dream of a technologically replete, living community. It was intended to represent a utopian vision of the future but, by the time it opened in 1982, several changes had been made to the original dream and Epcot opened as an educational center and permanent world's fair.

The 250-acre (100-ha) park is divided into two distinct halves: Future World with an emphasis on entertainment and education and World Showcase which represents the art, culture, and culinary expertise of different countries around the globe.

Test Track, one of the most popular rides at Epcot

TOP TIPS

• Early entry guests are allowed into the parks immediately to enjoy certain attractions, so it's a good idea to be at the turn-stiles at least 15 minutes before they open.
• Most people ride Spaceship Earth as soon as they arrive in Epcot and waiting times are therefore long. In the afternoon, however, you can walk on with virtually no wait.
• To avoid severe congestion at the end of the day, park in the visitor's car park of the Yacht and Beach Club hotels. Walk into World Showcase through the International Gateway and exit the same way after IllumiNations.

TACKLING THE PARK

Epcot is two and a half times the size of Magic Kingdom, which means that at least a day and a half are needed to cover most of the attractions here. World Showcase is not normally open until 11am so the early-morning crowds fill Future World and then gradually migrate to the rope between the two parks waiting for World Showcase to open. As with everything Disney, arriving early is the key to a successful visit. If you are entitled to early entry privileges, arrive one hour and 40 minutes before the official opening time.

Although there are really only a small number of rides in Future World, two of these – Test Track and Mission: SPACE – are besieged from the outset, so it's best to get to them early. Pick up a Fastpass for one and ride the other. To reach them, bear left through the huge Innoventions East building. It sometimes helps to think of

Future World as a clock face; if the main entrance is at 6 o'clock, then Mission: SPACE is at 9 o'clock and Test Track at 11 o'clock. This is roughly the equivalent of walking from the entrance of Magic Kingdom right through to Splash Mountain/Big Thunder Mountain Railroad.

After leaving the Mission: SPACE/Test Track area, retrace your steps back through Innoventions East, cross immediately through Innoventions West, and

emerge to the Imagination Pavilion to see Honey, I Shrunk the Audience (clock face position roughly 1 o'clock). After this, you can return to Spaceship Earth (6 o'clock) if the lines have shortened or make your way back across to the excellent Ellen's Energy Adventure (7 o'clock) and Wonders of Life (8 o'clock) pavilions. Though this seems like a lot of backtracking, you will have covered the main attractions very quickly and should enjoy a little glow of satisfaction when you see the lines snaking out of the entrances later in the day.

World Showcase holds far more interest for adults than children. However, there are Kidcot Fun Spots in several pavilions where kids can draw and have fun, and the diversionary tactic of buying

PIN TRADING

This answer to many a parent's prayer was introduced when Disney noticed that the lapel pins it had produced for special events were re-selling at several times the market value. In a flash of inspiration, they created Pin Stations, small booths in every park selling the hundreds of different Disney pins. Epcot's Pin Station Central, near Spaceship Earth, is the largest booth. The pins usually cost $6–$15 each. Following this with a stroke of genius, Disney created Pin Traders – cast members who could be persuaded to swap pins with guests – and surmounted the whole idea with a set of very simple trading rules, which cast members could break in favor of the guest. This has captured the imagination of children who happily spend hours tracking down the pin they don't have and swapping another for it.

Spaceship Earth, the 180-ft (55-m) geosphere at Epcot's entrance

each child a "passport" to have stamped can prove a blessing. There are minor rides – usually boat rides – in some pavilions and several others show films. The dining at some pavilions is excellent and can be booked ahead through your hotel. The transportation system in the park is not very efficient – you'll always get where you want faster by walking, so good, comfortable shoes are essential. There is also not much shade, so be sure to wear a hat.

FUTURE WORLD

As you enter the turnstiles, dominated visually by the giant geodesic dome that is home to the Spaceship Earth ride, you'll notice a new

feature: **Leave a Legacy**, which offers guests a chance to have an image of themselves engraved in metal and attached to a series of modern stone structures. Future World itself comprises a series of huge, modernistic buildings around the outside, the access to which is through Innoventions East and West. Some buildings house a single ride attraction while others afford the opportunity to browse various exhibits – usually hands-on – and enjoy smaller rides within the main pavilion. Most attractions here are sponsored by major corporations, which will be evident from the signs.

Spaceship Earth
Housed in a massive, 7,500-ton geodesic sphere, this continuously loading ride conveys you gently past superbly crafted tableaux and animatronic scenes portraying mankind's progress in technology. Almost as interesting as the ride is the dome which cunningly re-circulates rainwater into the World Showcase Lagoon.

Innoventions
Both buildings, East and West, form a hands-on exhibition of products of the near future which, through ties to consumer electronics manufacturers, is constantly updated.

TOP 10 ATTRACTIONS
① ILLUMINATIONS
② MISSION: SPACE
③ TEST TRACK
④ SOARIN
⑤ ELLEN'S ENERGY ADVENTURE
⑥ HONEY, I SHRUNK THE AUDIENCE
⑦ SPACESHIP EARTH
⑧ THE LIVING SEAS
⑨ MAELSTROM
⑩ THE RIVER OF TIME

Its structure – small, self-contained demonstration or game bays – make Innoventions an excellent "quick visit" you can return to throughout the day as you wait for your Fastpass time window or for lines to shorten. Though some of the original games have moved to Downtown Disney (see pp74–5), there's still plenty for kids to do, while parents take in the "live infomercials" that show off, and soft-sell, the latest gadgets.

1 DAY ITINERARY

1. Arrive 1 hour 40 minutes before the official opening time on an early entry day or an hour before on a normal day.
2. Head straight toward **Test Track** and pick up a Fastpass for later. Get in line for **Mission: SPACE**.
3. Upon leaving Mission: SPACE, use your Fastpass for Test Track, then cross the park to the **Imagination Pavilion** and see **Honey, I Shrunk the Audience**. Visit **Innoventions** if you have a bit of time to kill.
4. Upon leaving Honey, I Shrunk the Audience, head for **Spaceship Earth**.
5. Turn right from Spaceship Earth and head toward **Wonders of Life**. Ride **Body Wars** if operating (this is seasonal). Otherwise, you could visit Innoventions if you have not done so already.
6. Next, head to **Ellen's Energy Adventure**.
7. Head toward **World Showcase** and wait for the rope drop on the left.
8. At rope drop, head to **Mexico**. Ride **El Rio del Tempio**.
9. Leave to the right and go to **Norway**. Ride **The Maelstrom**.
10. Now it's time for a late lunch. Pick a pavilion other than the one you have in mind for dinner, and use the time after lunch to select and make dinner reservations. Time your reservation for two hours prior to the start of IllumiNations if possible. Once the reservations are made, visit **China** (movie), **France** (movie), and **Canada** (movie).
11. Return to Future World and visit **The Land** pavilion. Ride **Soarin** or, if the wait is too long, pick up a Fastpass for Soarin and experience the other attractions here while you wait.
12. Leave The Land pavilion to the left and head for **The Living Seas**.
13. Exit The Living Seas to the right, pass through both Innoventions East and West, and return to the Wonders of Life pavilion where you can see **Cranium Command** and **The Making of Me**, if operating.
14. Ride Soarin when your appointment time arrives and finish exploring Innoventions, or pick up a Fastpass for a repeat ride. Head for dinner, which should allow you a half-hour to find a good spot for **IllumiNations**.

Epcot: Mission: SPACE

One of the newest thrill rides at Epcot, Mission: SPACE takes guests on a journey to the heavens that culminates with a crash landing on Mars. This extremely popular attraction is the ultimate in simulator thrill rides, combining high-speed spinning – to simulate g-forces – with a simulator and a 3-D visual interactive storyline. The result is a mesmerizing and convincing rocket launch and high-speed trip to Mars, which also involves a ride around the moon. Particularly impressive are the wholly realistic re-creations of a liftoff into space and a problem-fraught landing. The most technologically advanced of Disney's attractions, the ride is a creation of Disney imagination, but is based on scientific fact and theory provided by astronauts, scientists, and engineers.

INTERNATIONAL SPACE TRAINING CENTER

The story is set at the International Space Training Center (ISTC) in the year 2036. In this future time of space exploration, many countries have joined together to train a new generation of space explorers. Mission: SPACE participants become astronaut candidates on their first training mission.

The ISTC building is a gleaming, metallic affair, complete with curved walls and a state-of-the-art, Space Age look. The curvy steel exterior surrounds the courtyard, called **Planetary Plaza** – from the moment visitors step into this courtyard, they are taken straight into a futuristic world. Huge replicas of Earth, Jupiter, and the moon fill Planetary Plaza, and its walls feature quotations from historical figures about space

travel and exploration. The moon model displays brass plaques indicating the location of every US and Soviet manned and unmanned touchdown during the 1960s and 70s. The interior of the ISTC is compartmentalized into various areas for different levels of training. There are four ride bays, with ten capsules in each bay; each capsule can hold four guests.

TRAINING

Before embarking on their flight, the explorers must follow a series of procedures in order to prepare for their "mission." These training and briefing sessions also go a long way in making the wait times for the show seem shorter, as they keep the crowds entertained prior to the actual ride portion of the show: the ambience is well-executed and slightly

militaristic – a rare feature at Disney parks. At the **ISTC Astronaut Recruiting Center**, explorers learn about training and view a model of the X-2 Trainer, the futuristic spacecraft they will board for their journey into space.

The second station of the mission is the **Space Simulation Lab**, a slowly spinning 35-ft (10-m) high gravity wheel containing work quarters, exercise rooms, sleeping cubicles, and dining areas for space teams. One of the highlights of the lab is an authentic Apollo-era Lunar Rover display unit on loan from the Smithsonian National Air and Space Museum, which describes mankind's first exploration of the moon.

Participants then enter the **Training Operations Room**, which bustles with the activity of various training sessions in progress. Several large monitors show live video feeds of ongoing ISTC training sessions. In **Team Dispatch**, a dispatch officer meets participants. Here, participants are split into teams of four people and sent to the **Ready Room**. This is the point at which each team member accepts an assignment: commander, pilot, navigator, or engineer. Each member is supposed to carry out the tasks associated with his or her assigned role

Replicas of planets standing out dramatically against the metallic façade of the Mission: SPACE building

during the flight. It is here that the explorers meet Capcom – the capsule communicator – who will act as the astronauts' guide through the flight. In the **Pre-flight Corridor**, explorers receive their final instructions for the mission. A uniformed flight crew member then escorts the team to a capsule – the X-2 Space Shuttle.

FLIGHT & LANDING

The team members board the X-2 training capsule and are securely strapped in, with individual "windows" just inches away. The countdown begins and then there is a pulse-racing liftoff: the roar of engines, the clouds of exhaust, and the motion of the capsule all combine to generate in the participants sensations similar to those that astronauts feel during actual liftoff.

The cabin's windows are actually state-of-the-art video flat screens that use a combination of LCD glass and electronic video cards to present an ultra-sharp full-motion video based on actual data taken from Mars-orbiting satellites. The spectacular

TOP TIPS

• *This is the first ride created with Disney's Fastpass system in mind. Avoid a lengthy wait at this popular attraction by using the Fastpass, which is available at the entrance to Mission: SPACE. Two times will be posted. If the wait is too long, guests can obtain a Fastpass ticket with an assigned return time.*
• *Read all the warning signs at the entrance to Mission: SPACE and take the ride only if you are sure you'll be able to handle it.*
• *The ride has a minimum guest height requirement of 3 ft 8 in (1.1 m).*
• *The entire Mission: SPACE experience, from pre-show to the Advance Training Lab, can last from 45 minutes to more than an hour. The ride to Mars lasts approximately 4 minutes from capsule door closing to it reopening.*

views of planets Earth and Mars that participants glimpse through the capsule windows, reinforce their illusion of traveling through space.

The members of the space team must work in unison, performing the roles of pilot, commander, navigator, and engineer in order to successfully face challenges and accomplish their mission to Mars. Throughout the flight, crew members receive instructions from Capcom regarding their duties, which consists of pressing buttons; the capsule obeys the commands very convincingly. Unexpected twists and turns keep participants on the edge of their seats, and call for tricky maneuvers with joysticks. Apart from the exhilarating "slingshot" around the moon, other thrills include a brief experience of "weightlessness" and dodging asteroids on the way to Mars.

The four-minute ride comes to a crashing finale with the Mars landing, complemented by superb sound effects that are achieved by the use of a stereo woofer built right into the back of the space capsules. Pioneering astronauts such as Buzz Aldrin and Rhea Seddon have taken their turn on the ride, comparing it favorably to actual space travel.

The g-forces that come into play during Mission: SPACE are, in fact, of lower intensity than in a typical roller coaster but they are of much greater duration.

ADVANCE TRAINING LAB

After the ride, guests can go around the Advance Training Lab, a colorful interactive play area where they can test their skills in space-related games for people of all ages. You can explore this area even if you choose not to go on the ride itself. There is no minimum height requirement here.

In **Space Race**, two teams are involved in a race to be the first to complete a successful mission from Mars back to Earth. The teams are

composed of up to 60 guests, who are required to work together to overcome numerous challenges and setbacks in their mission. **Expedition: Mars** is another fun endeavor at the Advance Training Lab. In this sophisticated video game, the player's mission is to locate four astronauts stranded on Mars. **Space Base** is targeted at junior astronauts. It is an excellent interactive play area where kids can climb, slide, crawl, explore, and get rid of excess energy. You can also send **Postcards from Space** at a kiosk in the Advanced Training Lab. Here, guests make a video of themselves in one of several space-related backdrops to create a fine memento of their Mission: SPACE experience, and can email the result to friends and family.

Beyond the Advance Training Lab is the **Mission: SPACE Cargo Bay**, a shopping area spreading over 1,500 sq ft (139 sq m). A 4-ft (1.2-m) high 3-D figure of Mickey Mouse dressed as an astronaut greets visitors, and the area is dominated by a 12-ft (3.6-m) mural depicting various Disney characters in space gear on the surface of Mars. Here, visitors can purchase a large variety of souvenirs, from inexpensive to costly, as a remembrance of their "space experience."

CAUTION

This ride is not for everyone, and certainly not for anyone prone to motion sickness or sensitive to tight spaces, loud noises, or spinning. Younger children may find it too intense, and expectant mothers and people with high blood pressure or heart problems would be well advised to forgo it. Remember: there is no backing out after liftoff.

FUTURE WORLD CONT...

Ellen's Energy Adventure

A passably entertaining film is enlivened by some fascinating technology and hosts Ellen DeGeneres and Billy Nye. The entire theater rotates before breaking into self-powered, moving sections, which take the audience through a prehistoric landscape, inhabited by some fairly convincing antediluvians.

The Living Seas

The technology behind this attraction is quite stunning in its own right, but the reason most come here is to visit Sea Base Alpha, Epcot's most ambitious research project. A pre-show presentation prepares you for your journey to the bottom of the ocean, after which you take the "hydro-lators" to the sea bed. There you board a continuously moving train of small cars, which carry you past astonishing views of sharks, dolphins, giant turtles, and manatees. On disembarking, the attractions include being able to watch the sealife through transparent walls and an interactive show based on the film *Finding Nemo*.

Wonders of Life

Operating only seasonally, this rambling, noisy pavilion deals with the functioning of the human body. **The Making of Me** is a pleasant film about the events preceding childbirth while **Cranium Command** is an amusing and often overlooked animatronic presentation about the operation of the brain. **Body Wars** – Epcot's first simulator thrill ride – takes you through the human body, having first miniaturized you. This, however, although popular, is a violent and jerky ride which induces motion sickness in quite a few people.

Test Track

One of the most popular rides at Epcot, Test Track uses the most sophisticated ride vehicle technology available, placing you in a simulator that moves on tracks at high speed. Essentially, you are the passenger in a six-seater prototype sports car being tested prior to going into production. Although the ride puts you through brake tests, hill climbs, sharp turns, near crashes, and paint spraying bays, the climax is the outside lap of the ride where the vehicle exceeds 66 mph (102 km/h) on a raised roadway around the outside of the Test Track building. However, the system has frequent stops – usually because the advanced safety systems have cut in and halted the entire run. While this may be reassuring, it results in the lines outside continuing to grow until, by the evening, you can expect a wait of between 90 minutes and two hours. The ride itself – just 4 minutes long – is so good you will want to try it again and again, but be aware that the Fastpass machines outside the entrance have normally exhausted their allocation by lunchtime.

TOP TIPS

• *Test Track is exceptionally popular but unreliable. To avoid the long lines, try to ride this first. On leaving, take a Fastpass ticket for another ride later.*

• *If a breakdown occurs during your ride, after disembarking ask the cast member if you can ride again, immediately.*

• *Because Test Track runs continuously – even when the park is closed – you can jump back on it for a repeat ride in the last minutes before park closing.*

• *Ellen's Energy Adventure show is exceptionally long (45 minutes). Take it in for a break from the heat or while you wait for a Fastpass ride window to become available.*

• *Although the lines for Ellen's Energy Adventure are long, it takes 600 guests every 17 minutes, so you won't have long to wait.*

• *The Land, with its giant produce, is an agriculturist's dream pavilion. It contains the new thrill ride Soarin, which appeals to all except the very young. Probably a better bet for them is The Living Seas, which has recently been modified to take advantage of Disney's monster hit Finding Nemo.*

The Imagination Pavilion

The Imagination Pavilion houses a show, a ride, and an interactive demo area. The show is the charming and funny 3-D presentation **Honey, I Shrunk the Audience**, the ride is **Journey into Imagination with Figment**, and the interactive showcase is a playground of audio-visual sensory games and demonstrations. Honey, I Shrunk the Audience is another example of the advances in sensory and visual 3-D storytelling. Dr. Nigel Channing, the always funny Eric Idle, hosts the Inventor of the Year Award Show, showing off the inventions that feature in the movie *Honey, I Shrunk the Kids!* – if things could just stop going wrong for a few moments. The clever plotline does indeed shrink the viewer and induces many laughs.

The Journey Into Imagination with Figment ride is an upbeat, light-hearted trip

Feeding time for the residents of The Living Seas

in search of ideas in the arts and sciences. However, it is overcomplicated and overlong. You move past several different animated scenes which present optical illusions and sound effects.

The **ImageWorks Lab** offers visitors a chance to manipulate sound and vision interactively, from making music by waving your arms to experimenting with fast- and slow-motion video to making music by doing aerobics. Highly recommended for the kids, it appeals to adults as well.

The Land

Ecology and conservation form the main themes and permeate the attractions housed around the fast food restaurant. As a consequence, these attractions become much busier during lunch-times. *The Lion King* charac-ters lead **The Circle of Life**, a hymn to conservation expressed through film and animation. Dangers to the

The tremendously funny "Honey, I Shrunk the Audience" show

environment as well as potential solutions are pre-sented through this enter-taining and inspirational show. **Living with the Land** is a cruise through the past, present, and future of US farming. A walking tour accompanies the boat ride.

The greatest attraction in the Land pavilion – and the newest thrill ride at Epcot – is **Soarin**. Passengers are lifted

high off the ground in this simulated hang glider. Wind whips through your hair, your feet dangle above treetops, and the scent of pine forests fills the air as you experience the sensation of flying over California's breathtaking natural wonders, including the Golden Gate Bridge and Yosemite National Park. Be warned that Soarin is not for those with a fear of heights.

RIDES & SHOWS CHECKLIST

This chart is designed to help you plan what to visit at Epcot. The rides and shows in Future World and World Showcase are listed alphabetically.

		WAITING TIME	HEIGHT/AGE RESTRICTION	BUSIEST TIME TO RIDE/ATTEND	FASTPASS	MAY CAUSE MOTION SICKNESS	OVERALL RATING
FUTURE WORLD							
R	BODY WARS	◗	3 ft 4 in	10am–2pm		✓	◆
R	JOURNEY INTO IMAGINATION WITH FIGMENT	◗		11am–2pm			◆
R	MISSION: SPACE	●	3 ft 8 in	All day	➡	✓	★
R	SPACESHIP EARTH	◗		9am–noon			★
R	TEST TRACK	●	3 ft 4 in	All day	➡	✓	★
S	CIRCLE OF LIFE	○		noon–2pm			▼
S	CRANIUM COMMAND	○					◆
S	ELLEN'S ENERGY ADVENTURE	◗		10am–1pm			◆
S	HONEY, I SHRUNK THE AUDIENCE	○		10am–5pm	➡		★
S	THE LIVING SEAS	○		11am–3pm			◆
S	LIVING WITH THE LAND	●		noon–2pm	➡		◆
S	THE MAKING OF ME	○					▼
R	SOARIN	●	3 ft 4 in	All day	➡	✓	★
WORLD SHOWCASE							
R	MAELSTROM	●		11am–5pm	➡		◆
R	THE RIVER OF LIFE	○		noon–3pm			▼
S	THE AMERICAN ADVENTURE	○					▼
S	IMPRESSIONS DE FRANCE	○					◆
S	O CANADA!	○					◆
S	REFLECTIONS OF CHINA	○					★

Key: Ride – R Show – S; Waiting Times Short – ○ Average – ◗ Long – ●;
Overall Rating Good – ▼ Excellent – ◆ Outstanding – ★

The gateway of the China pavilion

WORLD SHOWCASE

The temples, churches, town halls, and castles of these 11 pavilions or "countries" are sometimes replicas of genuine buildings, sometimes merely in vernacular style. But World Showcase is much more than just a series of architectural set pieces. Every pavilion is staffed by people from the country it represents, selling high-quality local products as well as surprisingly good ethnic cuisine.

At set times, which are given on the guide map, native performers stage live shows in the forecourts of each country: the best are the excellent acrobats at China and the bizarre and comic Living Statues at Italy. Only a couple of pavilions include rides, while a number have stunning giant-screen introductions to their country's history, culture, and landscapes. A few even have art galleries, though these often go unnoticed.

The fastest way to get around the 1.3 mile (2 km) perimeter is to walk, but the easiest way to get from the entrance to the back end, where the American pavilion is located, is to take the ferries that crisscross the lagoon, linking the Canada pavilion to the Morocco pavilion and Mexico to Germany.

Mexico
A Mayan pyramid hides the most remarkable interior at World Showcase. Musicians and stalls selling sombreros, ponchos, and papier-mâché animals (*piñatas*) fill a plaza bathed in a purple twilight. The backdrop to this is a rumbling volcano. Hidden among the splendor of the main area are little art galleries and an arts-and-crafts play space for children.

The tranquil **El Río del Tiempo** ("The River of Time") boat ride passes through Audio-Animatronics and cinematic scenes of Mexico, while the restaurant outside the pavilion offers a great viewing spot for IllumiNations (*see p52*) later in the day.

Norway
The architecture in this pavilion includes replicas of a stave church – a medieval wooden building – and the 14th-century fortress above Oslo harbor called Akershus Castle, arranged attractively around a cobblestone square.

You can buy trolls and sweaters and other native crafts, but the essential element here is **Maelstrom**, a short but exhilarating journey down fjords in a longboat into troll country, and across an oil-rig-flecked North Sea – before docking at a fishing port. The ride is followed by a short film about Norway. The film is not mandatory – you can pass through the theater and exit directly if you choose – but it is a well-done look at the past and present of the country.

China
In this pavilion the *pièce de résistance* is the half-size replica of Beijing's well-known landmark, the Temple of Heaven. The peaceful scene here contrasts with the more rowdy atmosphere in some of the nearby pavilions.

For entertainment, there is **Reflections of China**, a Circle-Vision film shown on nine screens all around the audience simultaneously, which makes the most of the country's fabulous, little-seen ancient sites and scenery. Note that you must stand throughout the film. China, the country, also sends a near-continuous stream of acrobatic and other performing troupes that put on mini-shows throughout the day all year long.

The pavilion's extensive shopping emporium sells everything from Chinese lanterns and painted screens to tea bags. Unfortunately, the restaurants are nothing to write home about.

The striking wooden structure at the entrance to the Norway pavilion

◁ **The unmistakable globe of Spaceship Earth, the focal point of Future World**

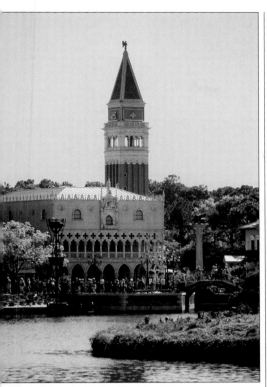

Architectural elements of Venice at the Italy pavilion

Germany

The happiest country in World Showcase is a mixture of gabled and spired buildings gathered around a central square, St. Georgsplatz. They are based on real buildings from all over Germany, including a merchants' hall in Freiburg and a Rhine castle. If you have children, try to time your visit so that it coincides with the hourly chime of the *glockenspiel* in the square.

An accordionist sometimes plays, and the shops are full of quirky or clever gifts such as beautifully crafted wooden dolls. However, you really need to dine here to get the full flavor of Germany.

Italy

The bulk of Italy's relatively small pavilion represents Venice: from gondolas moored alongside candycane poles in the lagoon to the tremendous versions of the towering redbrick campanile and the 14th-century Doge's Palace of St. Mark's Square; even the fake marble looks authentic. The courtyard buildings behind are Veronese and Florentine in style, and the Neptune statue is a copy of a Bernini work.

The architecture is the big attraction, but you should also stop off to eat at one of the restaurants or browse around the shops where you can pick up pasta, amaretti, wine, and so forth.

America

This is the centerpiece of World Showcase, but it lacks the charm found in most of the other countries. However, Americans usually find **The American Adventure** show, which takes place inside the vast Georgian-style building, very moving. For others, it will provide an interesting insight into the American psyche. The show is an openly patriotic yet thought-provoking romp through the history of the United States up to the present day. It incorporates tableaux on screen and some excellent Audio-Animatronics figures, particularly the author Mark Twain and the great 18th-century statesman, Benjamin Franklin.

WORLD SHOWCASE: BEHIND THE SCENES

If you'd like more than just a superficial view of Walt Disney World, its behind-the-scenes tours may appeal. In World Showcase, two-hour Hidden Treasures tours provide a closer look at the architecture and traditions of the countries featured in the park, while in the Gardens of the World tours the creation of the World Showcase gardens is explained; you are even given tips on how to create a bit of Disney magic back home. These tours cost around $25 per person. If you have $199 and seven hours to spare, you might want to sign up for the Backstage Magic tour, which includes all three theme parks. One of the highlights is the visit to the famous tunnel network beneath Magic Kingdom. Call up for information on all Disney tours (*see p77*).

The lovely architecture and landscaping at the Japan pavilion

ILLUMINATIONS: REFLECTIONS OF EARTH

The one Epcot show that you mustn't miss is the nightly IllumiNations. Presented near closing time around World Showcase Lagoon, it is a rousing *son et lumière* show on an unbelievably extravagant scale with lasers, fire- and waterworks, and a symphonic soundtrack that highlight the 11 featured nations. Best viewing spots are a seat on the veranda at the Cantina de San Angel in Mexico, the outside restaurant balcony in Japan, and the International Gateway bridge near the United Kingdom.

MORE PAVILIONS IN THE WORLD SHOWCASE

Japan

This is a restrained, formal place with a traditional Japanese garden, a Samurai castle, and a pagoda modeled on a seventh-century temple in Nara – whose five levels represent earth, water, fire, wind, and sky.

The Mitsukoshi department store, a copy of the ceremonial hall of the Imperial Palace in Kyoto, offers kimonos, wind chimes, bonsai trees, and the chance to pick a pearl from an oyster. Kabuki theater troupes and other performers appear throughout the day. However, Japan really only comes to life in its restaurants, where visitors can sample delicacies such as sushi and tempura. On the second level of the pavilion, chefs work dexterously with flashing knives, demonstrating the Japanese art of tableside cooking.

Morocco

Morocco's appeal lies in its enameled tiles, its keyhole-shaped doors, its ruddy fortress walls, and the twisting alleys of its *medina* (old city), which is reached via a reproduction of a gate into the city of Fez. The use of native artists gives the show a greater sense of authenticity.

Morocco offers some of the best handmade crafts in World Showcase. The alleys of the old city lead you to a bustling market of little stores selling carpets, brassware, leatherware, and shawls.

There are several interesting dining experiences on offer. The Tangerine Café serves a variety of Moroccan sandwiches and specialty pastries. Try the couscous, steamed and served with lamb or chicken, at the Restaurant Marrakesh. It is also the place to see belly dancers perform in a stimulating show.

France

A Gallic flair infuses everything in the France pavilion, from its architecture to its upscale stores. Architectural highlights include a one-tenth scale replica of the Eiffel Tower, Parisian Belle Epoque mansions, and a rustic village main street. Among the authentic products from France sold here are

Detailed replica of the famous prayer tower in Marrakesh at the Morocco pavilion, across a promenade

The Canada pavilion, featuring examples of Canadian architecture

perfumes – such as the famous Guerlain range – wine, and berets. Excellent French food can be sampled in a couple of restaurants in the pavilion and a patisserie selling sinfully rich croissants and cakes.

A film entitled **Impressions de France** is the main entertainment. The film, shown on five adjacent screens and set to the sounds of French classical music, offers a whirlwind tour through the country's most beautiful regions.

United Kingdom

The Rose and Crown Pub is the focal point in this pavilion. It serves traditional English fare such as Cornish pasties, fish and chips, and even draft bitter – chilled to suit American tastes. There's also a "chip shop" takeaway booth next door for those in a hurry or wanting a smaller, less expensive meal. The pub also sports a genuine singalong most evenings. Pleasant gardens surround the pub, as well as a medley of buildings of various historic architectural styles. These include a castle based on Hampton Court, an imitation Regency terrace, and a thatched cottage.

There is not much to do here in this pavilion other than browse around the shops, which sell everything from quality tea and china to sweaters, tartan ties, teddy bears, and toy soldiers. The terrace of the Rose and Crown, however, offers good views of IllumiNations.

Canada

A Native Indian village with a log cabin and 30-ft (9-m) high totem poles, a replica of Ottawa's Victorian-style Château Laurier Hotel, a rocky chasm, and ornamental gardens make up the large but rather staid Canadian pavilion.

The country in all its diversity, and particularly its grand scenery, comes to life much better in the Circle-Vision film **O Canada!** – though China's Circle-Vision film is even better. The audience stands in the middle of the theater and turns around to follow the film as it unfolds on no fewer than nine screens. Shops at Canada sell a wide range of Native Indian and Inuit crafts and various edible specialties, as well as wine. Le Cellier Steakhouse restaurant serves tasty Canadian seafood and steaks along with wines and beer from Canada.

EATING & DRINKING

Dining well is fundamental to visiting Epcot and particularly World Showcase. Some of the latter's pavilions have decent fast-food places, but the best restaurants (including those listed below unless otherwise stated) require reservations. Call Dining reservations *(see p77)* as soon as you know when you'll be at Epcot or book early in the day, using the TV monitors of the WorldKey Information Satellite, which provide up-to-date information on everything at Epcot. Most restaurants serve lunch and dinner; try unpopular hours such as 11am or 4pm if other times are unavailable. Lunch is usually about two-thirds of the price of dinner, and children's menus are available at even the most upscale restaurants.

Recommended in World Showcase are:
Mexico: the San Angel Inn serves interesting but pricey Mexican food. It is the most romantic place to dine at Epcot.
Norway: Restaurant Akershus offers a good-value *koldtbord* (buffet) of Norwegian dishes in a castle setting.
Germany: the Biergarten has a beer hall atmosphere, with a cheap and plentiful buffet and hearty oompah-pah music.
Italy: L'Originale Alfredo di Roma Ristorante is enormously popular and engagingly chaotic, with sophisticated dishes.
Japan: you can eat communally, either in the Teppan Yaki Dining Rooms around a grilling, stir-frying chef, or at the bar of Tempura Kiku for sushi and tempura (no reservations).
France: there are three top-notch restaurants here: the upscale Bistro de Paris (dinner only); Les Chefs de France, the most elegant restaurant in Epcot, with haute cuisine by acclaimed chefs *(see p151)*; and the terraced Chefs de France Steakhouse for steaks, escargots, and crêpes.
United Kingdom: Harry Ramsden's "chippy" booth sells only modest-sized, inexpensive pub fare; it makes for a great "lunch on the go" and the terrace adjoining it is the most relaxing spot in the World Showcase.

Recommended in Future World are:
The Land: the revolving Garden Grill passes a re-created rainforest, prairie, and desert.
The Living Seas: at the expensive Coral Reef you can eat fish and watch them through a transparent, underwater wall.

Disney-MGM Studios ❸

The smallest theme park in Walt Disney World Resort, Disney-MGM Studios was launched in 1989 as a full-fledged working film and TV production facility. In January 2004, however, the animation department was shut down, and the "working" side of the equation has been almost completely abandoned, although some film and TV production – mostly for the Disney cable channel – is still undertaken here. Regardless of these changes, the park remains a famed tourist destination, with top-notch shows and rides based on Disney and Metro-Goldwyn-Mayer films and TV shows, which offer a tribute to the world of Hollywood and showbiz. Constantly evolving, the park has introduced new and spectacular shows, such as Fantasmic! and Beauty and the Beast – Live on Stage, which have taken its popularity to new heights. Like its competitor Universal Orlando *(see pp88–99)*, Disney-MGM Studios' educational yet highly entertaining interactive experiences are geared toward adults and teenagers.

(see pp88–99)

TOP TIPS

- *The best place to watch the afternoon parade is on the bench nearest the popcorn and drinks stand located opposite Sounds Dangerous. You still, however, have to get there first.*
- *During the parades, most of the other attractions are quiet, but almost impossible to reach if you're not on the correct side.*
- *Avoid parking in the Disney-MGM or Animal Kingdom lots if you are visiting multiple parks throughout the day. Trams to these parking lots stop running long before the last show at the Magic Kingdom and it can take a long time for you to get back to your vehicle.*

TACKLING THE PARK

The layout of this park differs from that of the other theme parks, although Hollywood Boulevard takes on the role of "Main Street, USA" with the purpose of directing guests toward the numerous attractions.

Over the past few years, Walt Disney World has successfully expanded the scope and magnitude of the park's attractions, building some of the finest in Orlando. With scores of tourists lining up for the rides and shows, arriving early is the key to avoid waiting for long periods in line. It is also worth bearing in mind that some of the attractions might be particularly intense and can frighten young children.

The entertainment schedule changes frequently and streets can be closed off for either celebrity visits or in case of a live filming session. Although events such as these usually take place in winter, it's a good idea to find out about times, locations, and shows as soon as you enter the park from Guest Services, which is located on the left of the main entrance.

At about 3:30pm, the park holds its afternoon parade, usually based on one of Disney's recently animated movies. Be aware that, due to the open plan of the park, the heat can become quite uncomfortable for guests.

Fantasmic! takes place at night – once a night during the slow season and twice during peak periods. Despite seating about 10,000 people at a time, you may need to turn up quite early – up to two hours ahead of time – during peak periods to ensure a seat.

HOLLYWOOD BOULEVARD

Delightful Art Deco styled buildings vie with a replica of Mann's Chinese Theater to present an image of Hollywood that never was. It's here that your picture will be taken and you might see

Visitors heading for the Rock 'n' Roller® Coaster starring Aerosmith ride

The famous Hollywood Brown Derby Restaurant, Hollywood Boulevard

TOP 10 ATTRACTIONS

1. THE TWILIGHT ZONE TOWER OF TERROR™
2. FANTASMIC!
3. ROCK 'N' ROLLER® COASTER STARRING AEROSMITH
4. JIM HENSON'S MUPPET* VISION 3-D
5. STAR TOURS
6. INDIANA JONES™ EPIC STUNT SPECTACULAR!
7. WHO WANTS TO BE A MILLIONAIRE – PLAY IT!
8. VOYAGE OF THE LITTLE MERMAID
9. THE GREAT MOVIE RIDE
10. THE MAGIC OF DISNEY ANIMATION

some of the cast members, acting as reporters or police, chasing celebrities. Moreover, it is on the boulevard that the cast members will try to direct you to Echo Lake's Indiana Jones Epic Stunt Spectacular! – a live action show featuring stunts from the Indiana Jones films.

Halfway up the boulevard, a street breaks off to the right. This is known as Sunset Boulevard, and is home to two of Disney-MGM Studios' most popular rides: The Twilight Zone Tower of Terror and the Rock 'n' Roller Coaster starring Aerosmith.

At the junction of Sunset and Hollywood boulevards lies an enormous canopy that is shaped like Mickey's hat from *The Sorcerer's Apprentice*.

This is a combination store, shady spot, and pin station *(see p42)*, where budding traders can ambush the cast and swap badges.

At the top of Hollywood Boulevard lies the Central Plaza, which is dominated by the replica of Mann's Chinese Theater. Here you can experience **The Great Movie Ride**, a trip through movie history that features every film genre, ranging from musicals to horror films to gangster movies. Huge ride vehicles carrying 60 guests apiece track silently past the largest movie sets ever built for a Disney ride. As always, Disney's vast experience in the movie industry has led to the creation of some superb sets. Memorable cinematic

moments, such as Gene Kelly singing in the rain and Dorothy going down the Yellow Brick Road on her way to Oz, are re-created with the help of highly realistic Audio-Animatronic figures. Combined with old film clips, special effects, and some fun live action sequences, this is an enjoyable 25-minute ride that ends on a very upbeat and optimistic note. The Great Movie Ride is one of the few attractions where the queuing is almost as good as the ride itself.

1 DAY ITINERARY

1. Upon entering the park, immediately get a Fastpass to **The Twilight Zone Tower of Terror**.
2. Stroll back up Sunset Boulevard and get in line for **The Great Movie Ride**.
3. As you exit, head for Animation Courtyard and take in the various shows (which usually have minimal wait times) – **The Magic of Disney Animation, Voyage of the Little Mermaid**, and **Walt Disney: One Man's Dream**. Try and get a Fastpass for **Who Wants to Be a Millionaire – Play It!**
4. If your time window for the Tower of Terror has arrived, go back down Sunset to ride it. Wait in line for the **Rock 'n' Roller Coaster starring Aerosmith** after you ride the Tower (if the wait time is less than one hour; otherwise come back to it later).
5. Enjoy lunch in the large restaurant area on Sunset, or take in the **Beauty and the Beast – Live on Stage** show.
6. Attend your scheduled Millionaire show, then walk down to the southeast end of the park and get a Fastpass for **Star Tours**. Head to the **Jim Henson's Muppet Vision 3-D** show and walk down New York Street after you're done there.
7. Just before heading into Star Tours, get a Fastpass for the **Indiana Jones Epic Stunt Spectacular!**
8. Dine at your pre-reserved restaurant.
9. Head for your scheduled Indiana Jones show, then walk across the park for your last chance to re-ride either Tower of Terror or Rock 'n' Roller Coaster if the wait times have fallen to under one hour. Time this so that you emerge from the ride about 90 minutes to one hour prior to the start of **Fantasmic!**
10. As darkness descends on the park, head for the Amphitheater to catch Fantasmic! and end the day on a perfect note.

SUNSET BOULEVARD

Like Hollywood Boulevard, Sunset Boulevard is a rose-tinted evocation of the famous Hollywood street in the 1940s. Theaters and storefronts – some real, some fake – have been re-created with characteristic attention to detail. The Hollywood Tower Hotel lies at one end of the boulevard. This decrepit, lightning-ravaged hotel is home to one of Orlando's scariest rides – **The Twilight Zone Tower of Terror™**. The ride straps you into a runaway service elevator for a voyage inspired by the 1950s TV show *The Twilight Zone*. The pre-show area is a library into which you are ushered by a melancholic bellhop. From here you enter what appears to be the boiler room of the hotel and you walk through to board the freight elevators fitted with plank seats. The elevator doors sometimes open to allow glimpses of ghostly corridors. As you reach the 13th floor, the elevator actually trundles horizontally across the hotel. But it's hard to concentrate on anything other than the ghastly 13-story plunge that everyone knows will come – but not exactly when. The original single drop has now been increased to seven and, during the first drop, enormously powerful engines actually pull you down faster than free fall. Terrifyingly brilliant, this ride is a technological masterpiece. You can also enjoy a brief, fleeting view of the whole park, and indeed outside the park – a break with Disney tradition – before you begin the scary descent. The Tower of Terror ride is not to everyone's taste, but diehard enthusiasts and novices alike pack this ride from the outset.

An indoor extravaganza, the **Rock 'n' Roller® Coaster starring Aerosmith** ride accelerates from 0 to 60 mph (96 km/h) in just 2.8 seconds. Strapped into "stretch limos," guests experience 5G pulls as they hurl through the twists and turns. Replete with loops, steep drops, and corkscrew spins, the Rock 'n' Roller Coaster employs a fully synchronized and very loud soundtrack as it hurls you toward the neon-lit equivalent of oblivion. Those who enjoy sitting in the front can get to the seats via the lower ramp. The pre-show is a rather tame affair and presents a recording session of the popular American band, Aerosmith.

The boulevard also features two outdoor arenas for shows. The **Theater of the Stars** is a huge, covered amphitheater with 1,500 seats. The **Beauty and the Beast – Live on Stage** show is performed several times throughout the day here. The production is about 30 minutes long and has beautifully choreographed scenes adapted from the movie of the same title. The exquisitely detailed sets, and costumes are works of art. Since the show is extremely popular, go early to get a good seat. The gigantic **Hollywood Hills Amphitheater** is home to the spectacular and dazzling show, **Fantasmic!**

TOP TIPS

• *Fastpasses to the top rides – the Tower of Terror and the Rock 'n' Roller Coaster – are usually gone by early afternoon. If you do not arrive early at the park, your only chance to ride these rides will be to either wait in the "standby" line for up to two hours each, or stay in the park until it's nearly closing time, when the line wait times drop to around 45 minutes.*

• *In the boiler room of the Tower of Terror, take any open gateway to the lifts – don't worry if the other guests do not do the same. You'll get a better seat and a better view.*

• *Many people leave the park during bad weather or as night approaches, but this is in fact the best time to head for the Tower of Terror ride.*

Sunset Boulevard also offers a large seating area, where guests can choose from a wide range of food stands and restaurants. Visitors can opt for a quick snack, a light meal, or a full lunch. There is something to suit every budget.

FANTASMIC!

Each of the Disney parks aim to bring down the curtain with a spectacular show, but Disney-MGM's Fantasmic! extravaganza outdoes them all. It is, quite simply, the finest event of its kind in Florida. Combining lasers, fan fountain projection, animation, and a cast of more than a 100 actors and dancers, Fantasmic! manages to choreograph the entire event with split second accuracy to music, fireworks, and lighting. Set on an island in a lagoon meant to represent Mickey Mouse's imagination, the "story," such as it is, cleverly weaves elements of all the classic Disney films into a single battle between good and evil.

Illuminated boats, flying floats, and a lake that bursts into flames are but some of the remarkable features of this enchanting event. Playing to audiences of 10,000 per showing, Fantasmic! completely mesmerizes adults as well as children with incredible special effects and their interaction with live performers. The wide array of famous characters represented will bring squeals of recognition and delight from all ages.

As expected, the show is exceptionally popular with most visitors as a finale for the evening, which means that arriving early is a must if you want to sit near the front – be aware that you may get wet in the first few rows. Seating opens approximately two hours before showtime, and the earlier show tends to fill up faster than the final performance. Even in the quietest time of the off-peak season, all 10,000 places are taken up to 30 minutes before the show starts. However, this truly is one event you would never forgive yourself for missing.

◁ **The sinister exterior of The Twilight Zone Tower of Terror™, Disney-MGM Studios**

Bear and his friends at Playhouse Disney – Live on Stage!

ANIMATION COURTYARD

The original idea behind Animation Courtyard was not just to give visitors an inside look into the history and process of animation, but also a glimpse at all forthcoming Disney animated films as they were being made. With the shutting down of Disney's animation unit in January 2004, this area of the park is now less popular, but still has features worth visiting.

The **Magic of Disney Animation**, which used to be a tour of the working spaces in the Animation Department, is now a guided visit with a sole Disney artist and some films exploring Disney's rich history in animated films. The artist does live sketches on the spot and answers questions about how films are made. The "tour" concludes with the audience – mostly children – sitting at tables and working with the artist to create their own Disney character. For adults, the most interesting aspect of this attraction are the sketches from Disney classics, along with copies of the Academy awards the unit has won over the years.

The **Voyage of the Little Mermaid** show is enacted by cartoon, live, and Audio-Animatronic characters. Special effects use lasers and water to create the feel of an underwater grotto. It is one of the most popular shows in the park, though young children sometimes find the lightning storm scary.

Playhouse Disney – Live on Stage! is also geared toward youngsters and features singing and dancing Disney Channel characters. There's the lovable Bear in the Big Blue House and the cute and cuddly Winnie the Pooh. This 20-minute produc-tion encourages audience participation. Don't miss it.

MICKEY AVENUE

This connects Animation Courtyard to the **Disney-MGM Studios Backlot Tour**. Sound stages line the avenue and currently are the premises for **Who Wants to be a Millionaire – Play It!**, a re-creation of the ABC game-show phenomenon. Also, look out for Mickey, who may be signing autographs here.

Next door is the new attraction: **Walt Disney: One Man's Dream**. This could be dismissed as simple propaganda, but it is difficult not to admire Walt's great vision and risk-taking ability. A fascinating "museum" features collections of early Disney memorabilia, multi-media appearances of the man himself, and plenty of scale models and historical props from the parks. Wind your way to the cinema to see a film on Walt Disney. Despite the title, the film and photos make it pretty clear that Walt

SHOPPING

Most of the best shops are on Hollywood Boulevard, which stays open half an hour after the rest of the theme park has closed. Mickey's of Hollywood is the big emporium for general Disney merchandise. Celebrity 5 & 10 has a range of affordable movie souvenirs, such as clapper boards and Oscars®, as well as books and posters. More expensive is Sid Cahuenga's One-Of-A-Kind, where you can buy rare film and TV memorabilia such as genuine autographed photographs – of Boris Karloff and Greta Garbo, for example – or famous actors' clothes. Limited-edition "cels" in Animation Gallery in Animation Courtyard are also very expensive and will make an even bigger dent in your wallet; the same shop sells Disney posters and books too.

◁ **The electrifying Rock 'n' Roller® Coaster starring Aerosmith ride, Disney-MGM Studios**

Disney received extensive help from his family – particularly brother Roy, who worked arduously to complete and expand Walt Disney World after his brother's death in 1966. Especially admirable is Walt's enthusiasm for the expansion of his dream – the plans for Disney World and his dream project, Epcot. However, Walt would probably be fairly shocked at the size, scope and appeal of the company these days, having humbly said: "Never forget, it started because of a mouse."

Although it never fails to be entertaining, the half-hour Disney-MGM Studios Backlot Tour best comes to life when a film is actually being shot. The tour begins with a show explaining how the effects of controlling the weather and the forces of nature – such as the sea – are accomplished on film. Members of the audience are roped in for some of the demonstrations. A tram then takes you through various departments – props, makeup, costume, and so on – and finally down Residential Street, where different exteriors illustrate how the mood of a film is set. You also get to look in on three sound stages, where, if you're lucky, a TV show, commercial, or movie might be being filmed. If any actual television or film production happens to be taking place, the audience is usually allowed to walk onto the sound stage and observe the work in progress.

The most memorable part of the tour is a visit to the **Castastrophe Canyon**. Set in the American Southwest, this provides a highly realistic and terrifying journey through floods, explosions, earthquakes, and various other disasters. On leaving the canyon, you get a glimpse of the equipment used to create all these effects.

STREETS OF AMERICA

In this area the streets of New York, San Francisco, Chicago, and various other cities are recreated by movie sets. The bricks and stone are just painted on plastic and fiberglass, and the buildings' façades are propped up with girders. The sets are used for filming, but visitors can wander around freely.

Nearby is the **Lights, Motors, Action!™ Extreme Stunt Show**, in which visual thrills are supplied for 33 minutes, several times a day, by special cars and motorcycles.

Toy Story Pizza Planet Arcade is a trumped up arcade made to resemble Andy's favorite hangout. It is packed full of video games.

Jim Henson's Muppet™ Vision 3-D is a highly enjoyable, slapstick 3-D movie, starring the Muppets. The 25-minute show is a favorite with kids. Trombones, cars, and rocks launch themselves at you out of the screen; they are so realistic that children often grasp the air expecting to touch something. A full Muppet orchestra plays music in a pit. Audio-Animatronic characters and the excellent special effects, such as a cannon blowing holes in the walls of the theater, enhance the show's impact.

Visitors on an exhilarating ride through the Catastrophe Canyon, Disney-MGM Studios Backlot Tour

A giant ant at the Honey, I Shrunk the Kids Movie Set Adventure

ECHO LAKE

The interest here is focused on three shows and one thrill ride. Children also enjoy the sight of Gertie, the great green dinosaur, which houses an ice cream stand. The shows reveal the tricks of the film and TV trade.

In a nice change of pace, the audio portion of Hollywood's "magic" is given its due with the whimsical film **Sounds Dangerous – Starring Drew Carey**. Popular comedian/actor Drew Carey is a police detective who goes undercover with a hidden camera that keeps losing its picture, but never its sound. In an innovative twist, part of the film – about seven continuous minutes – takes place in complete darkness, leaving the audience with only the headphones to help them imagine what is going on.

The 12-minute pre-show is pure Muppet mischief. Here you will see Kermit and Miss Piggy at their best. In addition, the actual 3-D movie – hosted by Audio-Animatronic Statler and Waldorf – is full of playful comedy for all ages.

If you've got young children, don't miss the imaginative **Honey, I Shrunk the Kids Movie Set Adventure**. Everything is larger than life in this playground that is specifically designed for the younger set

to burn off their excess energy. As you enter, you are surrounded by 30-ft (9-m) high blades of grass, a slide made from a roll of film, and an ant the size of a pony. The huge tunnels, slides, giant spiders, and other props keep children amused for hours. Since the area is not very large, the playground can get very crowded, and it's a good idea to head for it early. Due to its popularity, parents find it difficult to get kids to leave.

Nearby, the **Academy of Television Arts and Sciences Hall of Fame** features the likenesses of many television legends, who have been honored for their outstanding achievements either in front of or behind the camera.

The storyline of the sensational ride **Star Tours** is based on the *Star Wars* films. Your spaceship, a flight simulator similar to those used to train astronauts, takes

An explosive scene from the Lights, Motors, Action!™ Extreme Stunt Show, Streets of America

a wrong turn and then has to evade meteors and fight in an inter-galactic battle. The craft's movements synchronize perfectly with the action on screen, adding to the illusion.

The large-scale show **Indiana Jones™ Epic Stunt Spectacular!** re-creates well-known scenes from the *Indiana Jones* movies to deliver lots of big bangs as well as daredevil feats to thrill the audience. Death-defying stuntmen leap between buildings as they avoid sniper fire, sudden explosions, and dangerous traps. As an educational sideline, the stunt director and real stunt doubles demonstrate how some of the action sequences are realized. Try to arrive early if you want to take part as an extra in the show.

Surrounding Echo Lake are many eating spots that have been designed to look like sets from films.

EATING & DRINKING

It is definitely worth going through the trouble of making a reservation at one of the full-service restaurants at Disney-MGM Studios, though more for their atmosphere than their food. You can reserve a table by calling *(see p77)*, or by going directly to the Dining Reservation Booth, at the crossroads of Hollywood and Sunset boulevards, or to the restaurants themselves.

The exclusive and costly Hollywood Brown Derby replicates the Original Brown Derby in Hollywood, where the stars met in the 1930s – right down to the celebrities' caricatures on the walls and the house specialties of Cobb Salad and grapefruit cake. Kids usually prefer the Sci-Fi Dine-In Theater Restaurant, a 1950s drive-in where customers sit in mini-Cadillacs to watch old science-fiction movies, while munching on popcorn, burgers, and sandwiches. In the 50's Prime Time Café, you are served in 1950s kitchens with the TV tuned to period sitcoms; the food – which includes items such as meatloaf, pot roast, fried chicken, and milk shakes – is homey. Adults in search of beverages can visit the Tune-In Lounge next door.

The best place to eat without a reservation is the self-service Art Deco-themed cafeteria Hollywood & Vine, where you can choose from a varied buffet that includes pasta, salads, seafood, ribs, and steaks. It also has an excellent selection of desserts. The recently opened Mama Melrose's Ristorante Italiano serves pizza, pasta, seafood, and other favorites in a typical Italian diner environment.

RIDES, SHOWS & TOURS CHECKLIST

This chart is designed to help you plan what to visit at Disney-MGM Studios. The rides, shows, and tours are listed alphabetically within each area.

		WAITING TIME	HEIGHT/AGE RESTRICTION	BEST TIME TO RIDE /ATTEND	FASTPASS	MAY CAUSE MOTION SICKNESS	OVERALL RATING
	HOLLYWOOD BOULEVARD						
R	**THE GREAT MOVIE RIDE**	○		Any			◆
	SUNSET BOULEVARD						
R	**ROCK 'N' ROLLER® COASTER STARRING AEROSMITH**	●	4 ft	➤11	➡	✓	◆
R	**THE TWILIGHT ZONE TOWER OF TERROR™**	●	3 ft 4 in	➤11	➡	✓	★
S	**BEAUTY AND THE BEAST – LIVE ON STAGE**	◗					◆
S	**FANTASMIC!**	●					◆
	ANIMATION COURTYARD						
S	**PLAYHOUSE DISNEY – LIVE ON STAGE!**	◗		Any			▼
S	**VOYAGE OF THE LITTLE MERMAID**	●		Any	➡		◆
T	**MAGIC OF DISNEY ANIMATION**	◗		Any			◆
	MICKEY AVENUE						
S	**WALT DISNEY: ONE MAN'S DREAM**	◗					▼
S	**WHO WANTS TO BE A MILLIONAIRE – PLAY IT!**	◗		Any	➡		▼
T	**DISNEY-MGM STUDIOS BACKLOT TOUR**	○		Any			★
	STREETS OF AMERICA						
S	**JIM HENSON'S MUPPET™ VISION 3-D**	●		Any			★
S	**LIGHTS, MOTORS, ACTION!™ – EXTREME STUNT SHOW**	●		➤11	➡		★
	ECHO LAKE		3 ft 4 in				
R	**STAR TOURS**	◗		➤11	➡	✓	★
S	**INDIANA JONES™ EPIC STUNT SPECTACULAR!**	●		Any			◆
S	**SOUNDS DANGEROUS – STARRING DREW CAREY**	◗		Any			▼

Key: Ride – R Show – S Tour – T; Waiting Times Short – ○ Average – ◗ Long – ●; Overall Rating Good – ▼ Excellent – ◆ Outstanding – ★; Time to Ride: Anytime – Any Before 11am – ➤11

Disney's Animal Kingdom® ❹

While the other Disney theme parks host a healthy collection of fish, birds, and other examples of nature, Disney's Animal Kingdom practically overflows with life and nature in all its forms. Quixotically, it is both the largest of the theme parks – five times the size of Magic Kingdom – and yet the easiest to cover, since a large portion of that extra space is accessible only by safari tour. Children and adults find great delight in the never-ending array of animals and exotic landscapes and architecture, both real and mythical, but teens and other thrill seekers have tended to find the rides too few and far-between for their tastes. To make the park a more enticing prospect for this group of visitors, it now features an exciting new attraction, Expedition Everest – opened in 2006. A thrilling high-speed train adventure, set in a reproduction of the mighty Himalayas, it offers thrills galore.

Carvings on the bark of The Tree of Life in Discovery Island®

TACKLING THE PARK

The park is divided into seven Lands: The Oasis, Discovery Island, Dinoland USA, Camp Minnie-Mickey, Africa, Asia, and Rafiki's Planet Watch. Navigation within the park is quite different from other parks. When you first pass through the turnstiles, you enter **The Oasis** – a foliage-festooned area offering several routes to the park's central hub, Safari Village. The Oasis contains many little surprises, most of which are missed by visitors who race through to reach the attractions. Time spent waiting quietly at the various habitats will be well-rewarded. The park has a strong emphasis on leisurely walks – with dozens of semi-hidden nature paths and byways filled with scenic views – and shows rather than rides, but

the rides Animal Kingdom does have are all outstanding and get very crowded.

There's plenty for young children to enjoy as well, with three areas of the park more or less dedicated to the little ones. If you love animals or are interested in conservation issues, this park is a heaven on earth, but time is needed to really absorb the experience – this is not a place for hurried tourists seeking quick excitement. Keep your camera charged and loaded – you'll want to take lots of stunning pictures.

DISCOVERY ISLAND®

As you emerge into the open space of the village, **The Tree of Life** looms – this is a massive, 14-story structure

that is the signature landmark of the park. It holds sway over a pageant of brightly colored shop fronts and a multitude of pools and gardens, each holding a variety of wildlife. The main shops, baby care, and first aid post all face The Tree of Life. Embedded in the tree and of endless fascination and

TOP TIPS

• *Upon entering the park, ignore The Tree of Life for now and head directly to the back of the park in order to get a Fastpass for the safaris, as they are often gone by early afternoon.*

• *Don't overlook the Oasis Exhibits in your rush to get to the rides and shows – children will be enthralled by being so close to the animals, and there's plenty of educational opportunity both here and in the DinoLand USA portion of the park.*

• *Too many tourists ignore the trails and treks throughout the park, but they are essential to a full enjoyment of Animal Kingdom and an integral part of the design philosophy of the creators. In addition to being well-stocked with wildlife, the vistas and greenery are amazingly beautiful and make for great photography.*

• *The dinosaur bones of Dino-Sue and inside the DINOSAUR ride are painstakingly exact replicas of real dinosaurs excavated in South Dakota, and the waiting room of the DINOSAUR ride is a wonderfully detailed simulation of the layers of the earth's crust.*

The It's Tough to be a Bug® show in Discovery Island®

The popular DINOSAUR ride, which brings dinosaurs back to life

TOP 10 ATTRACTIONS

1. KILIMANJARO SAFARIS®
2. FESTIVAL OF THE LION KING
3. IT'S TOUGH TO BE A BUG®
4. KALI RIVER RAPIDS®
5. DINOSAUR
6. TARZAN™ ROCKS!
7. FLIGHTS OF WONDER
8. PRIMEVAL WHIRL®
9. TRICERATOP SPIN
10. MICKEY'S JAMMIN' JUNGLE PARADE

delight to visitors are over 325 carvings or other images of various animals. While waiting in line for the shows or character greetings, children in particular spend time trying to identify them all. Under its branches lie the bridges that cross to the other Lands and within the trunk itself is the **It's Tough to be a Bug®** show. Held in a stunningly detailed "underground" theater, this 3-D film and sensory experience is one of the finest in the whole of Walt Disney World and not to be missed. Hosted by Flik and featuring many of the characters from Disney and Pixar's hit film *A Bug's Life*, the show combines animatronics and sensory enhancement to heighten the realism of the computer-animated 3-D. The show cleverly plays on our natural fear of insects and the audience is generally kept alternating between laughter and repulsion; the delightfully creepy finale keeps the crowd laughing right out the door.

DINOLAND USA®

This land is a mixed bag of children's play areas, rides, and serious exhibits of dinosaur artifacts. Fans of dinosaur lore will enjoy the actual dinosaur skeletons that lead you to the popular ride **DINOSAUR**, in which guests board a mobile motion simulator that travels back in time and bucks and weaves violently, trying to avoid carnivorous dinosaurs. Very young children may find the ride, which is mostly in the dark, quite scary. The pre-show is an excellent opportunity to educate yourself on Earth's past. The recreated layers of sedimentary soil and rock provide an insight into the history of the planet, and is accompanied by occasional narration from science entertainer Bill Nye.

Younger children will get a lot more fun, and dizziness, out of the carnival atmosphere of the outdoor rides, including the **Primeval Whirl®** and the **TriceraTop Spin**, a roller coaster with spinning cars. There's also **The Boneyard**, a playground where children can dig for dinosaur bones. For all-round family entertainment, the featured show in Dinoland USA is the **Tarzan™ Rocks!** extravaganza. This show is loud, rockin', and filled with stunts and songs that will impress. It has absolutely nothing to do with dinosaurs; however, children will be so taken with the in-line skaters, the gymnastic and aerialist stunts, and the high-energy performances of the singers, dancers, and musicians that it is very likely they won't care.

The thrilling Primeval Whirl® ride at Dinoland USA®

TOP TIPS

• *Check the start times of the Festival of the Lion King and Flights of Wonder – the times vary. See the attractions that run continously after you check out these scheduled shows.*
• *The Wildlife Express Train is a great way to get between Africa (on the northwest side of the park) and Rafiki's Planet Watch (on the northeast side). This ride is very relaxing in the hotter hours of the day.*

CAMP MINNIE-MICKEY

Designed primarily for guests to meet Disney characters, this Land also has the park's two live stage productions. Lines for the **Camp Minnie-Mickey Greeting Trails** – at the end of which the youngsters get to meet with the characters – can, predictably, become very long and sometimes become entwined with the lines for the stage shows.

A very popular show, and hands-down the finest live-action show in the whole of Walt Disney World, the **Festival of the Lion King** encourages cheering and singing like no other. Exceptionally well-choreographed and costumed, this colorful spectacle is one of the most elaborate shows to be performed outside Broadway. Particularly now that the theater is fully enclosed and

air conditioned, it's a must-not-miss attraction that is best seen at the beginning or the end of the day, though be prepared for wait times that are exceptionally long.

Pocohontas and Her Forest Friends lacks the punch of the Festival of the Lion King but is a favorite with little girls. The music is pleasant enough but the general feel is somewhat sugary. The theater is small and lines frequently long.

A daily parade that winds through the park, **Mickey's Jammin' Jungle Parade** brings a menagerie of abstract animal images to life in the form of towering animated puppets in fun costumes. Elaborate rickshaw taxis put selected guests in the middle of the parade, while party patrols of "animals" interact with guests and invite them to sing along with the music.

AFRICA

Entered through the village of Harambe, Africa is the largest of the Lands. The architecture is closely modelled on a Kenyan village and conceals Disney cleanliness behind a façade of simple, run-down buildings and wobbly telegraph poles.

The **Kilimanjaro Safaris®** is the park's busiest attraction, though it gets quieter in the afternoon. Guests board open sided trucks driven into an astonishing replica of the East

Lions and rhinos, to be glimpsed on Kilimanjaro Safaris®

African landscape. During this 20-minute drive over mud holes and creaking bridges you have the opportunity to see many African animals including hippos, rhinos, lions, and elephants, all roaming apparently free and undisturbed. It isn't unusual for a white rhino to get close enough to sniff the truck.

Affording an excellent opportunity to see gorillas close up, the **Pangani Forest Exploration Trail®** leads visitors into a world of streams and splashing waterfalls. It can get rather congested with guests exiting the safaris. The trail gets less busy in the late afternoon and you can actually spend some time watching the animals. The pleasant Wildlife Express, a re-creation of the African train system, takes you to **Rafiki's Planet**

Visitors savoring the sights of a re-created East African landscape on Kilimanjaro Safaris®

EATING & DRINKING

Disney's Animal Kingdom has only one full-service restaurant, the Rainforest Café near the entrance of the park, so reservations are a must. Character dining takes place at the amusing Restaurantosaurus, an all-you-can-eat buffet. Restaurantosaurus also features a full McDonald's. On opposite sides of Discovery Island are Pizzafari and the Flame Tree Barbecue lunch restaurants, while Africa boasts the Tusker House Restaurant. Asia offers only snack stands, which are also located throughout the other areas of the park. Feeding the animals or throwing coins in the water supplies is strongly discouraged.

The swirling water adventure ride, Kali River Rapids®

Watch, which features two educational programs, Conservation Station and Habitat Habit, and Affection Section, a shaded petting yard.

ASIA

This land features gibbons, exotic birds, and tigers set in a re-creation of post-Colonial Indian ruins. **Kali River Rapids®** offers you a chance to get completely drenched. This short ride presents some of the most striking and detailed surroundings in the park, which you may miss as yet

another wave saturates the parts still merely damp. Tapirs, Komodo dragons, and giant fruit bats can be found on the **Maharaja Jungle Trek**, the climax of which is undoubtedly the magnificent Bengal tiger roaming the palace ruins. Through glazed walled sections of the palace, you can get within arm's length of the tigers.

A campy, funny show with an unexpected amount of thrills, the **Flights of Wonder** showcases exceedingly beautiful birds demonstrating natural behavior with polished trainers and a clever "story." Be aware that the

birds fly extremely low and so graze the tops of the audience's heads, but ducking down just causes the birds to fly even lower.

Opened in 2006, **Expedition Everest** involves a high-speed train bound for Mount Everest, which takes passengers on a daring ride over rugged terrain and along icy slopes. The ride incorporates both roller coaster thrills and yeti mystique.

RIDES, SHOWS & TOURS CHECKLIST

This chart is designed to help you plan what to visit at Animal Kingdom. The major rides, shows, and tours are listed alphabetically within each area.

		WAITING TIME	HEIGHT/AGE RESTRICTION	BEST TIME TO RIDE/ATTEND	FASTPASS	MAY CAUSE MOTION SICKNESS	OVERALL RATING
	DISCOVERY ISLAND®						
S	IT'S TOUGH TO BE A BUG®	○		Any	➡		◆
	DINOLAND USA®						
R	DINOSAUR	➤	3 ft 4 in	Any	➡	✓	▼
R	PRIMEVAL WHIRL®	●	4 ft	➤11	➡	✓	◆
R	TRICERATOP SPIN	●		➤11		✓	★
S	TARZAN™ ROCKS!	➤		Any			◆
	AFRICA	➤		Any			◆
R	KILIMANJARO SAFARIS®	●		Any	➡	✓	★
T	PANGANI FOREST EXPLORATION TRAIL®	●		Any			◆
	ASIA			Any			
R	KALI RIVER RAPIDS®	➤	3 ft 2 in	Any	➡	✓	★
S	FLIGHTS OF WONDER	➤		Any			★
T	MAHARAJA JUNGLE TREK®	●		Any			◆
	CAMP MINNIE-MICKEY	●		Any			★
S	CAMP MINNIE-MICKEY GREETING TRAILS	●		Any			◆
S	FESTIVAL OF THE LION KING	➤		Any			★
S	POCOHONTAS AND HER FOREST FRIENDS	➤		➤11			▼

Key: Ride – R Show – S Tour – T; Waiting Time Short – ○ Average – ➤ Long – ●; Time to Ride: Anytime – Any Before 11am – ➤11; Overall Rating Good – ▼ Excellent – ◆ Outstanding – ★

Water Parks

Walt Disney World features two of the best water parks in the world, including the second-largest on record. A third water park, River Country – the first to be built in Walt Disney World – is now closed. While playing second fiddle to the major theme parks of the resort, the water parks manage to attract huge numbers of visitors, particularly during the hot summer months.

Typhoon Lagoon bears only a pretense of a theme, a whimsical pirate/nautical motif that features everything from thrilling slides to winding rapids to gentle rivers. Apart from the chance to snorkel with real sharks and other fish, it's a normal water park, only Disney-fied. On the other hand, Disney's Blizzard Beach is a wonderful working "flooded ski resort" that throws visitors into a "failed" winter wonderland and substitutes flumes and slides for skis and toboggans. This truly clever idea keeps the area covered in "snow" but with nice warm water almost all year round.

Sliding down Mount Gushmore at Blizzard Beach

A watery game of hide-and-seek in progress at Blizzard Beach

BLIZZARD BEACH **5**

During a "freak" winter storm – or so the legend goes – an entire section of the Disney property was buried under a pile of powdery snow. Disney Imagineers quickly set to work, building Florida's first ski resort, complete with ski lifts, toboggan runs, and a breathtaking ski slope. However, the snow started to melt quickly, and the Disney people thought all was lost until they spotted an alligator snowboarding himself down the mountainside. In a flash, they reinvented the ski resort as a water/ski park, Blizzard Beach; they turned luge runs into slides and the mountain into the world's longest and highest flume, and created creeks for inner-tube enthusiasts to paddle around in.

The centerpiece of Blizzard Beach is the 120-ft (36-m) high **Summit Plummet**, which rockets particularly brave visitors at speeds of over 60 mph (96 km/h). Incredibly popular with teens, it's too intense for children – you must be at least 4 ft (1.2 m) tall to ride it.

The Slush Gusher and Toboggan Racer are similar, but less frightening, water slides. There's also the Snow Stormers flumes and Downhill Double Dipper racing slides, a favorite with families.

The thrills continue with the **Teamboat Springs** white-water raft ride, a rollicking race through choppy waters that lasts far longer than you'd expect but leaves you wanting more anyway. The Runoff Rapids is another speedy trip through harrowing waterways, this time in an inner tube.

For those with a more relaxed agenda, there is the lovely chair lift to carry you up the side of **Mount Gushmore**, where you can go rock-climbing or hiking. Or you may choose to lazily float around the entire park by tubing down Cross Country Creek, enjoy the pool area called Melt-Away Bay, or take a slide down the mild Cool Runners.

Kids' areas include the Blizzard Beach Ski Patrol Training Camp, aimed at older children, and Tike's Peak for the little ones.

TOP TIPS

• Blizzard Beach and Typhoon Lagoon have their own, free, parking lots; Winter Summerland shares the Blizzard Beach lot. You don't need to wait for Disney transportation if you've got a vehicle – you can drive to the water parks and park right there.

Swimmers head almost straight down Summit Plummet

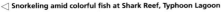

◁ **Snorkeling amid colorful fish at Shark Reef, Typhoon Lagoon**

TYPHOON LAGOON ❻

This water park offers less in the way of man-made thrills and more natural excitement, though it features some traditional water park favorites as well. Where Blizzard Beach trades on its novelty, Typhoon Lagoon revels in natural beauty and sealife encounters, and boasts a surf pool that is one of the world's largest, at 650,000 cu ft (18,406 cu m). The motif of this park is that of a shipwreck – the "Miss Tilly" which got caught in a storm so severe it landed on the peak of **Mount Mayday** – in a tropical paradise.

At the top of Mount Mayday are three whitewater raft rides of varying intensity – the thrilling Gang Plank Falls, the incredibly high and wild Mayday Falls, or the relatively tame Keelhaul Falls.

Also on Mount Mayday are the body-slide rides known collectively as Humunga-Kowabunga. Great fun but highly intimidating, these rides involve falls of roughly 50 ft (15 m) at speeds of 30 mph (48 km/h) almost straight down. The Storm Slides offer three flumes that go twisting and turning inside the mountain itself.

The newest addition to Typhoon Lagoon is Crush 'n' Gusher, in which torrents of gushing water take the most daring of raft riders on a

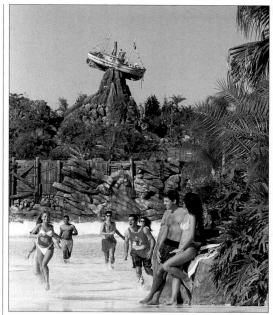

The Wave Pool, with "Miss Tilly" in the background

gravity-defying adventure through twisting caverns.

More relaxing is the powerful **Wave Pool** which offers 6-ft (1.8-m) high waves alternating with gentler periods. The other peaceful attraction is the meandering, relaxing, and stunningly beautiful **Castaway Creek**, where you can inner-tube your troubles away for what seems like forever. Children

can spend many happy hours at the aquatic playground, Ketchakiddee Creek, and the smaller wave pools. Of special note is the **Shark Reef**, where visitors can either observe tropical fish and live, small sharks from an "overturned freighter" or grab a snorkel and mask and swim with them. It is perfectly safe and offers lovely views of incredibly colorful sealife.

Getting up close and personal with sealife at Shark Reef

WINTER SUMMERLAND

Although Fantasia Gardens, on Buena Vista Drive, was the first themed mini-golf park on Disney property, Winter Summerland is unique in that it continues the motifs of the neighboring water parks, Blizzard Beach and Typhoon Lagoon, but adds a Christmas twist, with two elaborately-designed 18-hole courses – the Winter and Summer courses. The two courses were supposedly built by St. Nick's elves, who were divided into two camps – those who missed the North Pole and those who preferred the Florida heat.

Both courses feature plenty of interactive elements and are surprisingly challenging. Generally the most popular, the Winter Course is widely perceived as being slightly easier, with "snow" and holiday elements abounding. A few of the holes on each course are identical except for the substitution of sand for snow on the Summer holes. The Summer Course features surfboards, water sprays, and other tropical obstacles, including a sand-buried snoozing Santa. The two courses converge for the final two holes in a log cabin-style lodge.

Disney Cruise Line®

With a cruise line that offers two gorgeous, larger-than-average ships, private destinations, and an all-inclusive fare, Disney World, in 1998, extended its reach to the high seas of the Caribbean. In addition to the popular three- and four-night trips, there are now extended itineraries available to passengers, which offer more island ports and longer duration cruises. Disney's Cruise Line has a pair of powerful incentives no other cruise line can match: apart from its outstanding reputation for quality and comfort, it offers vacations that include stays at Walt Disney World as part of the total package.

A Disney Cruise Line® ship docked at a pier

A Disney Cruise Line® ship at Castaway Cay

THE SHIPS & THE DESTINATION

The two disney cruise ships, the **Disney Magic** and the **Disney Wonder**, have staterooms that are around 25 percent larger than those of most other cruise ships. The usual modern styling of most other ships are replaced with the stately elegance of European vessels of old, with an Art Deco theme for the Magic and Art Nouveau for the Wonder.

Dining in style at Palo restaurant aboard a Disney ship

Both ships offer theater, restaurants, spas, and fitness centers among several other amenities. **Castaway Cay**, Disney's own private island, is the end point of every Disney cruise, and is very much a tropical extension of Walt Disney World's hotels and resorts. There are uncrowded beaches, snorkeling, bicycling, glass-bottom boat tours, watersports, and much more on offer. In addition, there is always plenty to do for children on board and off – so much so that you may see very little of them during your trip.

THE SHORT (THREE–FOUR NIGHT) CRUISES

The itinerary on the shorter cruises for both ships is the same – after arriving at Port Canaveral by charter bus and checking in, you cast off and arrive in Nassau in the Bahamas the next day. The following day you arrive at Castaway Cay, and leave there in the evening to return to Canaveral at 9am the

following morning. The four-night cruise adds a day at sea with the occasional stop in Freeport before returning to Port Canaveral.

THE LONG (SEVEN–TEN NIGHT) CRUISES

Disney offers both an Eastern Caribbean and a Western Caribbean tour for their longer cruises, which include stops in St. Maarten and St. Thomas in addition to Castaway Cay for the eastern cruise, or Grand Cayman and Cozumel along with Castaway Cay for the western cruise. Plans are afoot for additional seven-night tours as well as a 10-night cruise that includes stops in Antigua, San Juan, St. Lucia, and Key West.

TOP TIPS

• Keep in mind that the all-inclusive fare does not include things such as tips for servers, stateroom hostess, assistant server, and head server. Other additional charges are for soft drinks at the pool, and alcoholic beverages. There is a $10 per person charge for eating in the adults-only specialty restaurant. Shore excursions are also extra significant charges – port charges as well as government taxes are added to the fee.

• It is a good idea to plan ahead for shore excursions to avoid waiting in a line to sign up for them once on the ship and taking a chance. You can log on to the website (see p77) to sign up for shore excursions.

Fort Wilderness Resort & Campground ➐

A campground would seem to be at odds with the provide-every-luxury mentality of most Disney World accommodations, but Fort Wilderness, which opened in 1971, still represents one of Walt Disney's aims – to foster an appreciation of nature and the outdoors. Located on Bay Lake in the Magic Kingdom resort area, it has more than 750 shaded campsites and over 400 cabins to provide various levels of "roughing it." While wildlife is fairly sparse in this area, amenities and even entertainment are plentiful. The center of Fort Wilderness is Pioneer Hall, home to several restaurants and the hugely popular dinner show, Hoop-De-Do Musical Revue *(see p75)*. There is convenient boat transportation to Magic Kingdom and motorcoach conveyance to all theme parks.

Riders enjoying a canter at Fort Wilderness Resort & Campground

A cabin at Disney's Fort Wilderness Resort & Campground

ACCOMMODATIONS & COMMUNITY AREAS

The campsites at Fort Wilderness are small but reasonably secluded, with electric and water "hookups" at all locations. All the cabins offer house-like comfort in confined quarters *(see p142).*

There are 15 air-conditioned "comfort stations" all around the campground, with facilities such as laundries, showers, telephones, and even ice machines, open 24 hours a day. Two "trading posts" offer groceries and rent out recreational equipment.

RECREATION

There is plenty to keep visitors happily occupied at Fort Wilderness Resort. The **Tri-Circle D Ranch** has two heated pools, guided horseback tours, and pony rides. Other recreational facilities include tennis, volleyball, and basketball courts, bike and boat rentals, fishing, an exercise trail, nightly wagon rides, horseshoes and shuffleboard, carriage rides, a petting zoo, and video arcades. You can also opt for skiing, parasailing, and wakeboarding. Equipment is usually available for rental. Reservations are required for the guided tours on horseback or for fishing.

In addition, Fort Wilderness offers a **Campfire** program with singalongs and outdoor movies. Available to all Disney guests – and not just Fort Wilderness residents – the program features an hour of singalongs complete with toasted marshmallows and the American delicacy "smores" – melted marshmallow and chocolate on graham crackers. Hosted in part by the Disney chipmunks Chip 'n' Dale, the singalong leads into the screening of a Disney animated feature. An additional attraction is the nighttime **Electrical Water Pageant** *(see p75)*, which goes by Fort Wilderness Resort at 9:45pm. There is a nice all-you-can-eat breakfast buffet at Pioneer Hall.

SPORTS AT WALT DISNEY WORLD

Besides Fort Wilderness, all Disney resorts have sports and fitness facilities, though available only for residents. In 1997, **Disney's Wide World of Sports**® complex was opened, primarily as a training camp and athletic haven for exhibition games, Olympic training, and other recreational activities *(see p178)*. While the DWWS experience is largely passive, the same cannot be said for what is Disney's most "hands-on" experience to date: **The Richard Petty Driving Experience** *(see p177)*, where visitors can train and become NASCAR-style race car drivers, actually driving real race cars at speeds in excess of 100 mph (161 km/h) around a race track. Unlike most Disney experiences, you are in full control of the vehicle. These cars boast over 600 horsepower engines so the thrill is most decidedly real. As might be expected, safety instruction takes top billing for this sport.

Downtown Disney® ⑧

Shopping, fine dining, exciting shows, and concerts and dancing 'til the last club closes at 2am, are on offer at Downtown Disney, giving visitors plenty to do at Walt Disney World Resort after the theme parks have closed. Three distinct areas collectively make up Downtown Disney – the Marketplace, a lovely outdoor mall; West Side, featuring stores, eateries, and concert venues; and the centerpiece of late-night Disney, Pleasure Island, a floating non-stop party complete with clubs, shows, and fireworks. Downtown Disney offers free parking, and the West Side and Marketplace areas have no charge for admission. Pleasure Island, which doesn't open until 7pm, requires separate admission unless you have the Ultimate Park Hopper or Park Hopper Plus passes (*see p76*); you must be at least 18 – or 21 for some venues – to enter. DisneyQuest, a five-story "indoor interactive theme park," also charges separate admission, except for Ultimate Park Hopper and Premium Annual pass holders. Buses run almost continually to the on-property resort hotels.

Fireworks at Pleasure Island in Downtown Disney®

PLEASURE ISLAND

This ultimate party zone consists mainly of eight nightclubs, each with a different theme. By far the most relaxing and surprising one is the **Adventurers Club**, which is more like a performance-art piece than a nightclub. Visitors walk into the year 1937 and a stately, exquisitely decorated British gentlemen's club where they are recruited as "new members." Club activities may involve a "radio broadcast" or a "balderdash" storytelling competition. There are odd surprises at every turn, from talking exotic masks to bar stools that raise and lower themselves.

Another all-time favorite is **The Comedy Warehouse,** which hosts hourly improvised comedy shows. The innovative decor of the club consists of "retired" Disney signage.

The most popular of the music clubs is **Mannequins Dance Palace**, which offers up-to-date music and DJs spinning the mostly electronica/techno rhythms alongside a stunningly elaborate light show. **Motion** is squarely aimed at the younger crowd and goes for the most popular sounds straight from the Top 40, played deafeningly loud. Older visitors can relive the rock era by visiting the **Rock 'n' Roll Beach Club**, which offers live bands re-creating the reliable crowd-pleasing hits of yesterday and today. The disco era is the theme of **8 Trax**, an accurate representation of 1970s styles and music. The **BET Soundstage Club** requires patrons to be 21 and up, and plays the latest hip-hop, reggae, and R&B music. Live entertainment can be found at the **Raglan Road Irish Pub and Restaurant**, which features authentic Irish food, drink, and music. There is a handful of shops on the island as well as a bevy of live street performers and outdoor stages, plus a daily New Year's Street Party, with a concert, countdown, and fireworks display at midnight.

WEST SIDE

Each store, restaurant, or business on Downtown Disney's West Side has a unique feel to it, making for a splendid evening's exploring. Among the do-not-miss shops are the gigantic **Virgin Megastore**, selling music, books, and paraphernalia; the **Magnetron** shop, with magnets and similar kitschy items; the **Magic Masters** trick shop, which features continuous live magic demonstrations; and the **Candy Cauldron** where sweets are made on the spot. There's also the state-of-the-art stadium-seating **AMC 24 Theatres**.

Full-service restaurants here include the popular Cuban and Latin fare of **Bongos Cuban Café**, the gourmet entrées of the upstairs **Wolfgang Puck's Café**, the Southern US cuisine of the **House of Blues** restaurant, and the American food

Downtown Disney® West Side glittering in the evening

Pirates of the Caribbean: Battle for Buccaneer Gold at DisneyQuest®

reality "rides" – you wear a special helmet with glasses – such as **Aladdin's Magic Carpet Ride**, **Ride the Comix**, and **Invasion!**, along with the two-man shooter rides such as **Pirates of the Caribbean: Battle for Buccaneer Gold.**

MARKETPLACE

An open-air mall with some excellent shops and a good variety of restaurants, the Marketplace makes for a relaxing walk when you're not pressed for time. Among the highlights, especially for children, is the **LEGO Imagination Center**, which features photo-op displays of wonderful LEGO con-structions, from a spaceship to a dragon in the pond next to the store. Also of interest to kids will be the **Once Upon a Toy** and **Disney's Days of Christmas** stores. Kids and adults alike will be awed by the sheer size of the **World of Disney** emporium, the largest Disney memorabilia store in the world and the "mother lode" for all Disney souvenirs. Restaurants include the colorful **Rainforest Café**, **Fulton's Crab House** with its superb seafood and riverboat ambience, and **Ghirardelli's Soda Fountain & Chocolate Shop** with its malt-shop atmosphere. Quick bites can be found at **Cap'n Jack's** floating restaurant and the **McDonald's**, **Wolfgang Puck Express**, and **Earl of Sandwich** chain eateries.

of movie-memorabilia-studded **Planet Hollywood**. Quick bites can be obtained from **Wetzel's Pretzels**, fea-turing hot pretzels and cold Häagen-Dazs ice cream, and the lower level of Wolfgang Puck's Café, which serves brick-oven pizzas and salads. The West Side has three special attractions that require separate admissions: the House of Blues concert hall – part of the national chain, which attracts major music acts – the **Cirque du Soleil®** show **La Nouba™**, and the electronic funhouse called **DisneyQuest®**.

In addition to regular shows by national artists – with a side stage for smaller acts – the House of Blues offers a Sunday Gospel Brunch that features live

La Nouba™ show
at Cirque du Soleil®

gospel performers showing off their uniquely American religious singing. The Cirque du Soleil show, which is a theatrical production based on a circus, is so popular that it is always sold out. This fabulous show has 64 performers on stage at the same time, performing a variety of gym-nastic feats. Reservations are a must. DisneyQuest is extremely popular with teens and younger kids and features state-of-the-art video arcades, virtual reality experiences, and other computer-driven and 3-D "interactivities" along with an assortment of traditional arcade games such as Skee-ball. Among the best of the various "zone" offerings are the virtual

AFTER DARK EVENTS

Apart from the Downtown Disney attractions, other prime after-dark entertainment includes **dinner shows** and the **Electrical Water Pageant**. A floating parade that wanders around park resorts such as Polynesian and Contemporary, the Electrical Water Pageant is best viewed from the unob-structed beach in Fort Wilderness. This kids' favorite show-cases 20 minutes of dazzling electrical animation – dolphins jumping out of the water, whales swimming by, even a fire-breathing dragon. Around since 1971, it often serves as an opening act or postscript for the Magic Kingdom and Epcot fireworks. Disney's two long-running dinner shows, Hoop-Dee-Doo Musical Revue and Disney's Spirit of Aloha, should not tempt visitors to leave the theme parks early but they are still enjoyable. The first is a popular Western comedy show at Fort Wilderness' Pioneer Hall; the second features authen-tic Polynesian music, dance, and food. Another show, Mickey's Backyard BBQ, provides country 'n' western fun.

The superbly constructed LEGO
dinosaur at the Marketplace

Essential Information

Spread over a large area of 47 sq miles (121 sq km) and brimming with attractions, Walt Disney World® Resort can provide entertainment for the whole family for at least a week. Guests who do not have much holiday time need to plan carefully to make the most of their visit to this dream vacationland. The information here is geared toward aiding them in this task.

WHEN TO VISIT

The busiest times of the year are Christmas, the last week of February until Easter, and June to August. At these times, the parks begin to approach capacity – some 90,000 people a day in Magic Kingdom alone. All the rides will be operating and the parks are open for longer periods. During off-season, 10,000 guests a day might visit the Magic Kingdom, only one water park may be operating, and certain attractions may be closed for maintenance. The weather is also a factor – in July and August, hot and humid afternoons are regularly punctuated by torrential thunderstorms. Between October and March, however, the temperatures and humidity are both more comfortable and permit a more energetic touring schedule.

BUSIEST DAYS

Each of the theme parks is packed on certain days. The busiest days are as follows: Magic Kingdom: Monday, Thursday, and Saturday. Epcot: Tuesday, Friday, and Saturday. Disney-MGM Studios: Wednesday and Sunday. Note, however, that after a thunderstorm, the water parks are often almost empty – even at the peak times of the year.

OPENING HOURS

When the theme parks are busiest, opening hours are the longest, typically 9am to 10–11pm or midnight. In less busy periods, hours are usually 9am to 6–8pm. Call to check. The parks open at least 30 minutes early for pass holders and guests at any of the WDW hotels and resorts.

LENGTH OF VISIT

To enjoy Walt Disney World to the full, you may want to give Magic Kingdom and Epcot two full days – or one and half days, with half a day at a water park – each, leaving a day for Disney-MGM Studios and Animal Kingdom. Set aside three nights to see Fantasmic!, IllumiNations, and Wishes firework displays.

THE IDEAL SCHEDULE

To avoid the worst of the crowds and the heat:
• Arrive as early as possible and visit the most popular attractions first.
• Take a break in the early afternoon, when it's hottest and the parks are full.
• Return to the parks in the cool of the evening to see parades and fireworks.

TICKETS & TYPES OF PASSES

There are several types of passes available for visitors. You can buy one- day, one-park tickets, but if you're staying for more than three days consider the **Park Hopper Pass**. This offers you one-day admission to each theme park on any four or five days. For most, one of these multi-day park hopper passes will suffice.

The **Park Hopper Plus** offers unlimited access to theme parks, water parks, and Pleasure Island on any five, six, or seven days.

However, one of the best passes is the **Ultimate Park Hopper Pass**, exclusively available to Disney hotel guests. It offers unlimited admission to theme parks, Pleasure Island, water parks, and the sports complex. Prices are determined by the length of your stay. Non-Disney guests visiting for more than ten days should consider the **Annual Pass** or the **Premium Annual Pass**, which costs little more than a seven-day Park Hopper. Separate Annual Passes are offered by the water parks, DisneyQuest, and Pleasure Island. Child ticket pricing applies to ages three through nine.

Passes are available at Disney stores, the airport, the Tourist Information Center on I-Drive, and the official Disney website. In addition, passes are sometimes included in package deals.

GETTING AROUND

An extensive, efficient transportation system handles an average of 200,000 guests each day. Even if you stay outside Walt Disney World Resort, many nearby hotels offer free shuttle services to and from the theme parks, but you can check this when you make your reservation.

The transportation hub of Walt Disney World is the **Ticket and Transportation Center (TTC)**. Connecting it to the Magic Kingdom are two monorail services. A third monorail links the TTC to Epcot. Ferries run from the TTC to the Magic Kingdom across the Seven Seas Lagoon.

Ferries connect the Magic Kingdom and Epcot with the resorts in their respective areas, while buses link everything in Walt Disney World, including direct links to the Magic Kingdom. All ticket holders can use the entire transportation system for free.

Although Disney transportation is efficient, you may wish to rent a car if you want to enjoy the entire area without inconvenience. The theme parks are spread out and, especially for visits to swimming attractions such as Blizzard Beach and Typhoon Lagoon, Disney transportation is not always the best option for children. Young children who are wet and tired from swimming will not welcome waiting for the Disney bus.

COPING WITH LINES

Lines tend to be shortest at the beginning and end of the day, and during parade and meal times. Lines for the rides move slowly, but the wait for a show is rarely longer than the show itself. The Fastpass (see p34) allows visitors to reserve time at 25 of the most popular attractions rather than wait in long lines. Disney parks fill rapidly after the first hour of opening. Until then, you can usually just walk onto rides for which you'll have to line up later.

DISABLED TRAVELERS

Wheelchairs can be borrowed at the park entrance and special bypass entrances allow disabled guests and carers to board rides without waiting in line. Staff, however, are not allowed to lift guests or assist with lifting for safety reasons.

VERY YOUNG CHILDREN

As Walt Disney World can be physically and emotionally tiring for children, try to adapt your schedule accordingly. If you've come with preschool-age kids, focus on Magic Kingdom.

The waiting and walking involved in a theme park visit can exhaust young children quickly so it's a good idea to rent a stroller, available at every park entrance. Each stroller is personalized when you rent it, but if it should go missing when you leave a ride, you can get a replacement with your rental receipt. Baby Care Centers for changing and feeding are located all around the parks.

In a system called "switching off," parents can enjoy a ride one at a time while the other parent stays with the child – without having to line up twice.

MEETING MICKEY

For many youngsters, the most exciting moment at WDW Resort is meeting the Disney characters. You will spot them in all the theme parks, but you can have more relaxed encounters in a number of restaurants, usually at breakfast. Each theme park and many of the resorts also offer "character dining," though you must call well ahead of time to make a reservation.

SAFETY

The resort's excellent safety record and first rate security force mean problems are rare and dealt with promptly. Cast members watch out for young unaccompanied children and escort them to lost children centers. Bags of all visitors are checked.

STAYING & DINING

Lodging in the Disney-run hotels and villa complexes is of a very high standard. However, even the lowest-priced places are more expensive than many hotels outside Walt Disney World. But do keep in mind that, apart from Disney quality, your money also buys:
• Early entry into the theme parks (up to 60 minutes).
• Guaranteed admission to the theme parks even when the parks are otherwise full.
• The delivery of shopping purchases made anywhere in Walt Disney World Resort.

For dining at any full-service restaurant in Walt Disney World, especially in Epcot, book a Priority Seating – the table booking equivalent of the Fastpass.

For more information, see pages 138–40 and 148–50.

PARKING

Visitors to Magic Kingdom must park at the TTC and make their way by tram or foot; Epcot, Disney-MGM Studios, and Animal Kingdom have their own parking lots. Parking is free for Disney resort residents – others must pay, but only once a day no matter how many times they move their vehicle. The lots are very large, so it's important to remember the character name and row of the section where you are parked.

DIRECTORY

GENERAL

General Information
Tel (407) 824-4321.
http://disneyworld.
disney.go.com/wdw/

Accommodation Information/ Reservation
Tel (407) 934-7639.

Dining Reservations (including Dinner Shows)
Tel (407) 939-3463.
Operational 7am–11pm Sat–Sun.

Disney Tours
Tel (407) 939-8687.

Golf Reservations
Tel (407) 939-4653.

THEME PARKS & ATTRACTIONS

Blizzard Beach
Tel (407) 560-3400.

Disney Cruise Line®
Tel (888) 325-2500.
www.disneytravelagents.com

Disney-MGM Studios
Tel (407) 824-4321.

Disney's Animal Kingdom®
Tel (407) 938-3000.

Disney's Wide World of Sports®
Tel (407) 828-3267.

Downtown Disney®
Tel (407) 828-3058.

Epcot®
Tel (407) 828-3058.

Fort Wilderness Resort & Campground
Tel (407) 824-2900.

Magic Kingdom®
Tel (407) 824-4321.

The Richard Petty Driving Experience
Tel (407) 939-0130.

Typhoon Lagoon
Tel (407) 560-4141.

ORLANDO'S OTHER THEME PARKS

With everything from roller coasters to performing killer whales, filmy fantasy to amazing shopping and dining experiences, the theme parks at Orlando provide endless entertainment options, and have catapulted the city into the ranks of the world's top vacation destinations. The pioneering effort was, of course, Walt Disney World in 1971; other parks quickly followed.

SeaWorld, the marine-based park, opened in 1973. With its range of educational and entertaining programs, the park brings visitors in close touch with whales, sea lions, manatees, and many other marine creatures. It also features sea-themed rides such as Kraken, one of the world's tallest and fastest floorless roller coasters. Located across from SeaWorld, Discovery Cove, which opened in 2001, is a tropical paradise where guests can swim with dolphins, snorkel with fish, and hand-feed exotic birds.

Universal Orlando, which came onto the scene in 1990 with the opening of its park, Universal Studios Florida, is going great guns. A lively entertainment venue, Universal CityWalk, followed in 1998; then came a second Universal theme park, Islands of Adventure. With its wildly exciting, high-tech rides and shows, based on blockbuster movies, Universal Orlando has emerged as serious competition to Disney. Another popular attraction is Wet 'n' Wild, the world's first water park in 1977, which now boasts a variety of thrill rides.

The theme parks are constantly evolving, with exciting areas and new, jazzy rides being added at regular intervals. For instance, SeaWorld recently opened The Waterfront, a 5-acre (2-ha) village suffused with the flavor and festivity of the most vibrant cities by the sea, while Universal Orlando's new Revenge of the Mummy ride showcases cutting-edge technology.

A mother-child pair of dolphins gamboling at Discovery Cove

◁ The 150-ft (46-m) high monster roller coaster, Kraken®, at SeaWorld® Orlando

Exploring Orlando's Other Theme Parks

Conveniently located in the area around International Drive *(see pp110–11)*, Universal Orlando, SeaWorld, Discovery Cove, and Wet 'n' Wild do not lag far behind Walt Disney World in the entertainment stakes. SeaWorld and Discovery Cove focus on the natural world with their beautifully re-created habitats that hold various creatures of the deep. SeaWorld's shows, such as Odyssea and Shamu Adventure, and its world-class rides provide plenty of excitement. The other two major theme venues are geared more toward older childen and adults. The water park Wet 'n' Wild is an out-and-out big-thrill rides experience, while Universal Orlando entices with two theme parks full of movie magic and amazing rides laden with special effects, as well as an exuberant entertainment district.

SIGHTS AT A GLANCE

Discovery Cove **2**
SeaWorld® Orlando **1**
Universal Orlando **3**
Wet 'n' Wild® **4**

Key West Dolphin Fest at SeaWorld® Orlando

Universal Orlando's Revenge of the Mummy – The Ride

SEE ALSO

- **Where to Stay** pp140–41

- **Where to Eat** pp150–51

GETTING AROUND

To the northeast of Walt Disney World, Orlando's other major theme parks are connected to each other and to Disney by I-4, the crucial artery of the Orlando region. Universal Orlando is at one end, situated off exits 29 and 30B from I-4. At the other end is Discovery Cove, across the road from SeaWorld, which is located at the intersection of I-4 and the Bee Line Expressway. Wet 'n Wild is situated off I-4, exit 75A.

Apart from the connections offered by the public bus service LYNX, there are private charters as well as free shuttle services provided by some hotels to the various theme parks. If you wish to cover a lot of ground in less time, the best option is to rent a car. However, keep in mind that I-4 is a high traffic zone. For more details, see pages 193–7.

KEY

	Interstate highway
	Major highway
	Secondary route
	Tourist Information

0 km   1

0 miles   1

A couple having fun at The Blast, a ride at Wet 'n' Wild®

SeaWorld® Orlando ●

In terms of scale and creativity, the world's most popular marine life adventure park is a match for any of Orlando's other theme parks. Opened in 1973, the park is home to thrilling rides as well as beautifully choreographed and flawlessly executed shows, including the highly popular Shamu Adventure show that stars Shamu, SeaWorld's mascot killer whale, and his many friends. Some attractions even allow you to touch or feed the marine life – an experience of a lifetime. The park also provides a platform for the promotion of educational, research, and conservation programs. Each presentation at the park illustrates ways and means by which people can protect and safeguard the environment and the wildlife that occupies it.

TACKLING THE PARK

Seaworld is usually less crowded than Orlando's other theme parks. Its gentler pace means that a visit after 3pm affords a cooler and less crowded experience. Try to set aside at least an entire day to cover all the attractions the park has to offer. Pick up a map from Guest Services, and plan your day. You can use the 400-ft (122-m) high Sky Tower as a point of reference while navigating the park.

Most of the presentations are walk-through exhibits or sit-down stadium shows. The stadiums seat so many that finding a good spot is seldom a problem. Bear in mind that if you sit near the front you may get wet. It is also worth noting that the shows are timed so that it's all but impossible to leave one show just in time for another. This is done to reduce crowding, but it is possible to get a seat in the Clyde and Seamore (Sea Lion and Otter) show if you leave the Shamu stadium about four minutes early – while all the performers are taking their bows at the end of the show.

During peak season, head for the Wild Arctic, Journey to Atlantis, Shark Encounter, and Kraken attractions early in the day as they get very crowded

later on and form long lines. Young children enjoy meeting the actors in furry suits who play the parts of Shamu and the crew – a killer whale, a penguin, a pelican, a dolphin, and an otter. They are usually found near the park's exit around closing time. SeaWorld also has several restaurants to choose from if you are hungry.

Tourists touching and feeding the friendly dolphins in a lagoon at Dolphin Cove®, Key West at SeaWorld®

Sea lions basking on the rocks at Pacific Point Preserve®

ANIMAL ATTRACTIONS

The meticulously designed habitats at SeaWorld offer a rare look at marine creatures, such as dolphins, penguins, and sharks, as they would be in their natural settings.

Key West at SeaWorld®

One of the park's most visited animal attractions, Key West at SeaWorld is a tropical paradise featuring animals of the Florida Keys. Spread over 5 acres (2 ha), the attraction's Dolphin Cove® and Stingray Lagoon® are home to several bottlenose dolphins and more than 200 stingrays. Guests can also experience the thrill of feeding and touching these animals. At Turtle Point®, various species of endangered and threatened sea turtles can be seen, and an underwater viewing area offers a peek at a beautiful coral reef.

Sunset Celebration, which takes place every night at Key West, is a colorful and festive affair abuzz with live music and entertainers.

Pacific Point Preserve®
Designed as a replica of the Northern Pacific coast, this 2.5 acre (1 ha) area has many beaches and rocky outcroppings. Visitors enjoy the antics of sea lions, harbor seals, and fur seals as they play, jump, and have a great time at this attraction. Don't miss the highly entertaining feeding sessions as the sea lions and other mammals dive around for food and swallow an entire fish in one gulp. Check at the information desk for timings.

Manatee Rescue
Named the country's best new zoological exhibit by the American Zoological Association, the attraction offers an up close and personal look at manatees. This highly educational exhibit includes a film show about the doleful and appealing herbivores. Injured manatees are brought to the park by an animal rescue team, and are released back into their habitat once they have recovered.

Penguin Encounter®
A re-creation of the polar regions, this glacial terrain is covered with snow and has a sub-zero temperature. Four

Rockhopper penguins on icy ledges at Penguin Encounter®

VISITORS' CHECKLIST

Road map E2. Orange Co. 7007 SeaWorld Drive, intersection of I-4 and Bee Line Expressway.
🛈 *(407) 351-3600.* 🚌 *8, 42 from Orlando.* ⏱ *9am–7pm daily; until 11pm in summer.*
♿ 🍴 📷 www.sea worldorlando.com

species of penguins – gentoo, rockhopper, chinstrap, and king – waddle along the rocky cliffs and swim gracefully in the icy waters, while puffins play close at hand. A 120-ft (35-m) long moving walkway passes through the habitat and gives guests a close view of the birds.

Shamu: Close Up!®
This research and breeding center facilitates the study of killer whales as part of SeaWorld's ongoing efforts to create awareness and educate people about these powerful creatures.
The Shamu Underwater Viewing area presents a massive 7 million gallon (26 million liter) habitat, which offers a close look at these giant mammals.

Shamu, the park's official mascot

Shark Encounter
Walk through an underwater tunnel surrounded by hair-raising creatures such as poisonous fish, scary barracudas, creepy eels, and predatory sharks. The 60-ft (18-m) long tunnel is made up of acrylic panels – each weighing almost 5000 lbs (2268 kg) – and offers a close but safe look at these dangerous animals.

Those looking for a more thrilling experience can try the interactive Sharks Deep Dive program, which is a part of the Shark Encounter. Here, visitors wear special wetsuits and snorkel or scuba dive in a shark cage while more than 50 sharks swim around them. This two-hour program is expensive and permits only two guests at a time. Note that children below the age of ten are not allowed.

MISTIFY®

Held each night at The Waterfront (*see p85*), SeaWorld's fireworks show Mistify is an absolutely stunning finale to a day at the park. The show uses laser projection techniques and highly advanced special effects to create 100-ft (30-m) tall fountains, giant displays of marine life, dancing flames, and a brilliant sky and underwater light show – all accompanied by dazzling fireworks. The best place to watch this spectacular event is from the shores of The Waterfront's seaport village.

RIDES & SHOWS

Spectacular stunts, hilarious animal antics, and exhilarating thrills characterize SeaWorld's rides and shows.

Wild Arctic®
Journey to the North Pole in a highly realistic simulated helicopter flight through blizzards and avalanches. At the end of this perilous "flight," visitors embark on an exploration of the frozen landscape. They also meet the region's animal inhabitants, such as giant walruses, frisky harbor seals, beautiful beluga whales, and two playful polar bears called Snow and Klondike.

Journey to Atlantis®
Unpredictable drops, twists, and turns are what riders can expect from this high-speed part water and part roller coaster adventure ride – the most thrilling being a terrifying drop, almost straight down, from a height of 60 ft (18 m). Eight riders, aboard an old Greek fishing boat, are pitchforked into a battle for the

lost city of Atlantis and face lugelike plunges and curves interlaced with amazing special effects as they fight their way through to safety.

Kraken®
Named after a giant mythical sea monster, the floorless roller coaster Kraken is one of the fastest coasters in Orlando.

SEAWORLD'S SERIOUS SIDE
The buzzwords at the nonprofit Hubbs-SeaWorld Research Institute are Research, Rescue, and Rehabilitation – the "three Rs." SeaWorld's animal rescue teams are on call 24 hours a day and have helped thousands of ill and injured whales, dolphins, manatees, and turtles. In fact, the park's manatee rescue program is the largest in the world. The animals are nursed and, if necessary, operated on in the park's rehabilitation center. Those that recover sufficiently are released back into the wild. SeaWorld also runs several educational tours, such as the Saving a Species tour, which offer a glimpse into their conservation programs.

SeaWorld's animal rescue team providing aid to a manatee calf

Riders are taken to a height of 149 ft (45.5 m) and then dropped 144 ft (44 m), while taking seven hair-raising loops that turn them upside down – all at an incredible speed of 65 mph (104 km/h). Adding to the thrill are the open-sided seats, offering only shouder restraints as support and leaving nothing for riders to hold on to as they are hurled through the air.

The Shamu Adventure®
The excitement of seeing a killer whale erupt out of the water carrying one of the SeaWorld trainers on its nose is hard to overstate. In Shamu Adventure, stunts such as this are supplemented by a giant video screen, ShamuVision, which provides close-ups of the action and footage of the huge mammals in the wild. The show is hosted by the famous animal expert, Jack Hanna, and features the killer whales performing remarkable acrobatic flips and jumps. Five orcas also perform.

Key West Dolphin Fest
Atlantic bottlenose dolphins and false killer whales perform with speed and amazing agility in this well choreographed and enjoyable show. The mammals leap, do back flips, and play with their trainers, as well as interacting with members of the audience. The show's highlight, however, is the dolphins' synchronized leaps over a rope.

Riders plummet down a sharp drop at the Journey to Atlantis® ride

A trainer performing tricks with a killer whale, Shamu Adventure® show

Clyde & Seamore Take Pirate Island®

Held at the Sea Lion and Otter Stadium, this hilarious show features two sea lions – Clyde and Seamore – otters, and a walrus, who, along with their trainer, embark on a swashbuckling adventure filled with lost treasure, pirate ships, and comical mix-ups at sea.

Odyssea

SeaWorld's Nautilus Theater hosts this mystical show, which takes viewers deep into the ocean with the help of stunning visual effects. Featuring spellbinding acrobatic feats, dramatic music, and imaginative costumes, this is one of the most sought-after attractions at SeaWorld.

Pets Ahoy!

This amusing show has an all-star cast of animals such as cats, birds, dogs, pigs, skunks, and many others performing amazing tricks and funny skits. Almost all of the animals have been rescued from animal shelters. Guests are also given tips on training pets at home.

Shamu Rocks America®

Blaring music greets visitors as they enter this nighttime rock 'n' roll show, held at the Shamu Stadium. SeaWorld trainers and killer whales perform astounding acrobatics to the beat of the music, complete with huge splashes of saltwater waves and excellent theatrical effects.

Blue Horizons

The power of the sea and the elegance of flight are conveyed through the truly spectacular show at Blue Horizons, featuring dolphins, false killer whales, exotic birds, and a cast of world-class divers and aerialists.

Tours & Other Attractions

Smaller exhibits at SeaWorld include Shamu's Happy Harbor®, a 3-acre (1.2-ha) play area for younger kids; Dolphin Nursery for new dolphin moms and their calves; and Clydesdale Hamlet, home to SeaWorld's famous Budweiser Clydesdales. The Polar Expedition Tour takes guests on a 60-minute educational exploration of the polar regions and a look at the Penguin Research Facility, while Adventure Express Tour offers reserved seats, guided tours of SeaWorld, animal feeding opportunities, and backdoor access to rides.

EATING, DRINKING & SHOPPING

A recent addition, The Waterfront at SeaWorld™ is a world-class dining, entertainment, and shopping area spread over 5 acres (2 ha), which offers merchandise and foods from all over the world. Guests may choose from nine restaurants, ranging from full-service to cafeteria-style. They include Voyagers Wood Fired Pizzas; The Seafire Inn, which offers stir fried dishes and hosts the Makahiki Luau show; the Sandbar pub, which serves sushi and martinis; and The Spice Mill, which features international cuisine. The Dine with Shamu restaurant, located at Shamu Stadium, allows guests to eat alongside killer whales, while at Sharks Underwater Grill (see p150), guests are served "Floribbean" fare as they eat just inches away from menacing sharks. The shops at The Waterfront include Allura's Treasure Trove, where kids can design their own porcelain dolls, and Under The Sun, which offers knick-knacks and several collectibles. Souvenirs are mainly soft toys and Shamu memorabilia; Shamu's Emporium has the largest selection.

Stuffed turtle and dolphin toys from SeaWorld shops

Discovery Cove ❷

Located just across the road from its big sister, SeaWorld, Discovery Cove is an enticing tropical paradise with beaches, reefs, and lagoons. Although the entry price is high enough to make all but lottery winners blink, the park's relaxing and tranquil setting offers some exceptional and unforgettable experiences, the highlight of which is a 30-minute opportunity to swim with Atlantic bottlenose dolphins. Forgoing the dolphin experience, however, can reduce the cost of a visit by almost half. In contrast to Florida's other theme parks, Discovery Cove has a capacity of only 1,000 guests a day – the car park takes only 500 cars – and it is advisable to make reservations well in advance.

Aquamarine lagoons surrounded by lush foliage at Discovery Cove

TACKLING THE PARK

White sandy beaches, lush green surroundings, and picturesque waterfalls create a serene atmosphere and allow guests to explore the park at a leisurely pace. Make sure you set aside an entire day to cover the park's animal attractions and enjoy the beaches.

The price is steep at $279 plus taxes per person – with no reductions for children – and include the Dolphin Swim experience, swimming and snorkeling gear, the use of beach amenities such as towels, umbrellas, and lockers, one main meal, and unlimited admission to SeaWorld or the Busch Gardens Tampa Bay for seven consecutive days. The price is reduced to $179 plus taxes if you choose not to do the Dolphin Swim. Note that children below the age of six are not permitted to swim with the dolphins.

Since admission is limited, the lack of crowds ensures attentive service as visitors are greeted by a personal guide, given a photo ID card, and taken on a familiarization tour through the park.

Cameras are allowed at most of the attractions except at Dolphin Lagoon, but avoid wearing jewelry as it might be distracting for the animals. Guests with disabilities are welcome and special outdoor wheelchairs, with oversized tires for easy maneuvering on the beach, are available.

There is only one restaurant but the food is good and you can eat on the beaches, too.

ATTRACTIONS

Discovery Cove is divided into five main areas – Coral Reef, the Aviary, Ray Lagoon, the Tropical River, and Dolphin Lagoon. These beautifully designed habitats are home to several exotic birds as well as marine life such as stingrays, tropical fish, and dolphins. The attractions provide a memorable interactive experience as guests are allowed to feed, touch, and even play with the animals.

Coral Reef
Explore an underwater world filled with hundreds of tropical fish as they swim through grottos, reefs, and the remains of an artificial shipwreck. Here, visitors have the unique opportunity to swim and snorkel alongside exotic fish and encounter giant stingrays. A transparent plexiglas partition that separates you from large sharks and barracudas, nevertheless creates the thrilling illusion of swimming with these predatory creatures.

Another striking feature of this artificially created habitat are the eye-catching colors of the coral reefs.

The Aviary
Trickling streams, stone tombs, bridges, and fountains create a beautiful setting for this bird sanctuary. Towering high above the rest of Discovery Cove, this recently expanded free-flight aviary is now home to more than 300 tropical birds. The new small bird sanctuary is filled with several types of finch, hummingbirds, and honeycreepers, which you

TOP 5 ATTRACTIONS

① **RAY LAGOON**

② **CORAL REEF**

③ **DOLPHIN LAGOON**

④ **AVIARY**

⑤ **TROPICAL RIVER**

Having fun with colorful, friendly birds at the Aviary

can feed by hand, while the large bird sanctuary features emus, toucans, and the red-legged seriema – some of the large birds are almost 4 ft (1.2 m) tall. The park's guides provide you with food for the birds, and introduce you to the various species, their habits, and the ongoing conservation programs.

The Aviary is accessible from the Discovery Cove beaches as well as from the waterfalls of the Tropical River.

Ray Lagoon
This large, secluded tropical pool is filled with several southern and cownose rays. Some of these rays are fairly large and can grow to almost 5 ft (1.5 m) in length and about 4 ft (1.2 m) in diameter. However, they are harmless and gentle creatures, and allow guests to swim and snorkel along with them. Those feeling more adventurous can even reach out and touch the surprisingly velvety skin of the rays as they softly glide past.

Tropical River
Following a serpentine route through most of Discovery Cove, the warm waters of this tropical river are inviting to say the least. Swimmers and snorkelers can float lazily past blue lagoons or take in the scenery around them as they wade through a thick rainforest. One of the most popular stopovers on the river are the cascading waterfalls, where guests can cool off from the heat of the Florida sun. Those

interested can also stop and take a look at various species of birds at the colorful Aviary. The river also features a specially designed underwater cave, which families can explore, as well as an underwater viewing window for a peek into Coral Reef.

Dolphin Lagoon
Discovery Cove's most famous attraction offers the amazing opportunity to swim and play with several bottlenose dolphins in Dolphin Lagoon. The experience begins with a 15-minute orientation program, held in beach cabanas, where trainers show a brief film on the habits and characteristics of the dolphins, and teach guests ways to communicate with the mammals by using special hand signals. Following this, groups of seven to eight guests are led into the shallow waters of the lagoon, which are home to around 30 of these friendly animals. The next 30 minutes, spent under the watchful eyes of the trainers, are simply unforgettable as you get the chance to talk to, hug, and even kiss the gentle dolphins.

Trainer for a Day
A new addition to the park's repertoire of offerings, this program allows up to 12 participants to work alongside

animal trainers, interact with the birds, tropical fish, sharks, dolphins, and other sealife, and take part in the behind-the-scenes animal training sessions at Discovery Cove for a day. Guests who wish to participate in the Trainer for a Day program must be physically fit and children below the age of six are not allowed. Note that the package is costly at $429 plus taxes.

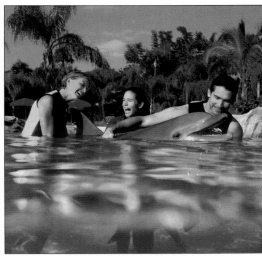

A family and a dolphin sharing a special moment at Dolphin Lagoon

Universal Orlando ❸

Once a single movie park, competing with the other local attractions, Universal Orlando has transformed into an expansive resort destination, which includes two theme parks, Universal Studios Florida and the Islands of Adventure; a 30-acre (12-ha) entertainment complex, Universal CityWalk; and three resorts *(see pp140–41)*. Together, these diverse options present a formidable reason to spend time away from Disney. Located off exits 29 and 30B from I-4, Universal's car parking brings guests through CityWalk on a series of moving walkways to a fork where they choose between the two parks.

TACKLING THE PARKS

The busiest times of the year at Universal Orlando are the same as at Walt Disney World *(see p76)*; the weekends are normally busier than the weekdays.

During peak season, the parks are open until late, and two full days are just about long enough to see everything at both of them. However, during off-season, they shut early, and you will need three to four days to cover all the attractions in the area.

Those staying for a longer duration can opt for any one of Universal's multi-day packages – such as 2-Day, 2-Park, 3rd Day Free Pass, the Bonus Pass, or the Annual Pass – which offer cost-effective admissions to the parks and CityWalk, as well as special discounts on hotel stays, food, and merchandise.

**Universal Orlando
Resort logo**

Lines at Universal can sometimes be even longer than those at Walt Disney World, and you might have to wait a considerable time for the best rides. One way of combating the lines is by purchasing the Universal Express pass, which operates in a similar manner to Disney's Fastpass *(see p34)*. Visitors can use this pass to make a reservation at an attraction – only one at a time – and skip the line on returning at the designated time. Moreover, guests staying at any of the Universal Orlando properties can use their room keys as Universal Express passes on all rides – with no limit – and also as a credit card throughout the park, charging food, gift shop items, and other expenditures to their room. On a busy day, visitors might like to consider indulging in the five-hour guided VIP Tour. Accommodating up to

12 people at a time, the tour provides priority admission to at least eight attractions, access to production facilities and sound stages, discounts, and a walk around backstage areas.

Most rides are likely to be too intense for very young children and of course some have minimum height restrictions; the exception to this is ET Adventure. The attractions designed to appeal to youngsters can be found at Woody Woodpecker's Kid Zone, and include A Day in the Park with Barney, and Animal Planet Live!.

Universal Orlando has made special provisions for families traveling with children, and for people with disabilities. Wheelchairs and strollers are available on rent near the entrance of both the parks. All the shopping and dining venues, and most of the attractions, are wheelchair friendly. The Family Service center also offers first aid and several restrooms with nursing and diaper-changing facilities.

The brightly illuminated world of Universal's Islands of Adventure

Exploring Universal Studios Florida®

Everything in this motion picture theme park is designed to take visitors into the magical world of movie-making. Built with the help of Steven Spielberg as a creative consultant, the park opened in 1990 and is home to several state-of-the-art rides, shows, and attractions – all based on popular films and television shows. Even the streets, shops, and restaurants are reminiscent of Hollywood sets, and the life-size reconstructions of New York and San Francisco are unbelievably realistic. The park is divided into six main sections – Production Central, New York, Hollywood, Woody Woodpecker's Kid Zone, World Expo, and San Francisco/Amity.

A scene from the animated Jimmy Neutron's Nicktoon Blast™ ride

LIVE FILMING

While there is no guarantee that you will be able to see live filming on the day you visit Universal Studios Florida, there is a slim possibility that cameras may be rolling on the backlot of the theme park itself. However, there is a good chance, especially from September to December, that you could be in the audience for the taping of a TV show. Those interested can also call ahead and check to find out which shows are being filmed during their visit. Tickets for the shows are issued on a first-come-first-served basis – on the day of filming – and are available at the Studio Audience Center located near Guest Services. Go there as soon as you enter the park to pick some up.

FRONT LOT

The entrance to Universal Studios Park is known as Front Lot because it has been created to resemble the front lot of a working Hollywood film studio from the 1940s. However, the shooting schedule notice board near the turnstiles, with the details of shows being filmed, is real enough.

Just inside the park, the palm-lined Plaza of the Stars has several shops (*see p93*), but do not linger here on arrival. Instead, you should immediately head off to the main attractions before the lines reach their peak.

PRODUCTION CENTRAL

Although this is the least aesthetic section of the park, two of Universal's most popular rides are located here. **Jimmy Neutron's Nicktoon Blast™** is a simulated adventure ride, which hurls you through space with the help of special effects, computer

Logo of the fun ride Shrek 4-D™

animations, and programmable motion-based seats. Evil egg-shaped aliens have stolen Jimmy's new invention, the Mark IV rocket, and are planning to take over the world. Now Jimmy needs your help to get it back. Blast off on a wild chase along with other favorite Nicktoons, including Fairly Odd Parents, Rugrats, Hey Arnold!, Goddard, Sponge Bob Square Pants®, and Jimmy's arch rival and nemesis, Cindy Vortex.

Shrek 4-D™, one of the newer attractions, is a fun-packed ride that features a 13-minute 3-D movie, in which Shrek and his friends set out to rescue Princess Fiona who has been kidnapped. The motion-simulated effects and special "OgreVision" glasses enable you to see, hear, and almost feel the action right in your seat. Starring the voices of Eddie Murphy, Mike Myers, John Lithgow, and Cameron Diaz, the ride is both a sequel to the original film *Shrek* and a bridge to the next instalment in the series, *Shrek 2*.

Amazing special effects enthrall the audience at Shrek 4-D™

Guests experiencing the forces of a tornado at Twister...Ride It Out®

NEW YORK

Universal's reproduction of the Big Apple is uncannily realistic and captures the minutest of details very effectively. The area is home *to more than 60 life-size façades, some of which replicate actual buildings in the city of New York, and others which reproduce those that have appeared only on screen. Macy's, the well-known department store, can be found here, as can Louie's Italian Restaurant, which was the location for a shootout in the original *Godfather* movie. Cutouts of structures such as the New York Public Library and the famous Guggenheim Museum cleverly create an illusion of depth and distance.

The washed out storefronts, warehouses, and even the stained and somewhat cracked cobblestone streets have been specially treated by a process called "distressing" to make them appear old.

New York is also host to the newest virtual reality ride at Universal Studios, **Revenge of the Mummy – The Ride**. Based on the phenomenally successful film, *The Mummy* and its equally popular sequel, *The Mummy Returns*, the ride combines extremely advanced special effects, such as space age robotics and high-speed roller coaster engineering, to take guests on a terrifying journey into the dark world of ancient Egypt. As they are swept through Egyptian tombs, passageways, and crumbling columns, riders have to face skeletal warriors and a giant animated figure of the menacing Mummy that jumps aboard the coaster. Fires, swarming bugs, and vengeful creatures add to the scare factor of this three-minute ride.

The other ride at New York is **Twister...Ride It Out®**, based on the movie *Twister*. Located inside a huge compound, the attraction pits visitors against Mother Nature at her most ferocious, as they stand just 20-ft (6-m) away from a graphically simulated tornado. Experience the overwhelming strength of the elements as cars, trucks, and even a cow are swirled up in the air by the ear-splitting, five-story-high funnel of winds.

Away from the rides, guests can also head down Delancey Street to take in **The Blues Brothers**, a 20-minute live music stage show, where Jake and Elwood perform a medley of their biggest hits. Relive moments from the original cult movie – starring John Belushi, Dan Aykroyd, Carrie Fisher, and Cab Calloway – as the brothers put on a show in an attempt to save their former school. There's plenty of audience participation, sing-alongs, dancing, and some outrageous humor.

The huge, scary skeletal warriors at Revenge of the Mummy – The Ride

Hollywood Boulevard, a fine example of the park's superbly created sets

TOP 10 ATTRACTIONS
① **REVENGE OF THE MUMMY – THE RIDE**
② **MEN IN BLACK™ – ALIEN ATTACK™**
③ **TWISTER...RIDE IT OUT®**
④ **JIMMY NEUTRON'S NICKTOON BLAST™**
⑤ **BACK TO THE FUTURE...THE RIDE®**
⑥ **SHREK 4-D™**
⑦ **TERMINATOR 2: 3-D BATTLE ACROSS TIME**
⑧ **EARTHQUAKE® – THE BIG ONE**
⑨ **FEAR FACTOR LIVE**
⑩ **ET ADVENTURE®**

HOLLYWOOD

Two of the most attractive sets at Universal Studios are the streets of Hollywood Boulevard and Rodeo Drive. While ignoring actual geography, these sets pay tribute to Hollywood's golden age from the 1920s to the 50s. The famous Mocambo nightclub, the luxurious Beverly Wilshire Hotel, the top beauty salon, Max Factor, and the movie palace, Pantages Theater, are just some notable examples of the wonderful re-creations lining these streets.

Shaped like a hat, the Brown Derby restaurant was once a fashionable eatery where the film glitterati used to congregate; Universal's own version is a fun hat shop. Schwab's Pharmacy, where hopefuls hung out sipping sodas and waiting to be discovered, is brought back to life as an old-fashioned ice cream parlor. The widely recognized Hollywood Walk of Fame, with the names of stars embedded in the sidewalk, just as in the real Hollywood Boulevard, has also been faithfully reproduced.

The top attraction in Hollywood is **Terminator 2: 3-D Battle Across Time**. Designed with the help of James Cameron, the director of the *Terminator* movies, this exciting ride uses the latest in 3-D film technology and robotics, along with explosive live stunts and giant screens, to catapult the audience into a battle with futuristic cyborgs. The fast-paced 3-D action features the star of the original films, Arnold Schwarzenegger, and other cast members. A typical sequence has a Harley-Davidson "Fat Boy" dramatically bursting off the screen and onto the stage. Note that young children may find this ride a bit scary.

Lucy – A Tribute acknowledges the talent of Lucille Ball, the queen of comedy and one of the world's favorite stage and television stars. The museum showcases clips, scripts, costumes, props, and other memorabilia from the comedian's hit TV show, *I Love Lucy*. The den of Lucy's Beverly Hills home and the set of her show have been meticulously replicated. The tribute also features an interactive game for trivia buffs to test their Lucy knowledge, as well as a gift shop where guests can pick up mementos. The museum is an ideal place to escape from the heat of the afternoon sun as well.

Another fascinating exhibit at Hollywood is the **Universal Horror Make-Up Show**. The attraction offers a behind-the-scenes look at how movies use makeup to create scary monsters and creepy effects. Props from films, such as the wax head from *The Exorcist*, the chambers where a man was merged with a fly in *The Fly*, and several masks, are on display. In addition, trained workers demonstrate the substitutes that can be used to resemble blood and slime. This partly gory and partly entertaining show takes place in a theater-like setting.

The audience face a giant robot, Terminator 2: 3-D Battle Across Time

ET and his alien friends on their colorful home planet, ET Adventure®

WOODY WOODPECKER'S KID ZONE

As the name suggests, this area caters specifically to preschoolers and younger children. Rides, shows, and attractions here have been designed to provide loads of fun with a minimum amount of scare factor.

Based on Steven Spielberg's 1982 movie, **ET Adventure®** is an enchanting, if rather tame, ride. Riders board flying bicycles and embark on a mission to save ET's home planet. Soaring high above a twinkling cityscape and through space, they fly past policemen and FBI agents before arriving at a strange world inhabited by aliens.

A must-see for animal lovers, the **Animal Planet Live!™** show features a talented troupe of dogs, cats, chimpanzees, birds, and other animals performing tricks and comical skits – some based on popular TV shows and movies. Animals playing the parts of canine superstars Beethoven and Lassie demonstrate how they are trained for film work. Audience participation and the antics of the animals make this an entertaining show.

A Day in the Park with Barney™ appeals only to very young children. A musical show set in a magical park, it features the lovable T-Rex Barney, who plays the lead in *Barney & Friends* – a top preschool-age TV show. The big purple dinosaur and his fun-loving friends, Baby Bop and BJ, sing, dance, and play with the children.

Inspired by the animated films *An American Tail* and *An American Tail: Fievel Goes West*, **Fievel's Playland®** features a playground as seen through the eyes of a mouse. Larger-than-life props, such as a cowboy hat, boots, glasses, cans, and a teacup have been used to construct tunnel slides, a 30-ft (9-m) spider web climbing area, and a 200-ft (61-m) twisting water slide.

Other attractions at Kid Zone are **Woody Woodpecker's Nuthouse Coaster®** – a gentle and child-friendly introduction to the world of roller coasters – and **Curious George Goes to Town** – a colorful playground with lots of water for kids to splash around in, as well as a ball area where they can play with hundreds of foam balls.

WORLD EXPO

Architecturally inspired by the Los Angeles 1984 Olympics Games and Expo '86 in Vancouver, World Expo has two major attractions. **Men in Black™ – Alien Attack™**, based on the *Men in Black* films, is an addictive ride in which visitors join Agent J (as played by Will

Guests fending off an attack by bug-eyed monsters at the Men in Black™ – Alien Attack™ ride

smith) in a simulator, battling aliens who have escaped after their shuttle crashed on Earth. This ride-through interactive video game is filled with 360-degree spins and lots of gunfire and infrared bullets, as well as plenty of noise. Each person has their own laser weapons and smoke bombs, and can earn bonus points by hitting certain aliens. The scores reflect the team's ability to destroy aliens.

Located nearby, **Back to the Future...The Ride®** is one of Orlando's most intense rides. No knowledge of the eponymous films is needed to enjoy this journey in a time-traveling sports car. The car's movements are synchronized to the action on a gigantic wraparound screen, making it seem as though you really are plunging over a flow of molten lava, skimming ice fields, and flying right into the mouth of a giant dinosaur.

SAN FRANCISCO/ AMITY

Most of this area is based on San Francisco, notably the city's Fisherman's Wharf district. For instance, the Chez Alcatraz snack bar is modeled to resemble the ticket booths for tours to Alcatraz Island. San Francisco's main draw is the amazing special effects ride, **Earthquake® – The Big One**. The ride has a low start with an educational how where the audience sees how earthquakes can be simulated using detailed models, and how actors are superimposed onto dramatic scenes. Things start picking up as you board a subway

Visitors on a catastrophic train journey in Earthquake® – The Big One

train for a short ride. Suddenly, an earthquake, measuring 8.3 on the Richter scale, hits the train station, and you are trapped amid collapsing ceilings, underground floods, colliding trains, and a burning oil tanker. When it's all over, you can watch the entire set put itself back together.

Amity, the other half of this corner of Universal Studios, is named after the fictional village in New England that was the setting for *Jaws*. The **JAWS®** ride (now only operating seasonally) begins as a serene cruise around the bay, but soon the deadly dorsal fin appears, and then a 32-ft (9.7-m) long mechanical great white shark is tearing through the water at a terrifying speed and lunging at your boat.

Beetlejuice show's sign

A tremendously popular new attraction is **Fear Factor Live**, the first ever theme park experience based on a reality TV show. Casting takes place 75 minutes before the show, which tests the courage and strength of participants.

Of more limited appeal is **Beetlejuice's Graveyard Revue**™, a live rock 'n' roll dance concert featuring Beetlejuice, Dracula, and the Frankenstein monster, literally pounding out hit songs.

EATING, DRINKING & SHOPPING

The food at the restaurants in Universal Orlando's theme parks is generally good, and there are plenty of options. Advance reservations are advisable for Lombard's Seafood Grille, specializing in fish dishes, and the Universal Studios Classic Monster Café, which offers Italian and Californian cuisine and has a good value buffet. Mel's Drive-In is definitely the place to go for fast food and shakes; the wonderful 1950s diner is straight out of the 1973 movie American Graffiti.

Most of the shops at the parks stay open after official closing times, and offer a wide range of themed souvenirs. The Universal Studios Store in the Front Lot sells everything from fake Oscars to oven mitts bearing the Universal logo, and you can buy autographed, but extremely expensive, photographs of your favourite movie star at the On Location store. Most of Universal Orlando's attractions have their own store.

MEETING THE STARS

Actors in wonderful costumes can be seen all along the streets of Universal Studios, playing the likes of Jake and Elwood from *The Blues Brothers*, Ghostbusters, Frankenstein, the Flintstones, as well as legends of the silver screen such as Marilyn Monroe and the Marx Brothers. They usually tend to congregate at the Front Lot.

Daily during the high season, and twice a week in off-season, guests can eat with the stars at a Character Breakfast in the park an hour prior to the scheduled opening time.

Exploring Islands of Adventure

Logo of Islands of Adventure

One of the world's most technologically advanced theme parks, Islands of Adventure is home to some of the most thrilling roller coaster and water rides in Florida. Spread over an area almost as vast as Universal Studios Florida, the park consists of five themed zones – Marvel Super Hero Island, Toon Lagoon, Jurassic Park, The Lost Continent, and Seuss Landing – all positioned around a central lagoon. Each Island has a creative and imaginative layout, which serves as an introduction to famous comic book, cartoon, and movie characters. Visitors will need to set aside an entire day to cover all the attractions on offer at Islands of Adventure.

TOP 5 RIDES
① **AMAZING ADVENTURES OF SPIDER-MAN®**
② **INCREDIBLE HULK COASTER®**
③ **DOLPHIN LAGOON®**
④ **POPEYE & BLUTO'S BILGE-RAT BARGES®**
⑤ **JURASSIC PARK RIVER ADVENTURE**

Incredible Hulk Coaster®

MARVEL SUPER HERO ISLAND®

Super heros and villains from the Marvel Comics' stable of characters are the inspiration behind this Island's four main attractions.

Arguably the best coaster in Florida, the **Incredible Hulk Coaster®** is a green leviathan that accelerates from zero to 40 mph (64 km/h) in just two seconds. Riders are taken 110 ft (33.5 m) in the air, turned upside down, and sent plummeting down a terrifying 105-ft (32-m) drop. With seven inversions and two drops into deep watery trenches, this stimulating ride is guaranteed to leave you breathless.

Highly advanced 3-D film technology, spectacular special effects, and motion simulated action makes the **Amazing Adventures of Spider-Man®** one of the most sought-after rides at the park. Guests are cast into a battle between Spider-man and villains, as the super hero leaps from tall buildings, saving damsels in distress and others. A scary 400-ft (122-m) simulated free fall is the highlight of this exciting, edge-of-your-seat ride. **Doctor Doom's Fearfall®** catapults its riders high into the air before plunging them down a 150-ft (46-m) fall. The ride also offers a great view of the entire park. **Storm Force Accelatron®** is a more intense version of the Mad Tea Party ride *(see p39)* at Disney.

TOON LAGOON®

Favorite cartoon characters come to life against this Island's colorful backdrop. The Comic Strip Lane, at the entrance, is lined with life-size images of toons such as Betty Boop, Olive Oyl, and Beetle Bailey; the island also hosts scheduled performances of the fun-filled Toon Lagoon Beach Bash.

Based on the Rocky and Bullwinkle cartoons, **Dudley Do-Right's Ripsaw Falls®** is a thoroughly drenching and enjoyable flume ride. Be prepared for the 15-ft (4.5-m) dive into a deep lagoon. **Popeye & Bluto's Bilge-Rat Barges®** is a whitewater raft ride where visitors are squirted and splashed by water guns fired from the nearby shores and playgrounds.

Children love exploring **Me Ship, The Olive**, a play area with bells, organs, ladders, tunnels, and whistles. The ship also overlooks the raft ride and offers water cannons to soak riders below.

JURASSIC PARK®

Step into a lush, tropical, and jungle-like setting as you enter this Island, where all the attractions are based on the *Jurassic Park* films. The **Jurassic Park River**

Fantastic special effects at the Amazing Adventures of Spider-Man®

◁ **Tourists flocking to the entrance of Universal Studios Florida**

Visitors under attack at the Jurassic Park River Adventure®

giant flames, and explosions, as Sinbad embarks on a journey to find treasure.

The best show, however, is **Poseidon's Fury®**, which features a battle between the King of the Seas and the King of the Gods. Visitors walk through a tunnel surrounded by a giant swirling whirlpool, while massive waves crash around them and the gods throw flaming fireballs at each other.

SEUSS LANDING®

Based on the popular Dr. Seuss children's books, this Island appeals mainly to the young and fans of the books.

Those with no experience of Dr. Seuss might find **The Cat in the Hat™** a somewhat bewildering and chaotic ride. A spinning and whirling couch takes you on a trip with the mischievous cat and characters such as Thing 1 and Thing 2. Some children may find the cat's sudden pounces at the corners scary.

Younger kids enjoy riding **One Fish, Two Fish, Red Fish, Blue Fish™** as they spin around on a remote controlled fish that moves up and down, and try to avoid being squirted by water jets.

Caro-Seuss-El is a merry-go-round with lovable Dr. Seuss characters, such as Dog-alopes, Aqua-MopTops, cow-fish, and elephant-birds among others, as the horses.

If I Ran The Zoo is another playground and the ideal place for kids to burn off energy.

Adventure® starts out as a peaceful cruise along a river, where you encounter friendly dinosaurs before an accidental raptor breakout. Suddenly you are faced with a menacing T-Rex and the only escape route is a 85-ft (26-m) drop into a lagoon.

Jurassic Park Discovery Center® is an interactive exhibit, with realistic replicas of dinosaurs, a Beasaurus area, which allows visitors to see and hear things as dinosaurs did, and several games and quizzes. It also offers a virtual demonstration of a raptor egg hatching in the lab.

The remaining three draws at the island are **Pteranodon Flyers®**, a slow sky ride over Jurassic Park, **Camp Jurassic®**, a playground with caves and buried fossils for kids, and the **Triceratops Discovery Trail**, where youngsters can tickle a 24-ft (8-m) Triceratops robot that moves when patted.

THE LOST CONTINENT®

Enter a magical world that is inspired by mythical and supernatural creatures, and has mysterious fortune tellers as well as a talking fountain. A favorite with coaster addicts,

Dueling Dragons® has two coasters – Fire and Ice – racing toward each other in a battle to see who will arrive back first. Riders come within inches of each other as the dragons go through several inversions and sharp corners. There is a separate, and longer, line for those who want to sit in the first car of the coasters.

A less thrilling ride, designed primarily for young children, is the **Flying Unicorn®** – a pleasant and non-frightening introduction to roller coasters.

An exciting stage show, **The Eighth Voyage of Sinbad®** is filled with stunts,

Riders miss each other by inches at the Dueling Dragons® ride

Exploring Universal CityWalk®

Logo of Universal's CityWalk

The gateway to Universal Orlando's offerings, CityWalk is a 30-acre (12-ha) entertainment, dining, and shopping complex that offers visitors the opportunity to continue their Universal experience long after the parks have closed – most of the places remain open from 11am to 2am. Restaurants, shops, concerts, nightclubs, and a movie theater present a range of options for an exciting night out. The banks of a sparkling lagoon running through CityWalk are perfect for an after-dinner stroll. While admission to the complex itself is free, most clubs have a cover charge. However, guests can visit all the clubs for the price of one with Universal's Party Pass.

home. Nightly performances by local and national reggae bands are the highlight here and can be enjoyed along with Jamaican and Caribbean food.

Another outstanding nightclub, **CityJazz®** features rare instruments belonging to the legends of jazz music, and hosts live concerts every night.

Some of the biggest bands in the music world perform at the **Hard Rock Live!® Orlando** coliseum-shaped concert hall. Guests can call ahead to find out which group will be playing during their visit.

RESTAURANTS

Citywalk offers a delectable selection of international cuisines to choose from.

Award-winning chef Emeril Lagasse's **Emeril's® Restaurant Orlando** *(see p151)*, serves delicious, but expensive, New Orleans Creole-based cuisine. Those looking for excellent Caribbean, Cajun, and fresh Florida fare should visit **Jimmy Buffett's®; Margaritaville®** *(see p151)*, which also offers live entertainment every night.

Munch on tasty Hispanic food from 21 nations at **Latin Quarter™**, while a dance troupe performs the salsa. At the family-style **Pastamoré Ristorante**, you can dine on superb Italian cuisine, with dishes such as grilled eggplant and chicken parmigiana as well as panini.

More than 1,000 pieces of rock memorabilia can be seen at the famous **Hard Rock Café® Orlando** *(see p150)*. The café serves up great

American food at reasonable prices. At **Bubba Gump Shrimp Co.**, shrimp is served in numerous ways, just as Forrest Gump would like it. The staff ask trivial questions about the movie.

The **NASCAR Café®**, an officially sanctioned NASCAR eatery, features authentic racing memorabilia along with a menu of steaks, BBQ, shrimp, chili, and salads. Voted Orlando's best theme restaurant, **NBA City** offers a large viewing area with screens, where basketball fans can watch games while enjoying burgers, steaks, pastas, and sandwiches.

ENTERTAINMENT

Live music, concerts, and hot dance floors fill the many clubs at CityWalk with energy and a sense of festivity.

Bob Marley – A Tribute to Freedom is a replica of the famous musician's Jamaican

One of CityWalk's most popular dance clubs is **the groove**. The lively atmosphere offers a mixture of hip-hop, rock, and dance music that is played live through the night on the club's impressive sound system.

Duplicating the famed New Orleans watering hole, **Pat O'Brien's®** is a much-celebrated bar, known for its specialty drinks, such as the Hurricane, and the "dueling piano" bar.

Catch a movie at any of the 20 theaters in the state-of-the-art **Universal Cineplex**. In addition, the outdoor stages and areas are settings for street performances and art festivals.

The world's largest Hard Rock Café® and music venue, at CityWalk®

A live music concert in progress at Hard Rock Live!® Orlando

TOP 5 ATTRACTIONS

① **HARD ROCK LIVE!®
   ORLANDO**

② **BOB MARLEY – A TRIBUTE
   TO FREEDOM**

③ **THE GROOVE**

④ **LATIN QUARTER™**

⑤ **JIMMY BUFFETT'S®;
   MARGARITAVILLE®**

CITYWALK VENUES

All Star Collectibles ⑯
Bob Marley – A Tribute to
   Freedom ③
Bubba Gump Shrimp Co. ②
Cartooniversal ㉑
Cigarz at CityWalk ⑲
CityJazz® ⑨
Dapy® ⑱
Elegant Illusions ⑳
Emeril's® Restaurant Orlando ⑧
The Endangered Species Store ⑫
Fossil® ⑭
Fresh Produce® ⑮
Glow!® ⑰
Hard Rock Café® Orlando ㉓
Hard Rock Live! Orlando ㉔
Jimmy Buffett's®; Margaritaville® ⑦
Latin Quarter™ ⑥
NASCAR Café® ㉒
NBA City ㉕
Pastamoré Ristoranté ⑪
Pat O'Brien's® ④
Quiet Flight® Surf Shop ⑬
the groove ⑤
Universal Cineplex ①
Universal Studios Store® ⑩

SHOPS

The central area features several stores with an extensive choice of merchandise (see p161). Interesting stores include **Glow!®**, which sells clothes, accessories, and home decor items that glow in the dark, and **The Endangered Species Store®**, which has merchandise aimed at raising eco-awareness. **Fresh Produce®** sells apparel in bright vegetable and fruit dyes, and beach products are available at **Quiet Flight® Surf Shop**. **Cartooniversal** offers souvenirs and clothes inspired by lovable cartoon characters, while **Dapy®** features lava lamps and novelty gifts. Souvenir hunters will also enjoy shopping at **Universal Studios Store®**, which offers a vast collection of products from the park. Sports fans can choose from an impressive selection of sports memorabilia and gifts at **All Star Collectibles**, while watches, leather items, and sunglasses can be purchased at the **Fossil®** store. A superior range of cigars and accessories are available at **Cigarz at CityWalk**. If you want a diamond ring or necklace, but don't want to pay megabucks for it, check out **Elegant Illusions**, which sells affordable copies of designer jewelry.

0 meters   25

0 yards   25

KEY

▢ Restaurants

▢ Entertainment

▢ Shops

The well-stocked sports store at NBA City

Wet 'n' Wild® ❹

Wet 'n' Wild logo

One of Central Florida's top attractions, Wet 'n' Wild opened in 1977. It focuses on rides of the hair-raising variety, boasting an awesome collection of high-velocity rides – multi-passenger as well as solo, on toboggans, rafts, or inner tubes, down slides and chutes or through tubes. There are activities for smaller kids as well, with miniature versions of the park's popular adult attractions on offer at Kids' Park. A range of family activities and a beach party atmosphere add to Wet 'n' Wild's appeal. Several outlets offer fast food; visitors can also bring in their own picnic hamper.

Knee Ski
Ride a surfboard on your knees in this cable-operated, half-mile (0.8-km) course on the park's lake. You can also wakeboard at the lake.

Black Hole®
Hang on for dear life in a two-person raft propelled by a blast of water through 500 ft (150 m) of twisting tubes in total darkness.

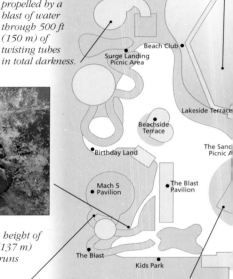

Beach Club ●
Surge Landing
Picnic Area
Lakeside Terrace
Beachside
Terrace
The Sand
Picnic A
● Birthday Land
Mach 5 ● Pavilion
● The Blast
Pavilion
The Blast
Kids Park

Surf Lagoon, a 17,000-sq ft (1,580-sq m) wave pool, features 4-ft (1.2-m) high waves and a waterfall.

The Flyer
Four-seater toboggans descend from a height of 40 ft (12 m), plowing through 450 ft (137 m) of banked curves and racing straight runs in this exhilarating watery ride.

Mach 5
Riders navigate this solo flume ride on a foam mat. On tight turns, ride the flowing water as far up the wall as possible. You can choose from three different twisting-and-turning flumes.

TOP TIPS

• Steps to the rides and asphalt walkways can get very hot. Wear non-slip footwear as protection.
• High-speed rides can leave you uncovered. Ladies should avoid wearing bikinis or consider adding a T-shirt.
• Rides have a 36-inch (91-cm) minimum height requirement for kids riding solo.
• Be sure to carry sunscreen.

Hydra Fighter

Strapped back-to-back in a swing, armed with water cannons, and in control of the swing's movement, two riders are supposed to create their own ride. A zestful water fight between riders in all eight swings provides loads of fun.

Blue Niagara®, a six-story drop through 300-ft (92-m) long twisting, interwoven tubes, ends in a bracing fall into a splash-landing tank.

Bomb Bay

A six-story plunge down a nearly vertical slide from a bomb-like capsule, this is one of Wet 'n' Wild's most sensational rides. Der Stuka is a slightly less scary version.

Bubble Up

Topped by a fountain that squirts water over the surface, this huge, colorful, slippery balloon makes a fun area for kids to climb, jump, and slide on.

Ski
ock

ba Tub
vilion

Lazy River
Picnic Pavilion

International
Pavilion

Lazy River®, a mile-long (1.6-km) circular waterway, lets you swim or float gently past swaying palms, orange groves, and waterfalls – a lovely re-creation of Old Florida.

Bubba Tub®

A raft large enough to hold five is the just the thing for watery splashes and fun for the family as it hurtles down a six-story slide with three big drops.

The Storm

Plummet down a chute with mist, thunder, and – at night – lightning effects, then drop into a huge open bowl, to swirl out with a splash into a lower pool in this exciting ride.

ORLANDO & CENTRAL FLORIDA

T*he thrills available at the numerous theme parks attract the majority of visitors to Orlando but the city and its surrounding region have much more to offer the discerning tourist, from beautiful beaches – quiet, unspoilt havens as well as bustling spots – to lush forests and serene lakes, to the space-related attractions at Cape Canaveral and a plethora of cultural activities.*

As late as the first half of the 20th century, Orlando and neighboring towns such as Kissimmee were small, sleepy places dependent on cattle and the citrus crop. Everything changed with the arrival of Disney World. Its booming entertainment industry, which has spawned several new and exciting entertainment venues, has made Orlando one of the country's fastest growing areas. But quieter pleasures are still available within Orlando, in its numerous museums and leafy suburbs. Outside Orlando, the landscape becomes more bucolic, with huge agricultural fields interspersed between the highways. The charming towns of Sanford and Mount Dora to the north provide a glimpse of Central Florida of a few decades ago. West of the St. Johns River lies the wooded expanse of the Ocala National Forest and, farther west, the world's largest artesian spring, Silver Springs. Along the Atlantic Coast, broad white sandy beaches flank the popular resort of Daytona Beach, which has been synonymous with car racing ever since the likes of Henry Ford and Louis Chevrolet raced automobiles on the beach during their winter vacations. Farther down, Cocoa Beach is another lively beach, famous for surfing. In between, along the Space Coast, the barrier islands across the broad Indian River boast 72 miles (116 km) of stunning sandy beaches, and there are two enormous nature preserves rich in bird life. Amid all this, set in a preserved marshy vastness beneath giant skies and in surprising harmony with nature, is the Kennedy Space Center, from where rockets are launched dramatically out of the earth's atmosphere.

The busy beach north of Main Street Pier, Daytona Beach

◁ Silver Glen Springs, Ocala National Forest

Exploring Orlando & Central Florida

The primary reason thousands of vacationers come to Central Florida is its theme parks, but the region has many other options for enjoyment. Smaller entertainment venues abound, and Orlando itself has 35 museums which house a diverse range of art. A wealth of retail stores and boutiques will satisfy the most discriminating shopper. Beaches in Central Florida range from empty, wild sands to the action-packed Daytona Beach and the buzzing surfing mecca of Cocoa Beach. Inland, the Ocala National Forest offers dozens of hiking trails, boating, and fishing; snorkeling and diving are also popular pursuits in crystal-clear springs. Kennedy Space Center, on the Space Coast, competes sharply with Orlando's attractions for excitement.

Sign for the town of Sanford

KEY

=== Highway

=== Major road

— Secondary route

=== Minor road

— Main railway

SIGHTS AT A GLANCE

Blue Spring State Park **4**
Canaveral National Seashore **23**
Cocoa **20**
Cocoa Beach **19**
Cypress Gardens Adventure Park **16**
Daytona Beach **7**
DeLeon Springs State Park **6**
Dinosaur World **15**
Fantasy of Flight **13**
Florida Southern College **14**
Gatorland **10**
Historic Bok Sanctuary **17**
Kennedy Space Center **25**
Kissimmee **11**
Merritt Island National Wildlife Refuge **24**
Mount Dora **3**
Ocala National Forest **8**
Orlando **1**
Sanford **2**
Silver Springs **9**
Southern Cassadaga Spiritualist Camp **5**
US Astronaut Hall of Fame **22**
Valiant Air Command Warbird Museum **21**
Yeehaw Junction **18**
A World of Orchids **12**

0 km   25

0 miles   25

SEE ALSO

• *Where to Stay* pp141–5

• *Where to Eat* pp151–5

Juniper Springs at Ocala National Forest

Jacksonville ↖
Ormond-by-the-Sea
Ormond Beach
DAYTONA BEACH 7
ville
DELEON SPRINGS STATE PARK
Port Orange
Wilbur-by-the-sea
Ponce Inlet
Ponce de Leon Inlet
e Land
New Smyrna Beach
SOUTHERN CASSADAGA SPIRITUALIST CAMP 5
Edgewater
Apollo Beach
DeBary
Deltona
BLUE SPRING STATE PARK 4
SANFORD 2
Saint Johns River
Geneva
Altamonte Springs
Oviedo
Winter Park
ORLANDO 1
Conway
GATORLAND
KISSIMMEE
Saint Cloud
ake
ekaligo
Holopaw
Deer Park
FLORIDA'S TURNPIKE
Lake Kissimmee
Lake Marian Highlands
Kenansville
Indian Lake Estates
YEEHAW JUNCTION 18
West Palm Beach ↘

Mosquito Lagoon
CANAVERAL NATIONAL SEASHORE 23
Playalinda Beach
Mims
MERRITT ISLAND NATIONAL WILDLIFE REFUGE 24
Titusville
US ASTRONAUT HALL OF FAME
VALIANT AIR COMMAND WARBIRD MUSEUM 21 22
KENNEDY SPACE CENTER 25
Sharpes
Cape Canaveral
Cape Canaveral
COCOA 20
Merritt Island
Rockledge
COCOA BEACH 19
Satellite Beach
Eau Gallie
Indian Harbour Beach
Melbourne
Melbourne Beach
Palm Bay
Micco
Sebastian
Gifford
Vero Beach
West Palm Beach ↘
Blue Cypress Lake

GETTING AROUND

With a huge network of divided highways, Central Florida offers fast driving – rent a car to best explore the region. The Space Coast is an hour east from Orlando on Route 528 (Bee Line Expressway). I-95 is the main north–south route along the coast. LYNX buses *(see p196)* serve most tourist sights in Greater Orlando. Apart from Orlando, only Sanford and Daytona Beach have international airports. Sanford – the terminus of the Auto Train *(see p196)* – Winter Park, Kissimmee, and Orlando have Amtrak stations.

A boardwalk trail at Blue Spring State Park

Orlando ❶

Not much more than a sleepy provincial town until the 1950s, Orlando's fortunes were transformed by its proximity to Cape Canaveral and the theme parks. Downtown Orlando's glass-sided high-rises mark a busy business district; it also has a burgeoning arts and culture scene. In the evening, Orange Avenue, Orlando's main street, pulsates with an exciting nightclub scene. Another bustling street is International Drive, with its many attractions, plenty of shopping opportunities, and excellent restaurants. Winter Park, one of Orlando's most elegant neighborhoods, boasts a bevy of cultural attractions from art museums to scenic boat tours; the nearby suburbs of Eatonville and Maitland feature quiet attractions, which make a pleasant change from the thrills and spills of the theme parks.

VISITORS' CHECKLIST

Orange Co. 180,000. Orlando International Airport, 1 Airport Blvd, 9 miles (14 km) SE of Downtown. Amtrak Station, 1400 Sligh Blvd. Greyhound Lines, 555 N John Parkway. 8723 International Dr, Suite 101, (800) 551-0181.

Charles Hosmer Morse Museum of American Art *in Winter Park features a lovely collection of glass by famed designer Louis Comfort Tiffany (see p112).*

Zora Neale Hurston National Museum of Fine Arts *in Eatonville exhibits the works of contemporary African-American artists. It is named after African-American writer Zora Neale Hurston, who grew up in Eatonville (see p113).*

Winter Park, Eatonville & Maitland
(see pp112–13)

0 km 30
0 miles 20

Downtown Orlando
(see pp107–109)

Ripley's Believe It Or Not! Orlando Odditorium, *with its fantastic collection of the world's strangest odditites collected by Robert Ripley during his travels around the globe, is a major attraction on International Drive (see p111).*

I-Drive
(see pp110–11)

Lake Eola Park, *a quiet haven in Downtown Orlando, has an ornate fountain set in the center of a picturesque lake (see p108).*

Exploring Downtown Orlando

The city's first designated historic district, Downtown Orlando encompasses eight square blocks and more than 80 buildings constructed between 1880 and 1940, which offer visitors a window into the city's past. Today, these buildings house offices, restaurants, and trendy galleries and boutiques. The crown jewel of Downtown Orlando, Lake Eola Park, separates the historic downtown district from Thornton Park, Orlando's center of new urbanism, with its collection of eclectic shops. The broader downtown area, especially the natural and cultural retreat Loch Haven Park to the north, features several unique and top-quality visual and performing arts centers and museums.

Sculpture at the Mennello Museum of American Folk Art

🏛 Orlando Science Center

777 E Princeton St, Loch Haven Park. **Tel** *(407) 514-2000.* ⏲ *9am–5pm Tue–Thu; 9am–9pm Fri & Sat, noon–5pm Sun.* 🅿 ☐ ☐ ♿
www.osc.org

Originally called the Central Florida Museum when it was opened in 1960, the museum acquired its current name in 1984. Covering 207,000 sq ft (19,200 sq m) of floor space, the present building was opened in February 1997.

The aim of the center is to provide a stimulating environment for experiential science learning, which it achieves by presenting a huge array of exciting, state-of-the-art interactive exhibits, designed to introduce kids of all ages to the wonders of science. The center's four floors are divided into ten themed zones dealing with subjects that range from mechanics to math, health and fitness to

lasers. The Body Zone, for instance, allows guests to explore the intimate workings of the human body. Other fascinating attractions include the DinoDigs exhibit with its collection of dinosaur fossils, which is very popular with children, as is the ShowBiz Science exhibit, which reveals some of the effects and tricks used in the movie business.

The gigantic Dr. Phillips CineDome surrounds visitors with amazing images and films on a range of topics such as Egyptian treasures and ocean life; it is also a planetarium.

🏛 Orlando Museum of Art

2416 N Mills Ave, Loch Haven Park. **Tel** *(407) 896-4231.* ⏲ *10am–4pm Tue–Fri, noon–4pm Sat & Sun.* 🌐 *public hols.* 🅿 ☐ ♿
www.omart.org

One of Southeastern USA's finest arts museums, the Orlando Museum of Art has a

superb permanent collection that includes pre-Columbian artifacts, with figurines from Nazca in Peru; African art; and American paintings of the 19th and 20th centuries. These are supplemented by traveling exhibitions from major metropolitan museums, and smaller shows of regional or local significance. Music, food, and the works of local artists are on offer at a lively get-together on the first Thursday evening of every month.

🎭 John & Rita Lowndes Shakespeare Center

812 E Rollins St, Loch Haven Park. **Tel** *(407) 447-1700.* **Orlando-UCF Shakespeare Festival**
www.shakespearefest.org

Spread over 50,000 sq ft (4,645 sq m), the elegant Shakespeare Center features the 350-seat Margeson Theater and the smaller Goldman Theater. Since February 2002, this state-of-the-art venue has been host to the nationally recognized **Orlando-UCF Shakespeare Festival**, which has been performing since 1989. It mounts high-quality performances throughout the year – its annual spring festival at Lake Eola Park (*see p108*) is very popular.

🏛 Mennello Museum of American Folk Art

900 E Princeton St, Loch Haven Park. **Tel** *(407) 246-4278.* ⏲ *10:30am–4:30pm Tue–Sat, noon–4:30pm Sun.* 🌐 *major hols.* 🅿 ♿
www.mennellomuseum.com

This small, lakeside museum houses an unusual collection of paintings by curio-shop owner and Floridian folk artist, Earl Cunningham (1893–1977), and traveling exhibitions of the works of other folk artists. Quirky sculptures are scattered throughout the grounds.

The sparkling exterior of the Orlando Science Center

A bridge across a rocky stream at Harry P. Leu Gardens

🌺 Harry P. Leu Gardens

1920 N Forest Ave. **Tel** (407) 246-2620. ⬡ 9am–5pm daily. ⬤ Dec 25. 🖼 🖾 🎫 🛒 ♿
www.leugardens.org

The Harry P. Leu Gardens offer 50 acres (20 ha) of serene, beautiful greenery to stroll in. Features such as Florida's largest rose garden are formal while, elsewhere in the park, there are mature woods of spectacular live oaks, maples, and bald cypresses, festooned with Spanish moss; in winter, seek out the mass of blooming camellias. Other attractions are a herb garden and one filled with plants that attract butterflies. Visitors can also tour the early 20th-century Leu House and its gardens, which local businessman Harry P. Leu donated to the city of Orlando in 1961.

🏛 Ivanhoe Row

N Orange Ave.

Shops 10am–5pm Mon–Sat. Stretching from Colonial Drive to Lake Ivanhoe, this row of antiques shops features an interesting mix of the old and the unconventional. Vintage linens, clothing, jewelry, and various collectibles are on offer here, as is also period furniture ranging from Victorian to Art Deco. The Wildlife Gallery sells original paintings and sculptures of animals, while Art's Premium Cigars offers a range of cigars and smoking paraphernalia. The prices are on the high side, but you might find some unusual treasures here.

Sign for Ivanhoe Row

🌺 Thornton Park

E of Lake Eola.

Close to the city's business center, hip and artsy Thornton Park offers a blend of trendy cafés, unique boutiques, stylish eateries such as HUE Restaurant, which serves world-class cuisine, and pretty B&Bs. Most active after 6pm, it is a popular neighborhood for locals to unwind in after work. One of the area's most happening hangouts is Dexter's of Thornton Park (see p151), with its chrome vinyl stools, terrazzo floors, contemporary art, and gourmet food. Other attractions include Urban Think!, a bookshop that features author readings, art shows, and a bar, and Marie-France, a chic jewelry boutique.

🌺 Lake Eola Park

N Rosalind Ave & E Washington St. **Tel** (407) 246-2827. ⬡ 5am–sunset daily. **Boat rentals Tel** (407) 658-4226. ♿

Orlando's most visited park, Lake Eola Park is spread over 43 acres (17 ha) and is encircled by a 0.9-mile (1.4-km) pedestrian-only path. This charming park in the heart of the city offers a lovely view of the downtown skyline. Cruise the lake on two-person swan-shaped paddle boats, or feed the swans, drifting along in the lake's shallow water.

The park hosts several annual and seasonal events, including the Fourth of July fireworks show and the superb UCF-Shakespeare Festival. The plays and concerts are performed against the stunning backdrop of the Walt Disney Amphitheater, a band shell with excellent acoustics. The Terrace in the Park restaurant serves fine cuisine, not the usual park fare.

SIGHTS AT A GLANCE

KEY

▬▬	Interstate highway
▬▬	Major highway
▬▬	Highway
▬	Railroad

0 km   1

0 miles   1

A scene in progress from Les Liaisons Dangereuses, Mad Cow Theatre

Mad Cow Theatre

105 S Magnolia Ave. **Tel** *(407) 297-8788.*
www.madcowtheatre.com

Started in late 1997 as a simple project between a band of actors and some directors in a former blueprint studio in Maitland, this theatrical group has developed a reputation for outstanding productions performed at different settings for several years. In 2004, it acquired a permanent home in the heart of Downtown Orlando, at a venue that seats an audience of around 160.

The Mad Cow Theatre presents a quality range of classics, musicals, and original works, and produces an annual Orlando Cabaret in July. Past productions have ranged from Chekhov and T.S. Eliot to Neil Simon. The group also offers educational shows and workshops.

Orange County Regional History Center

65 E Central Blvd. **Tel** *(407) 836-8500, (800) 965-2030.*
10am–5pm Mon–Sat, noon–5pm Sun.
www.thehistorycenter.org

Housed in the former Orange County Courthouse, the Orange County Regional History Center sits on nearly 2 acres (0.8 ha) of land in Heritage Square, the old town center. It has four floors of exhibits and interactive areas for visitors of all ages, offering a glimpse into the history and environment of Central Florida. Everything, from wildlife, and the first Native Americans in the area, to Walt Disney and the space program, is covered here. Highlights include replicas of a Seminole settlement and an early Florida Pioneer Cracker home. Visitors can also wander though a re-created Timucuan village. The museum has an interesting exhibition on the training of aviators, from World War II pilots to NASA astronauts. The center also offers several educational programs and school field trips for children, and organizes get-togethers such as concerts on a regular basis.

Wells' Built Museum of African American History & Culture

511 W South St. **Tel** *(407) 245-7535.* *9am–5pm Mon–Fri, Sat 10am–2pm.*
www.pastinc.org

The Wells' Built Hotel was constructed in 1912 by Orlando's first African-American physician, Dr. William Monroe Wells, as a lodging for performers on the Chitlin' Circuit, a network of locations throughout southern United States where African Americans stayed and performed music. Many of the day's top black entertainers, including Billie Holiday, Ray Charles, Benny Carter, and Duke Ellington, have stayed here at different times. The building was converted into a museum in 1999. The museum contains artifacts, photographs, and exhibits relating to Orlando's African-American communities, focusing on locals who were the first African Americans to attain positions of prominence in their professions and the community. There is a photo display of the Chitlin' Circuit.

SAK Comedy Lab

380 W Amelia St. **Tel** *(407) 648-0001.* **www**.sak.com

One of the best places for live comedy in Orlando, SAK Comedy Lab stages two hilarious shows per night. The later show is slightly racier, but obscene material is strictly avoided, and the high-energy improvization comedy is a great option for families looking for laughs. Especially popular are the series shows, such as *Duel of Fools*. The 215 seats of the theater are wrapped around the stage, giving all members of the audience a good view. Comedians who have performed here include Wayne Brady – one of the stars on the *Whose Line is it Anyway?* TV show.

Wells' Built Museum of African American History & Culture

Exploring International Drive

Garish and glittering International Drive, generally known as I-Drive, is a 3-mile (5-km) ribbon of innumerable attractions, including five major theme parks *(see pp78–101)*. Several of the entertainment venues are open day and night, making the area a zone of frenetic activity 'til late at night. I-Drive brims with hotels and restaurants catering to all budgets, and shopping malls and stores where tourists can pick up souvenirs as well as go in for serious discount shopping. Also located here is Orlando's excellent Official Visitor Information Center, which has coupons for many of the city's attractions, hotels, and restaurants. The most convenient way to take in I-Drive's sights is to hop onto the I-Ride Trolley *(see p197)*.

SIGHTS AT A GLANCE

Air Florida Helicopters ②
Holy Land Experience ⑦
Ripley's Believe It Or Not®!
  Orlando Odditorium ⑤
Skull Kingdom and a Chamber
  of Magic ⑥
SkyVenture ④
Titanic – The Experience ③
  WonderWorks ①

KEY

▬▬▬	Interstate highway
▬▬▬	Major highway
▭▭▭	Highway

```
0 km            2
0 miles         2
```

🏛 WonderWorks

Pointe Orlando, 9067 International Dr. **Tel** *(407) 351-8800.* ◯ *9am–midnight daily.* 📷 🔲 �ⅈ 🚻
www.wonderworksonline.com

One of the most striking buildings on International Drive, WonderWorks looks as though a three-story tall, Neo-Classical building has landed upside down atop a 1930s brick warehouse. This interactive entertainment center boasts numerous hands-on exhibits – some incorporating virtual reality – and demonstrations that the whole family can enjoy. Visitors can experience hurricane-force winds and an earthquake, or even play basketball with a very tall simulated opponent. Other favorites include the Wonder-Coaster, where guests can design and ride their own roller coaster in a simulator, and the laser tag video arcade.

✈ Air Florida Helicopters

8990 International Dr.
Tel *(407) 354-1400.* ◯
10am–5:30pm daily 📷
www.airfloridahelicopters.com

Get a bird's-eye view of Sea World, Discovery Cove and other theme parks with Air Florida Helicopters. They operate a fleet of Robinson R44s which offer exceptional visibility and panoramic views for all passengers. The pilot narrates each tour and there are nine to choose from. Tours can also be designed to meet personal requests. Flights start at $20 with a minimum of two passengers per flight. The most expensive tour takes tourists over local celebrity mansions and to Lake Apopka where alligators, osprey and bald eagles can be seen.

The Grand Staircase at Titanic – The Exhibition

🏛 Titanic – The Experience

The Mercado, 8445 International Dr. **Tel** *(407) 248-1166.* ◯ *10am–10pm daily. Ticket office: 10am–8pm daily.* ◯ *public hols.* 📷 🔲 🚻
www.titanictheexperience.com

This exhibition allows visitors to re-live the *Titanic*'s mes-merizing drama as it unfolded, share in the inspirational personal stories of those aboard, and marvel at the splendor of one of the finest ships ever built. The doomed ship is impressively re-created here with the help of modern

The upside down façade of WonderWorks

◁ **The Sun Trust building towering over Church Street, Downtown Orlando** echnology, reproductions of he ship's rooms – including he Grand Staircase – historic rtifacts, and interactive nterpretations by storytellers n period costume. The xhibit also contains props nd memorabilia from three najor Titanic movies, ncluding an outfit worn by .eonardo Di Caprio in the :001 version.

Holy Land Experience, a reconstruction of biblical Jerusalem

SkyVenture
805 Visitors Circle. *Tel (407) 903-*
150. ☐ *10am–midnight daily.*
www.skyventureorlando.com
ioar like a bird on a column
of air moving at 120 mph (80
mph). SkyVenture's vertical
vind tunnel opened in 1998
nd since then more than
00,000 visitors have enjoyed
he high adventure of
kydiving without
naving to pack a
parachute or jump
out of a plane. The
hour-long session
ncludes a training
class and two one-
minute jumps which
re more than enough
o exhaust a novice. Kids
is young as three can fly
although there are some
weight restrictions. It is
possible for visitors who
do not wish to jump to
vatch participants floating
and spinning (and usually
grinning) in colorful jumpsuits.

**Logo of
SkyVenture**

(1893–1949) in the course
of his travels. Housed in a
building that appears to be
sinking, the Orlando branch
is one of the best of the 27
Ripley's, with 16 galleries of
the unusual. Highlights
include a 1907 Silver Ghost
Rolls Royce – with
moving engine parts
– that was made
from 63 pints of
glue and 1,016,711
ordinary matchsticks,
a version of the *Mona
Lisa* made out of toast,
and a holographic
1,069-lb (485-kg) man. The
replicas of human and animal
odditites on display may make
some cringe. There is also a
gift shop with collectibles for
visitors who wish to take some
unusual souvenirs home.

Ripley's Believe It Or Not® Orlando Odditorium
8201 International Drive. *Tel (407)*
863-4418. ☐ *9am–1am daily.*
www.ripleysorlando.com
showcasing the bizarre and
he extraordinary, Ripley's
worldwide chain of attractions
displays the fantastic odditities
discovered by Robert Ripley

⌂ Skull Kingdom and a Chamber of Magic
5931 American Way. *Tel (407) 354-*
1564. ☐ *10:30am–11:30pm daily.*
for kids. (limited).
www.skullkingdom.com
A two-story haunted castle,
fronted by a gigantic skull,
Skull Kingdom is a fantastic
combination of old-fashioned
sideshow scares and cutting-
edge special effects. Robotics,
detailed light and sound

effects, and superb, won-
derfully made-up actors keep
your spine tingling at every
turn as you make your way
through caverns, mazes, and
haunted hallways. Families
are led through the castle by
a staff guide to ensure everyone makes it safely to the end
of the tour. There are day and
night horror shows, with the
latter being more intense. The
Chamber of Magic Show and
Dinner features a magic
entertainment show and all-
you-can-eat pizza, beer, and
soda for a set price.

⌂ Holy Land Experience
4655 Vineland Rd. *Tel (407)*
367-2065. ☐ *10am–5pm*
Mon–Sat. *Thanksgiving,*
Dec 25.
www.holylandorlando.net
Opened in 2001, this biblical
history museum which
spreads over 15 acres (6 ha)
re-creates in elaborate and
authentic detail the city of
Jerusalem and its religious
importance between the years
1450 BC and AD 66. Guides
in period costume, dramatic
enactments of stories from
the Old and New Testaments,
and high-tech presentations
bring Jerusalem to life in this
religious theme park. Among
the highlights of Holy Land
Experience are recon-
structions of Jesus's tomb
and the limestone caves
where the Dead Sea Scrolls
were discovered. There are
also displays of rare Bibles
and biblical manuscripts.
While the museum makes no
bones about being a Christ-
centric institution, visitors of
all faiths can enjoy its very
evocative journey back in
time. A Middle-Eastern-style
café serves "Goliath burgers."

The dramatic sinking home of Ripley's Believe It Or Not! Odditorium

Exploring Winter Park, Eatonville & Maitland

Greater Orlando's most refined neighborhood, Winter Park took off in the 1880s, when wealthy northerners came south and began to build lavish winter retreats here, along the area's waterways. Excellent stores and classy cafés afford ample opportunities for strolling and window-shopping, and there are several intriguing museums. Nearby Eatonville, the first incorporated African-American municipality in the USA, has an interesting museum on African-American culture, while Maitland, to the north, has beautiful homes and gardens and boasts an excellent art center.

SIGHTS AT A GLANCE

Albin Polasek Museum & Sculpture Gardens ④
Audubon Center for Birds of Prey ⑦
Central Park ②
Charles Hosmer Morse Museum of American Art ①
Cornell Fine Arts Museum ③
Holocaust Memorial Resource & Education Center of Central Florida ⑨
Maitland Art Center ⑧

Winter Park Scenic Boat Tour ⑤
Zora Neale Hurston National Museum of Arts ⑥

| 0 km | | 2 |
| 0 miles | | 2 |

KEY

≡ Interstate highway

≡ Major highway

― Highway

⏛ Charles Hosmer Morse Museum of American Art
445 N Park Ave. **Tel** (407) 645-5311. ◯ 9:30am–4pm Tue–Sat, 1–4pm Sun. ● public hols. (Sep–May: 4–8pm Fri free) www.morsemuseum.org
The imposing, windowless walls of this museum rather ironically contain an outstanding collection of beautiful stained-glass windows and objects by the American designer, Louis Comfort Tiffany (1848–1933). Other highlights include American ceramics and representative collections of the late 19th- and early 20th-century American and European paintings, graphics, decorative arts, furniture, and jewelry.

♣ Central Park
Downtown Winter Park. **Tel** (407) 599-3334. ◯ daily. &
Located alongside Winter Park's main street, Park Avenue, Central Park is a lovely shaded area that hosts numerous events throughout the year. Tall oaks, pretty fountains, and a splendid rose garden provide a scenic backdrop to monthly concerts on Sunday evenings by the Orlando Philharmonic. Other events include monthly jazz concerts, the Winter Park Sidewalk Art Festival in March, screening of film classics, month-long Christmas festivities, and school activities. Many carry their own blankets and even chairs to enjoy the various musical events. Sculptor Albin Polasek designed the beautiful fountain called "Emily." Benches are scattered throughout and parking is free at the two lots adjacent to the park.

⏛ Cornell Fine Arts Museum
100 Holt Ave. ◯ 10am–5pm Tue–Sat, 1–5pm Sun. **Tel** (407) 646-2526. www.rollins.edu/cfam
Located on the scenic Rollins College campus, this small but elegant museum houses Florida's oldest art collection. The diverse and distinguished collection features European and American paintings, sculptures, and decorative arts from the Renaissance to the 20th century, including the works of artists such as Cosimo Roselli, Henry Moore, William Merritt Chase, and Louis Sonntag.

⏛ Albin Polasek Museum & Sculpture Gardens
633 Osceola Ave, Winter Park. **Tel** (407) 647-6294. ◯ 10am–4pm Tue–Sat, 1–4pm Sun. ● public hols, July & Aug. & www.polasek.org
Listed on the National Register of Historic Places, the home of Czech-American sculptor Albin Polasek (1879–1965) is a beautifully maintained, serene spot spread over 3 acres (1 ha). The house and its lovely gardens showcase

Albin Polasek Museum & Scuplture Gardens

Winter Park Scenic Boat Tour, along Winter Park's waterways

works spanning the career of the artist who specialized in the European figurative technique. The four galleries within the house also feature works by some other artists.

🚤 Winter Park Scenic Boat Tour
E end of Morse Blvd, Lake Osceola. **Tel** (407) 644-4056. ⬤ *tours depart on the hour 10am–4pm daily.* ⬤ *public hols.* ◉
www.scenicboattours.com

Spend a very pleasant hour cruising along Winter Park's lovely lakes overhung with hibiscus and bamboo on this narrated pontoon boat ride. Running since 1938, this part-nature trip and part-local history lesson takes in landmarks such as Rollins College and huge lakeside mansions with green sweeping lawns, as well as cypress swamps where nature lovers can take a gander at birds such as herons and ospreys.

🏛 Zora Neale Hurston National Museum of Arts
227 E Kennedy Blvd, Eatonville. **Tel** (407) 647-3307. ⬤ *9am–5pm Mon–Fri, Sun by request only.* ⬤ *public hols.* ◉ ◉
www.zoranealehurston.com

One of the brightest stars of the Harlem Renaissance of the 1920s and 30s, writer, anthropologist, and folklorist Zora Neale Hurston was born in Eatonville in 1891. Many of her most famous writings – including the 1937 novel, *Their Eyes Were God* – reflected life in her hometown. This modest museum keeps her memory alive, offering maps for a self-guided walking tour to the remaining literary landmarks of her neighborhood. There are exhibitions centered on Hurston and the Eatonville of days gone by. The museum also has rotating exhibits of a range of works by contemporary African-American artists.

🦅 Audubon Center for Birds of Prey
1101 Audubon Way, Maitland. **Tel** (407) 644-0190. ⬤ *10am–4pm Tue–Sun.* ⬤ *public hols.* ◉ *(donation requested).*
⬤ **www**.audubonofflorida.org/conservation/cbop.htm

Audubon Center for Birds of Prey

One of the largest bird rehabilitation centers in Southeastern US, this sanctuary for birds, created by Florida Audubon Society, is a great place to get up close and personal with eagles, owls, hawks, vultures, and other raptors. The center takes in about 700 birds annually and releases about 40 percent of them. Guests are not allowed to witness the rehabilitation process. Those birds that cannot survive being released into the wild are kept here, living a pampered existence in this lovely lakeside location, while helping to educate visitors about wildlife issues and conservation. Guided tours are available for groups, and there is a wide-ranging volunteer program.

🏛 Maitland Art Center
231 W Packwood Ave, 6 miles (9.6 km) north of Downtown Orlando. **Tel** (407) 539-2181. ⬤ *9am–4:30pm Mon–Fri, noon–4:30pm Sat & Sun.* ⬤ *public hols.* ◉ *(donation requested).*
⬤ 🏛 **www**.maitartctr.org

Founded in the 1930s by artist André Smith, this was originally an artists' colony, with studios and living quarters. It is now an art museum and teaching center managed by the Maitland Historical Society. The studios are still used by working artists, and there are exhibitions of contemporary American arts and crafts as well as art classes taught by professional artists. Set around courtyards and gardens, the buildings are interesting, with murals and carvings that make abundant use of Mayan and Aztec motifs.

🏛 Holocaust Memorial Resource & Education Center of Central Florida
851 N Maitland Ave, Maitland. **Tel** (407) 628-0555. ⬤ *9am–4pm Mon–Thu, 9am–1pm Fri, 1–4pm Sun.* ⬤ *public & Jewish hols.* ◉ ◉
www.holocaustedu.org

Set up with the aim of preventing the oppression of minority groups in future by learning from the Holocaust, this small museum's permanent exhibit has 12 segments, each introducing a major theme of the Holocaust. The museum features multimedia displays on the history of the Holocaust as well as photographs and artifacts.

There is also an extensive library on the subject, with more than 5,000 volumes and 500 videotapes, some of which contain oral histories of survivors of the Holocaust. The library also stocks a selection of juvenile books on this tragic event.

Decoration inspired by the Aztecs, at the Maitland Art Center

S-32—Park Avenue and Municipal Zoo from the Band Shell on Lake Monroe, Sanford, Fla.

A postcard of Sanford, showing Lake Monroe

Sanford ❷

Seminole Co. 45,000.
400 E 1st St, (407) 322-2212.
www.sanfordchamber.com

Located to the north of Orlando and on the southern shores of Lake Monroe, Sanford was founded in the 1870s by Henry S. Sanford, near Fort Mellon, the US Army post built during the Seminole Wars *(see p14)*. The construction of a railway station thereafter added to Sanford's prosperity and the thriving town soon became a major inland port thanks to the commercial steamboat services, which also brought the city's early tourists.

Sanford town sign

Restored downtown Sanford dates from the 1880s, which was the height of the steamboat era. Several of the lovely old red brick buildings – a rarity in Florida – are home to antiques shops, and the area can easily be explored on foot in a couple of hours. Today's visitors are more likely to arrive on the Auto Train *(see p196)* than by river, but short pleasure cruises are also available.

Mount Dora ❸

Lake Co. 11,000.
341 Alexander St, (352) 383-2165. www.historicmountdora.com

Set among the citrus groves of Lake County, this town is one of the prettiest Victorian settlements left in the state.

Its name comes from both its relatively high elevation of 184 ft (56 m) and the small lake on which it sits. Mount Dora was originally known as Royellou, after Roy, Ella, and Louis, the three children of the first postmaster.

Mount Dora's attractive tree-lined streets are laid out on a bluff above the lakeshore. Visitors can refer to the 3-mile (5-km) historic tour map, which is available at the town's chamber of commerce. The tour takes a scenic route around the quiet neighborhoods of late 19th-century clapboard homes and the wonderfully restored downtown historic district, which has an array of stores and antiques shops.

On Donnelly Street, you will find the grand **Donnelly House**, now a Masonic Hall. A notable example of ornate "steamboat architecture," the building is aesthetically decorated with pinnacles and a cupola. Nearby, the small **Royellou Museum** showcases local history exhibits. Water sports and fishing are on offer at Lake Dora.

🏛 **Royellou Museum**
450 Royellou Lane. **Tel** (352) 383-0006. 1–5pm Thu–Sun. Jan 1, Thanksgiving, Dec 25. limited. www.historicmountdora.com

Blue Spring State Park ❹

Volusia Co. 2100 W French Ave, Orange City. **Tel** (386) 775-3663.
8am–sundown daily.
www.floridastateparks.org/bluespring

One of the country's largest first-magnitude artesian springs, Blue Spring pours out around 100 million gallons (450 million liters) of water a day. The temperature of the water is at a constant 68°F (20°C), and consequently the park is a favorite winter refuge for manatees. From November to March, when the manatees escape from the cooler waters of the St. Johns River, you can see them from the park's elevated boardwalks. Activities such as snorkeling and scuba diving are available in the turquoise waters of the spring head, as is canoeing on St. Johns. **Thursby House**, atop one of the park's ancient shell mounds, was built in the late 19th century.

Environs

Just about 2 miles (3 km) north as the crow flies is wooded **Hontoon Island State Park**. Reached by a free passenger

Shingles and gingerbread decoration on Donnelly House, Mount Dora

Children playing in front of Thursby House, Blue Spring State Park

ferry from Hontoon Landing, the island has an 80-ft (24-m) observation tower, pic-nic and camping areas, and a nature trail. Fishing skiffs and canoes can also be rented.

The original inhabitants of the park were the Timucua Indians. In 1955, a rare wood-en owl totem was found here.

Hontoon Island State Park
2309 River Ridge Rd, DeLand. **Tel** (386) 736-5309. ◯ 8am–sundown daily. www.floridastateparks.org/hontoonisland

Southern Cassadaga Spiritualist Camp ➎

1325 Stevens St, Cassadaga. **Tel** (386) 228-3171. ◯ 10am–5pm daily. Office: 9am–4pm Mon–Thu. www.cassadaga.org

Founded by a group of spiritualists in 1894 to study the philosophy, science, and religion of Spiritualism in greater depth, the Southern Cassadaga Spiritualist Camp is one of the oldest active religious communities in the United States. In 1991, the center was earmarked as a Historic District by the National Registry of Historic Places.

Spread over 57 acres (23 ha), the community is home to numerous certified and prac-ticing healers, clairvoyants, mediums, and psychics, who offer healing sessions to those suffering from ailments of the body and the spirit. Visitors can arrange a session with any of the spiritual counselors for a specified fee. Accom-modation is available on the premises. The center also organizes activities and classes on aspects of Spiritualism.

The Cassadaga Spiritualist Bookstore and Information Center has a vast collection of spiritual reading matter, CDs, and tapes, as well as gift articles such as crystals, jewelry, and ethnic artifacts.

DeLeon Springs State Park ➏

601 Ponce DeLeon Blvd. DeLeon Springs. **Tel** (386) 985-4212. ◯ 8am–sundown daily. www.floridastateparks.org/deleonsprings

The springs at this State Park were once believed to be the legendary fountain of youth. Today, they provide a pristine setting for various forms of outdoor recreation.

Swimming is one of the most popular activities here, with the springs being dammed to create a fine bathing area where the water remains at a pleasant 72°F (22°C). Numerous nature and hiking trails take visitors through beautiful, thickly wooded areas typical of Florida's habitat, and there are lovely picnic spots and pavilions. Fishing, boating, kayaking, and canoeing are permitted – you can rent kayaks and canoes at the park. At the **Old Spanish Sugar Mill** restaurant, guests can cook their own pancakes.

Adjoining the park is **Lake Woodruff National Wildlife Refuge**, a preserve for endan-gered birds and animals. Explore the lakes and marshes of the refuge in a canoe.

Lake Woodruff National Wildlife Refuge
2045 Mud Lake Rd, DeLand Springs. **Tel** (386) 985-4673. ◯ daylight hours daily.

The Old Spanish Sugar Mill amid the lush greenery and lakes of the DeLeon Springs State Park

Daytona Beach **7**

Volusia Co. 🏛 *64,000.* ✈ 🚉
ℹ️ *126 E Orange Ave, (386) 255-0415.* www.daytonabeach.com

Noisy Daytona Beach calls itself the "World's Most Famous Beach." This 23-mile (37-km) long beach is one of the few in Florida where cars are allowed on the sands, a hangover from the days when motor enthusiasts raced on the beaches: the first timed automobile runs took place just north of Daytona Beach, on the sands at Ormond Beach – the official "Birthplace of Speed" – in 1903.

Daytona is still a mecca for motorsports fans. The nearby **Daytona International Speedway** draws huge crowds, especially during the Speedweeks in February and the motorcycle racing events in March and October. Eight major racing weekends are held annually at the track, which can hold more than 110,000 spectators. The speed-way hosts NASCAR (National Association for Stock Car Auto Racing) meets – the Daytona 500 being the most famous – and sports car, motorcycle, and go-karting races. Events include charity bike-a-thons, vintage car rallies, superbike spectaculars, and production car tests. A tram tour around the speed-way track is available on days

The Daytona 500, held each February at Daytona International Speedway

when no races take place. Tickets for each Daytona 500 are usually sold out a year in advance, but visitors can relive the experience at DAYTONA USA, a popular attraction at the visitor center. One of the main exhibits is a film featuring spectacular in-car camera shots and behind-the-scenes action from a recent Daytona 500 race.

A race car at Daytona International Speedway

The beach, lined with hotels, bustles with frenzied activity. On offer are jet skiing, wind-surfing, buggy rides, gondola sky-rides above Ocean Pier. The old-fashioned boardwalk on the seafront is nostalgic, with bandstands, arcades, go-karts, and cotton candy.

Downtown Daytona, known simply as "Mainland," lies across the Halifax River from the beach. The restored downtown area is home to the **Halifax Historical Society**

Museum. Located in a 1910 bank building, the museum is decorated with fancy pilasters and murals. Local history displays include a model of the boardwalk as it was in 1938.

Close by, **Jackie Robinson Ballpark and Museum** – named after the baseball legend – is the home field of the Daytona Cubs.

West of downtown, the excellent **Museum of Arts & Sciences** has exhibits that cover a range of subjects, from Florida prehistory to fine and decorative arts from 1640–1920. There is a notable Cuban and African art collection. The 1907 **Gamble Place**, run by the same museum, is a hunting lodge with period furnishings. Tours of the house require reservations, and also include the Snow White House – built in 1938 and an exact copy of the one in the 1937 Disney classic.

Daytona International Speedway
1801 W International Speedway Blvd. **Tel** *(386) 253-7223.* ⬜ *daily.* ⬤ *Dec 25.* 📷 🎫 ♿ www.daytonainternationalspeedway.com

🏛 **Halifax Historical Society Museum**
252 S Beach St. **Tel** *(386) 255-6976.* ⬜ *10am–4pm Tue–Sat.* ⬤ *public hols.* 📷 🎁 ♿ www.halifaxhistorical.org

Jackie Robinson Ballpark and Museum
105 E Orange Ave. **Tel** *(386) 257-3172.* www.daytonacubs.com

🏛 **Museum of Arts & Sciences**
1040 Museum Blvd. **Tel** *(386) 255-0285.* ⬜ *9am–5pm Mon–Sat, 11am–5pm Sun.* ⬤ *Thanksgiving, Dec 24, Dec 25.* 📷 ♿ www.moas.org

Cars cruising the hard-packed sands of Daytona Beach

Beaches of the East Coast

The wide, sun-soaked sandy beaches of Central Florida's Atlantic Coast, with their warm waters and an average daytime temperature of 73°F (23°C), attract millions of visitors annually. The 72 miles (116 km) of the Space Coast feature lovely beaches, several being contiguous with lush nature preserves. Most are on barrier islands, and range from the pristine white beaches of the

Ponce de Leon Inlet lighthouse

Canaveral National Seashore and the Indian River, to boisterous resorts such as Cocoa Beach. To the north of the Space Coast are Ormond Beach and the highly popular Daytona Beach, both associated with automobile racing. Most of the East Coast beaches are family-friendly, with picnic areas and restrooms, and also offer a wide range of water sports.

Ormond Beach ①
This resort offers small town charm along with water activities on its many rivers and lakes, as well as the ocean.

Ponce Inlet ④ is a vehicle-free beach with several nature trails. It also has an observation deck, and offers tours of its lighthouse.

New Smyrna Beach ⑤ has a tranquil stretch of sand and gentle waves. Highlights include nature trails and quaint stores along the nearby streets.

Daytona Beach ②
Proximity to an auto racing mecca, glittering nightspots, and a surfeit of water sports make this Florida's busiest beach.

Daytona Beach Shores ③ is a popular family destination, more peaceful than Daytona Beach.

Indian River Beaches ⑧ offer uncrowded stretches of sand and access to Merritt Island National Wildlife Refuge.

Melbourne Beach ⑨ is a quiet spot, with superb sunsets and several beachfront parks.

Titusville

Kennedy Space Center

Cocoa

Melbourne

92
95

Playalinda at Canaveral ⑥
One of Florida's few nude beaches, it offers a great view of Kennedy Space Center's rocket launches (*see p124–7*).

Cocoa Beach ⑦ offers a range of fun-filled activities, such as surfing, scuba diving, and waterskiing, as well as dining and shopping options (*see p122*).

0 km   10

0 miles   10

Ocala National Forest ⓾

Lake Co/Marion Co. ⓘ *3199 NE Co. Rd, (352) 236-0288.* ⏰ *8am–sunset daily.* 🚫 *to campsite & swimming areas.* ♿ ⛺ **Juniper Springs canoe rental *Tel* (352) 625-2808.** **www**. ocalacc.com/visitor-center/forestry.asp

Located between Ocala city and the St. Johns River, this is the world's largest pine forest, covering an area of 366,000 acres (148,000 ha). The forest is crisscrossed by spring-fed rivers and dozens of hiking trails. One of the last refuges of the endangered Florida black bear, it is also home to many more common animals such as deer and otter. Several birds, including barred owls, bald eagles, ospreys, the non-native wild turkey, and various species of waders – which frequent the river swamp areas – can all be spotted here.

The numerous hiking trails in the forest vary in length from boardwalks to short loop trails of under a mile (1.6 km) to a 66-mile (106-km) stretch of the cross-state National Scenic Trail. Bass fishing is popular on the many lakes scattered through the forest, and there are swimming holes, picnic areas, and campgrounds at recreation areas such as Salt Springs, Fore Lake, and Alexander Springs.

Canoes are easily available for rental. The 7-mile (11-km) canoe run down Juniper

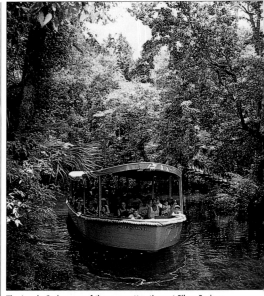

The Jungle Cruise, one of the many attractions at Silver Springs

Creek from the **Juniper Springs Recreation Area** is one of the finest in the state. Book in advance as it is an extremely popular tourist destination. The Salt Springs Trail provides an excellent vantage point for bird-watching, and wood ducks congregate on Lake Dorr.

You can pick up guides and information at the main visitor center on the western edge of the forest, or at the smaller centers at Salt Springs and Lake Dorr, both on Route 19.

Silver Springs ⓾

Marion Co. *5656 E Silver Springs Blvd. Tel (352) 236-2121.* ⏰ *10am–5pm daily.* 🚫 ♿ *limited.* **www**.silversprings.com

Glass-bottomed boat trips at Silver Springs have been revealing the natural wonders of the world's largest artesian spring since 1878. Today, Florida's oldest commercial tourist attraction offers not only the famous glass-bottomed boat rides but also jeep safaris and jungle cruises, which take you on a trip through the Florida out-back. The early Tarzan movies starring Johnny Weismuller were filmed here.

Another popular attraction here is the Alligator & Crocodile Encounter at Cypress Island: this 5-acre (2-ha) area is home to 13 of the 23 species of alligators and crocodiles. Nearby, Wild Waters is a lively family-oriented water park.

Environs
The **Silver River State Park**, 2 miles (3 km) southeast, offers a lovely walk through a hardwood hammock and cypress swamp area, leading to a swimming hole in a bend of the crystal-clear river.

FLORIDA'S BUBBLING SPRINGS

Most of Florida's 320 known springs are located in the upper half of the state. The majority are artesian springs, formed by waters forced up through deep fissures from underground aquifers (rock deposits containing water). Those that gush over 100 cu ft (3 cu m) per second are known as first-magnitude springs.

Filtered through the rock, the water is extremely pure and sometimes high in salts and minerals. These properties, plus the sheer beauty of the springs, have long attracted visitors for recreational and health purposes.

Juniper Springs in Ocala National Forest, adapted for swimmers in the 1930s

The gaping jaws of an alligator marking the entrance to Gatorland

Silver River State Park

1425 NE 58th Ave, Ocala. **Tel** (352) 236-7148. ◯ 8am–sunset daily. www.floridastateparks.org/silverriver

Gatorland ❿

Orange Co. 14501 S Orange Blossom Trail, Orlando. (800) 393-5297. Orlando. Orlando. ◯ 9am–5pm daily. www.gatorland.com

Spread over an area of 110 acres (44 ha), this park opened in the 1950s as a huge working farm, and has a special license to raise alligators for their hides and meat. Gatorland's breeding pens, nurseries, and rearing ponds are home to thousands of alligators that range in size from infants that fit into the palm of your hand to 12-ft (4-m) monsters. They can be observed from a boardwalk and tower as they bask in the hallows of a cypress swamp.

The shows are somewhat contrived but still fun. They include alligator wrestling and the Gator Jumparoo, in which huge alligators leap out of the water to grab chunks of chicken from the hands of the trainers. In addition, the park features close encounters and handling demonstrations of Florida's poisonous snakes.

The park's other highlights include an aviary, a bird breeding marsh, and a petting zoo. Gatorland's restaurant offers unique delicacies, such as Gator nuggets and ribs.

On sale at Gatorland

Kissimmee ⓫

Osceola Co. 41,000. 1925 E Irlo Bronson Memorial Hwy, (407) 847-5000. www.floridakiss.com **Old Town** 5770 W Irlo Bronson Memorial Hwy. **Tel** (407) 396-4888. www.old-town.com

This cattle boom town, whose name means "Heaven's Place" in the language of the Calusa Indians, had cows freely roaming its streets in the early 1900s. Now the only livestock visitors are likely to encounter are those that appear in the twice-yearly rodeos at Silver Spurs Arena, and the more down-to-earth rodeos held every Friday night at **Kissimmee Sports Arena & Rodeo** (see p179). Most visitors headed for Walt Disney World often stop at Kissimmee for the many inexpensive motels on the busy, traffic-ridden US 192.

One of the typically offbeat shops in Kissimmee's Old Town

Kissimmee's **Old Town** is a re-created pedestrian street of early 20th-century buildings with some unusual and eccentric shops, offering psychic readings, tattoos, Irish linen, candles, and so forth. There is also an entertaining haunted house and a small fairground with antique equipment.

Warbird Adventures, by the Kissimmee municipal airport, gives visitors the unforgettable opportunity to fly in an original World War II advanced T-6 navy trainer or a classic MASH helicopter. Whether you want a thrilling acrobatic adventure or a smooth sightseeing flight, visitors can take the controls and learn about flying one of these historical aircraft from an experienced instructor.

Kissimmee Sports Arena & Rodeo

1010 Suhls Lane. **Tel** (407) 933-0020. ◯ for shows 8pm Fri. Dec. www.ksarodeo.com

Warbird Adventures

Tel (407) 870-7366, (800) 386-1593 ◯ 9am–5pm Mon–Sat, Sun by appointment only. www.warbirdadventures.com

A World of Orchids ⓬

Orange Co. 2501 Old Lake Wilson Rd, Kissimmee. **Tel** (407) 396-1887. ◯ 9:30am–4:30pm Mon–Sat. Sun & public hols. www.aworldoforchids.com

Varieties of gorgeous orchids bloom through-out the year in this huge conservatory – complete with streams and waterfalls – spread over 3,000 sq ft (279 sq m). Also showcased here are several species of tropical plants, including palms and bamboo, as well as exotic birds and small animals, such as Asian squirrels and chameleons. Rare species of colorful fish are on display in beautifully set-up aquaria. Visitors can enjoy nature walks and guided tours, and stop at the gift shop to carry home a couple of these spectacular plants. Plan to spend at least an hour in this lovely setting.

Fantasy of Flight ⑬

Polk Co. 1400 Broadway Blvd SE, Polk City. *(863) 984-3500.* Winter Haven. Winter Haven. 10am–5pm daily. Thanksgiving, Dec 25. www.fantasyofflight.com

This aviation center gains an advantage over similar attractions in Florida by being the only one to provide the very sensations of flying. The Fightertown section, for instance, allows visitors to ride in a World War II fighter aircraft simulator in a dogfight over the Pacific. Firstly, you receive a pre-flight briefing, and then once you are in the cockpit the control tower advises you about takeoff, landing, and the presence of enemy aircraft.

Other attractions include a series of vivid walk-through exhibits, which take you into a World War II B-17 Flying Fortress during a bombing mission, and into World War I trenches in the middle of an air raid. A hangar holds an impressive collection of vintage airplanes in mint condition, such as the first widely used airliner in the US, the 1929 Ford Tri-Motor, which appeared in the film *Indiana Jones and the Temple of Doom*, and the Roadair 1, a combined plane and car that flew just once, in 1959.

Florida Southern College ⑭

Polk Co. 111 Lake Hollingsworth Dr, Lakeland. **Tel** *(863) 680-4111.* Lakeland. Lakeland. daily. Jan 1, Jul 4, Thanksgiving, Dec 25. **Visitor Center** 10am–4pm Mon–Fri, 10am–2pm Sat.

Located in the picturesque town of Lakeland, Florida Southern College has the world's largest collection of buildings designed by Frank Lloyd Wright, one of America's most eminent architects. Amazingly, the college president managed to persuade Wright to design the campus with the promise of little more than the opportunity to express his ideas, and payment when

The light and spacious interior of the Annie Pfeiffer Chapel

the money could be raised. Work began in 1938 on what Wright, already famous as the founder of organic architecture, termed his "child of the sun." His aim of blending the buildings with their natural surroundings was achieved by using glass to bring outdoor light to the interiors. The original plan was for 18 structures, but only seven had been completed by the time Wright died in 1959; five were finished or added later.

The **Annie Pfeiffer Chapel** is a particularly fine expression of his ideas. Stained-glass windows break the monotony of the building blocks, and the entire edifice is topped by a spectacular tower in place of the traditional steeple. Wright called this tower a "jewel box."

On the whole, the campus has the light and airy feel that Wright sought to achieve. The buildings are linked to each other by the Esplanades – a covered walkway, stretching for 1.5-miles (2 km), in which light, shade, and variations in height draw attention from one building to the next.

You can wander around the campus at any time, but the interiors can be explored only during the week. The Frank Lloyd Wright visitor center at **Thad Buckner Building** has examples of Wright's drawings and furniture.

FLORIDA SOUTHERN COLLEGE

Annie Pfeiffer Chapel ⑥
Benjamin Fine Building ②
Emile Watson Building ①
J. Edgar Wall Waterdome ③
Lucius Pond Ordway Building ⑨
Polk County Science Buildings ⑧
Raulerson Building ④
Thad Buckner Building ⑤
William Danforth Chapel ⑦

KEY

Esplanades

Parking

Information

0 meters 100
0 yards 100

Dinosaur World ⓕ

Hillsboro Co. 5145 Harvey Tew Rd,
Plant City. *Tel (813) 717-9865.*
◯ 9am–5pm daily. 🖼 📷 👤
www.dinoworld.net

Tyrannosaurus rex and
around 150 other life-size
dinosaurs tower over vegetation in the lush park setting
of this outdoor museum.
Made of styrofoam and metal,
these realistic-looking and
scientifically accurate models
of prehistoric creatures are
arranged in a chronological
order throughout the park.

A museum displays fossils
and other dinosaur-related
objects. Other highlights
include a film on the world
of dinosaurs and a display
that explains the elaborate
process used by the park to
create its dinosaurs.

Dinosaur World offers many
hands-on activities for kids: at
a fossil dig, they can use little
shovels or dip their hands in
the sand to come up with tiny
treasures that are dinosaur
related; at the Boneyard, they
can hunt for dinosaur bones.
Picnic areas abound, and
there is a gift shop with fun
but pricey products.

Cypress Gardens Adventure Park ⓰

Polk Co. 6000 Cypress Gardens Blvd,
Winter Haven. *Tel (863) 324-2111.*
🚃 Winter Haven. ◯ daily. ●
Good Fri, Thanksgiving, Dec 25. 🖼
👤 **www.**cypressgardens.com

Relying on the unlikely twin
elements of flowers and
waterskiing to attract the
crowds, Florida's first theme
park, Cypress Gardens,
opened in 1936. Closed in
2003, the park was rescued
by grants from the state of
Florida and Polk County. The
new park, opened in 2004,
combines the charm of the
original with the excitement
of various new thrill rides.

The park retains the original
splendor of the botanical
gardens, which feature 8,000
varieties of plants set beside a
massive cypress-fringed lake.
Also restored are the amazing
waterskiing and ice-skating

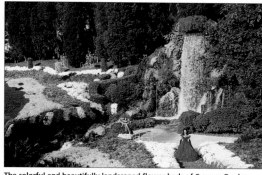
The colorful and beautifully landscaped flower beds of Cypress Gardens

stunt shows, the Wings of
Wonder butterfly arboretum,
topiary gardens, and animal
exhibits. New attractions
include a huge concert
amphitheater and around
38 water, thrill, and roller
coaster rides. A lovely
carousel, a 100-ft (30-m)
Ferris wheel, and bumper
cars are other highlights.

Cypress Gardens is still
undergoing reconstruction,
with ever-more attractions
being added to the park.

Historic Bok Sanctuary ⓱

Polk Co. 1151 Tower Blvd, Lake Wales.
Tel (863) 676-1408. 🚃 Lake Wales.
🚃 Winter Haven. ◯ 8am–5pm
daily. 🖼 👤 **www.**boksanctuary.org

Edward W. Bok arrived in the
US from Holland in 1870
at the age of six, and subse-
quently became an influential

The striking pink marble Singing
Tower at Historic Bok Sanctuary

publisher. Shortly before his
death in 1930, he presented
128 acres (52 ha) of beautiful
woodland gardens to the
American public "for the
success they had given him."

Sitting at the highest spot in
peninsular Florida – at 298 ft
(91 m) above sea level – the
gardens are spread over 250
acres (102 ha) around the
Singing Tower that soars
above the treetops. Bok's
grave is at its base. Visitors
are not allowed to climb the
tower; but try to attend its 45-
minute live carillon concert,
which is rung daily at 3pm.

Yeehaw Junction ⓲

Osceola Co. Desert Inn, 5570
S Kenansville Rd, Yeehaw Junction.
Tel (407) 436-1054. ◯ daily. 👤
www.desertinnrestaurant.com

Located at the crossroads of
US 60 and the Florida
Turnpike, quaintly named
Yeehaw Junction harks back
to the Florida of a couple of
centuries ago. It is known
for its motel and restaurant,
Desert Inn, which served as a
watering hole for lumbermen
and cowboys driving herds of
cattle from the center of the
state to the reservations and
plantations on the coast. Now
listed on the National Registry
of Historical Places, the 1880s
wooden building offers a
fascinating look into the
history of Cracker Country.
The restaurant serves gator-
and turtle-burgers, and also
has a large outdoor area for
festivals – mostly bluegrass
music – and barbecues.

The grand Porcher House, on the edge of Cocoa's leafy historic district

Cocoa Beach ⑲

Brevard Co. ⓘ *400 Fortenberry Rd, Merritt Island.* **Tel** *(321) 459-2200.* ⚑ *14,000.* ⚑ *Merritt Island.* **www.** cocoabeachchamber.com

Located on a barrier island adjoining the Atlantic Ocean, this is one of the most popular beaches on the Space Coast. Known as the East Coast's surfing capital, bustling Cocoa Beach hosts several surfing festivals during Easter and the Labor Day weekends. Motels, chain restaurants, and the odd strip joint character-ize the main throughfare. The best-known attraction here is the **Ron Jon Surf Shop**, a neon palace-like store with a huge T-shirt collection and surfboards *(see p163).* Tour the Banana River Lagoon fringing Cocoa Beach to see marine and bird species. Or go fishing at the dock at Ramp Road Park, one of the state's best fishing spots.

🏠 Ron Jon Surf Shop
4151 N Atlantic Ave. **Tel** *(321) 799-8820.* ⏱ *24 hrs daily.* ♿
www.ronjons.com

Cocoa ⑳

Brevard Co. ⚑ *20,000.* ⚑ ⓘ *400 Fortenberry Rd, Merritt Island, (321) 459- 2200.*

The most appealing of the sprawling communities along the Space Coast mainland, the vibrant town of Cocoa is located close to the Indian River. Its historic district, Cocoa Village, has buildings dating from the 1880s, replica gas streetlamps, and brick sidewalks. On Delannoy Avenue, on the eastern edge of the village, is the Classical Revival **Porcher House**, built of coquina stone in 1916 by a leading citrus plantation owner. Another not-to-miss site is the **Brevard Museum of History & Science**, which has nature trails that represent different ecosystems – pine sandhill, freshwater marsh, and hardwood hammock.

🏛 Brevard Museum of History & Science
2201 Michigan Ave. **Tel** *(321) 632-1830.* ⏱ *10am–4pm Mon–Sat, noon–4pm Sun.* 🎟 ♿
www.brevardmuseum.com

Valiant Air Command Warbird Museum ㉑

Brevard Co. 6600 Tico Rd, Titusville. **Tel** *(321) 268-1941.* ⚑ *Titusville.* ⏱ *10am–6pm daily.* ⬤ *Jan 1, Thanksgiving, Dec 25.* 🎟 🎫 ♿
www.vacwarbirds.org

This museum is home to an enormous hangar that fea-tures an impressive collection of military aircraft from World War II and later, all restored to flying condition. The pride of the collection is a Douglas C-47 called Tico Belle, which became the official carrier for the Danish royal family at the end of the war. An air show is held in March each year.

Tico Belle, the prize exhibit at the Warbird Air Museum

US Astronaut Hall of Fame® ㉒

Brevard Co. Junction of Rte 405 & US 1. **Tel** *(321) 269-6101.* ⚑ *Titusville.* ⏱ *10:30am–6:30pm daily.* ⬤ *Dec 25.* 🎟 ♿ **www.** kennedyspacecenter.com/visitKSC/ attractions/fame.asp

Set up to commemorate the country's astronauts, the facility showcases a fascinat-ing collection of their personal memorabilia and other related artifacts. The center also offers

The Ron Jon Surf Shop in Cocoa Beach, with everything for the surfing or beach enthusiast

eractive experiences in the
rm of a simulated ride in a
ck space shuttle. On the
me site, the US Space Camp
fers some specially designed
urses for children interested
learning about space.

Canaveral National Seashore ㉓

evard Co. Rte A1A, 20 miles (32 km)
of Titusville or Rte 402, 10 miles (16
n) E of Titusville. **Tel** (321) 267-1110.
Titusville. ☐ *Beaches 6am–*
m Apr–Oct, 6am–6pm Nov–Mar.
for shuttle launches. 🎥 ♿
www.nps.gov/cana

pread over an area of 57,000
cres (23,000 ha), Canaveral
ational Seashore located on
barrier island, features an
stounding range of fauna
nd a wide range of habitats,
ncluding marshes, saltwater
stuaries, hardwood ham-
nocks, and pine flatwoods.
he bird life makes the
reatest visual impact.

The park incorporates
lorida's largest undeveloped
barrier island beach – a
magnificent 24-mile
39-km) stretch
backed by barrier
dunes. Apollo
Beach, at the
northern end, is
accessible along
Route A1A, while
Playalinda Beach is
reached from the south,
along Route 402. Note
that this is a popular
spot for nude bathing.

An alligator in the wild

Behind Apollo Beach, the
Turtle Mound is a 40-ft (12-m)
high midden of oyster shells
created by Timucua Indians.

Merritt Island National Wildlife Refuge ㉔

Brevard Co. Route 406, 4 miles
(6.5 km) E of Titusville. **Tel** (321)
861-0667. 🚌 ☐ *sunrise–sunset*
daily. 🚌 *for shuttle launches.*
www.merrittisland.fws.gov

Experience an incredible
variety of marine and wild-life
at this expansive nature
preserve adjoining Canaveral
National Seashore. Covering
an area of 140,000 acres
(56,656 ha), the Merritt Island
National Wildlife Refuge is
a seaside haven for several
endangered and threatened
species of animals and birds,
including manatees, sea
turtles, Eastern indigo
snakes, American alligators,
otters, falcons, terns, ospreys,
woodpeckers, owls, and many
more. The refuge also
provides sanctuary to
thousands of plant
species typical of
Florida's ecosys-
tems and habitats.
By far the best way to
explore the local
wildlife is to follow the
7-mile (11-km) Black Point
Wildlife Drive – a self guided
tour through salt- and freshwater marshes. An excellent
leaflet, available at the track's
start near the junction of
Routes 402 and 406, explains
such matters as how dikes
help control local mosquito
populations – although it is
a good idea to come armed
with insect repellent in
summer. Halfway along the
drive, you can stretch your
legs by following the 5-mile
(8-km) Cruickshank Trail,
which starts nearby and has
an observation tower.

East along Route 402, to-
ward Playalinda Beach, the
Merritt Island Visitor Information Center offers educational
displays and a short film
about the refuge. A mile
(1.6 km) farther east, the Oak
Hammock and Palm Hammock
trails have short boardwalks
across the marshland for bird-
watching and photography.

A large part of the refuge
lies within Kennedy Space
Center (see pp124–7) and is
out of bounds to the public.

SPACE COAST BIRD LIFE

The magnificent and abundant bird life
of the Space Coast is best viewed early
in the morning or shortly before dusk.
Between November and March, in
particular, the marshes and lagoons
teem with migratory ducks and waders,
as up to 100,000 arrive from
colder northern climes.

Sandhill crane

Brown pelican

Royal tern

Black skimmer

Scenic view from Black Point Drive, Merritt Island National Wildlife Refuge

Kennedy Space Center ㉕

NASA insignia

Situated on Merritt Island Wildlife Refuge, just an hour's drive east of Orlando, the Kennedy Space Center is the only place in the Western Hemisphere from where humans are launched into space. It was from here, with the launch of *Apollo 11* in July 1969, that President Kennedy's dream of landing a man on the moon was realized. The center is the home of NASA (National Aeronautics and Space Administration), whose space shuttle *(see pp22–3)* can often be seen lifting off from one of the launch pads. With a scale and popularity comparable to Orlando's other theme parks, the Visitor Complex aims to both inform and entertain.

Spacemen
Staff dressed up as spacemen may put in a surprise appearance at any time, providing ideal photo opportunities for children.

★ **Apollo/Saturn V Center**
A Saturn V rocket, of the kind used by the Apollo missions, is the showpiece here. There is also a reconstructed control room where visitors experience a simulated launch (see p127).

Astronaut Encounter

Children's Play Dome

★ **Rocket Garden**
You can walk through a group of towering rockets, each of which represents a different period of space flight's history.

Nature & Technology Universe Theater

Exploration in the New Millennium

Entrance

P   **P**

STAR FEATURES

★ Apollo/Saturn V Center

★ Rocket Garden

★ KSC Bus Tours

★ IMAX® Theater

VISITOR COMPLEX

All visitors to the Kennedy Space Center must stop at the Visitor Complex, which was established in 1966 to offer bus tours of the area. It is now an extensive attraction with many exhibits.

★ KSC Bus Tours
A bus tour makes a circuit of the center's launch pads, passing the Vehicle Assembly Building and the "crawlerway," along which the shuttle is slowly maneuvered into position.

★ IMAX® Theater
The IMAX® Theater runs films about spac e exploration. Footage from the shuttle missions offers some breathtaking views of Earth from space (see p126).

Astronaut Memorial

Space shop

Shuttle Plaza

Launch Status Center
Interactive exhibits re-create the space shuttle's complex prelaunch, liftoff, and flight procedures.

Information Central	Robot Scouts	Departure point for bus tours

0 meters   25

0 yards   25

KEY

🅿 Parking

💲 ATM (cash machine)

🍴 Restaurant

KENNEDY SPACE CENTER PLAN

(402) Apollo/Saturn V Center

Launch pad 39b

Shuttle Runway

Launch pad 39a

INDIAN RIVER   MERRITT ISLAND

Vehicle Assembly Building

(405)

Visitor Complex

Space Center Headquarters

Air Force Space Station

0 km   (3) 10

0 miles   5

(A1A)

PORT CANAVERAL

Exploring the Kennedy Space Center

Built in 1967 for astronauts and their families to view space center operations, today the Visitor Complex is host to more than 2 million tourists each year. The 131-sq-mile (340-sq-km) facility offers guests a full-day, comprehensive space experience, including excellent IMAX® films at the Visitor Complex, live-action shows, astronaut encounters, and the Apollo/Saturn V Center – the climax of the narrated, video-enhanced bus tour. The go-at-your-own-pace tour enables visitors to stop and explore each of the major destinations. One all-inclusive admission ticket takes visitors on the KSC Tour, both IMAX® space films, and all exhibits.

Kids enjoy the Robot Scouts at the Imax® Theater

VISITOR COMPLEX

The place where everyone heads first is the **IMAX® Theater**, where two back-to-back IMAX® theaters put on stunning films on screens more than five stories high. For some people this is the highlight of their visit.

Top of the bill is *Magnificent Desolation: Walking on the Moon 3-D.* Narrated by Tom Hanks, this film takes audiences to the lunar surface to walk alongside the 12 astronauts who have been there. Rarely seen NASA footage, computer-generated images, and live-action renditions all feature. The other film on offer at the IMAX® Theater is *Space Station 3-D,* which

shows astronauts from Europe and America on board a space station. It provides great footage of those amazing views that only astronauts get to see.

The 300-seat Universe Theater at the Visitor Complex shows the inspirational film *Quest for Life,* which highlights the need for future space exploration to search for life in our galaxy. The **NASA Art Gallery**, inside the IMAX® Theater, offers more than 200 artworks by some famous artists, including Andy Warhol, Robert Rauschenberg, and Annie Leibovitz.

Kids will probably prefer to see the latest planetary explorer robots, and learn

about their interplanetary adventures as revealed in **Robot Scouts**. The **Astronaut Encounter** show offers visitors the rare opportunity of meeting a real astronaut.

In Shuttle Plaza, guests can climb aboard and enjoy a close-up view of **Explorer** – a replica of the space shuttle. The **Launch Status Center** alongside has displays of genuine flight hardware and rocket boosters. Nearby, a "Space Mirror" reflects sunlight onto the names inscribed on the **Astronaut Memorial**. This honors the 16 astronauts, from the *Apollo 1* to the Space Shuttle *Columbia* missions, who have died in the service of space exploration. The new **Space Shuttle Launch Experience** gives visitors the opportunity to experience the reality of a launch.

Exploration in the New Millennium offers a film, lecture, and informative exhibits on what the future holds for space exploration. Guests can see and touch a piece of a Mars meteorite.

The *Explorer*, a life-size replica of the space shuttle

TIMELINE OF SPACE EXPLORATION

1955	1960	1965	1970	1975
1958 First American satellite, the *Explorer 1,* is launched (Jan 31)	**1962** John Glenn orbits the earth in *Mercury* spacecraft	**1969** Neil Armstrong and Buzz Aldrin *(Apollo 11)* walk on the moon (Jul 24) **1966** *Gemini 8* makes first space docking (Mar 16)		**1977** The Space Shuttle *Enterprise* is tested aboard a Boeing 747 (Feb 18)
	1961 On May 5, Alan Shepherd becomes the first American in space. Kennedy commits nation to moon landing *John Glenn*	**1965** Edward White is the first American to walk in space (Jun 3)	**1968** *Apollo 8* orbits the moon (Dec 24) **1975** American *Apollo* and Russian *Soyuz* vehicles dock in orbit (Jul 17)	

Buzz Aldrin

Space Shuttle Colu

Canceled

KENNEDY SPACE CENTER — page 127

KSC EXHIBITS & BUS TOURS

The entrance gate, modeled after the International Space Station, welcomes guests to the Visitor Complex. Once inside the complex, there is a fascinating walk-through exhibit, which shows visitors a comprehensive history of the major missions that provided the foundation for the space program. The all-glass rotunda leads to **Early Space Exploration**, which showcases key figures from the early days of rocketry. In the **Mercury Mission Control Room**, visitors view from an observation deck the actual components and consoles from which the first eight manned missions were monitored. Footage and interviews with some of the personnel are highlights of this area. Next to it are displays of some of the authentic *Mercury* and *Gemini* spacecraft, which enable visitors to relive some of the excitement and intensity of early space exploration. KSC Tour buses leave every few minutes from the Visitor Complex and offer an exceptional tour of the space center's facilities. The tour encompasses two major facilities at the space center: the LC 39 Observation Gantry and the Apollo/Saturn V Center. The tour takes guests into secured areas, where guides explain the inner workings of each of the facilities. Visitors can take as long as they wish to explore each sight.

There are two additional special-interest tours that visitors can take at the center: **Cape Canaveral: Then & Now Tour**, which is a historic tour of the *Mercury, Gemini,* and *Apollo* launch pads; and the **NASA Up Close Tour**, which provides an insider's view of the entire space shuttle program. The NASA Up Close Tour includes within its ambit the International Space Station Center. Here, guests can walk through and peer inside the facility where each shuttle's components are assembled for launch.

The Vehicle Assembly Building, which dominates the flat landscape

Rockets on display at the Cape Canaveral Air Station

SPACE CENTER TOUR

Each self-guided tour can take anything between two and six hours to fully explore the two facilities on the KSC Tour. Visitors can get a spectacular bird's-eye view of the gigantic launch pads from the 60-ft (18-m) observation tower at the first stop, the **LC 39 Observation Gantry**. Back on the ground, a film and a range of exhibits tell the story of a NASA space shuttle launch and landing.

A commemmoration of the first moon landing of 1969, the spacious **Apollo/Saturn V Center** features an actual 363-ft (110-m) Saturn V moon rocket. Guests can watch the historic launch of *Apollo 8*, the first manned mission to the moon, in the Firing Room Theater. They can follow this up by viewing a film at the Lunar Theater, which shows actual footage of the moon landing. The only place in the world where guests can dine next to a genuine moon rock is also here, at the Moon Rock Café.

Timeline: 1984 First American woman, Kathryn Sullivan, walks in space (Oct 11). The first woman into space, Space Shuttle Challenger. 1986 The Challenger explodes, killing all its crew (Jan 28). 1988 Discovery, the first shuttle since the Challenger disaster, is launched (Sep 29). 1990 Hubble telescope is launched (Apr 24). 1995 The Atlantis docks with Russian Mir space station (Jun 29). Atlantis–Mir insignia (Jun 1995). 1996 Mars Pathfinder gathers data from Mars. 2001 Dennis Tito pays US$20 million for one week on the International Space Station. 2003 Space Shuttle Columbia explodes on re-entry into Earth's atmosphere (Feb 1). 2005 Discovery, the first mission since the Columbia disaster, arrives home safely after dramatic spacewalk repairs.

The bright lights of Universal CityWalk® at night

TRAVELERS' NEEDS

WHERE TO STAY

With an extensive range of available accommodations and more than 100,000 hotel rooms in the area, Orlando caters to every budget and taste. A visitor can choose from neighborhood bed-and-breakfasts, off-the-beaten-track motels, resorts with in-room Jacuzzis and championship golf courses, ultra-luxurious penthouse suites, buildings shaped like giant guitars, and even rooms that overlook wandering herds of zebra and wildebeest. Outdoor enthusiasts, looking forward to sleeping under the stars, can access any of the

Logo of the Hard Rock Hotel

many campgrounds and trailer parks. If you are planning a long trip or are traveling in a big group, there are plenty of condos available for hire. The listings on pages 138–45 recommend a variety of places in Central Florida, all representing the best of their kind and in all the price ranges, from reasonable to extravagant. However, the prices tend to fluctuate depending on the season and the location. The Orlando/Orange County Convention & Visitors Bureau website can provide more detailed information on rooms and availability.

The opulent interior of the renowned Peabody Hotel, International Drive

HOTELS & RESORTS

Most of the larger hotels and resorts in the area are fairly new or have been recently renovated. The smaller hotels, on the other hand, tend to be older and are well-established.

Widely prevalent and extremely popular, chain hotels have the advantage of at least being predictable – although prices vary depending on the location. Every chain is represented, from the high-end Radisson and Marriott hotels through the mid-range Holiday Inns to the budget Days Inn chain.

Resorts are large hotel complexes, usually set by the water and surrounded by acres of immaculately kept grounds. Prices are high, but these resorts provide various amenities, from swimming

pools and exercise rooms to shops and a wide range of world-class restaurants to choose from. With their well-equipped games rooms and special children's programs,

Disney's Palm Course, golfing paradise for amateurs and pros

these resorts can be a good option for families. Golf is a major attraction in Central Florida, and many resorts offer championship-level courses and instructors for private lessons. Themed resorts, designed around a particular era or activity such as sports or the films of the 1950s, are very popular.

Also designed to entertain are the traditional hotels, such as the Sheraton Safari with its African motif, the Red Horse Inn, decked out in Southwestern style, and the Doubletree Castle, with its towering spires and the Renaissance era music.

Only lacking the manicured acreage of the resorts, the grand hotels of Orlando are impressive in all other aspects. The Peabody Hotel, for instance, offers a fully-equipped athletic club with an Olympic-sized pool, tennis courts, and two excellent gourmet restaurants.

THE THEME PARK EXPERIENCE

When the Disney theme parks set up resorts right on their properties, it opened a whole new world of vacation possibilities (see p133 & pp134–5). With several hotels literally within walking distance of a theme park or the Disney shopping area, the goal is to keep the attractions always in sight of

The hotels mentioned here are listed on pp138–45

The brilliant exterior of the Hard Rock Hotel, Universal Studios

...he entertainment-hungry visitor. Special package plans often include entry to the parks and transportation. Several shuttles and water-taxies connecting the parks and hotels are exclusively available for hotel guests.

In case parents equate theme parks with kid stuff, Disney property is also home to five 18-hole, PGA championship courses and training camps for the Atlanta Braves, the Orlando Rays, and the Tampa Bay Buccaneers ballteams. Recreational activities – such as surfing at the famous Typhoon Lagoon water park, golf, tennis, swimming, para-sailing, and horseback riding – are all included and within easy reach of the hotels.

Universal Orlando is oriented more toward older children and adults than Disney. This is reflected in the main attractions of the two theme parks, and the "themes" of the three hotels on Universal property *(see p133 & p135)*. The Jurassic Park rides, The Amazing Adventures of Spider-Man, Back to the Future...The Ride, and Terminator 2: 3D are not for the Mickey Mouse-aged crowd. The lure of the Hard Rock Hotel, Portofino Bay, and the Royal Pacific Resort is also definitely adult oriented. The absence of any sports or recreational facilities here is more than made up by the shopping and dining options at Universal CityWalk. Placed between the two parks, it can make for an entertaining and exciting destination.

SPA HOTELS

Disney is the trendsetter of all things spa in Orlando, and hosts three world-class retreats on its property – the Saratoga Springs Resort & Spa, the Grand Floridian Resort & Spa with 900 rooms on an expansive 40-acre (16-ha) spread, and the 9,000-sq-ft (836-sq-m) Wyndham Palace Resort & Spa *(see p139)*. Although all these are highly expensive stays compared to traditional hotels, the amenities provided here are difficult to

A relaxing massage at the Grand Floridian Resort & Spa

find anywhere else. Grand Floridian, in particular, offers beauty shops, facial, massage and water therapy, and a white-sand beach for relaxing.

The facilities at Westgate Lakes, just outside the Disney main gate on Lake Buena Vista, are typical of what local spas have to offer – personal attendants, facials, massages, steam rooms and saunas, whirlpools, and a full beauty salon. The Canyon Ranch Spa Club at the new Gaylord Palms Resort offers guests use of cardiovascular equipment, haircuts, and manicures along with body wraps and saunas. The internationally-renowned Mandara Spa from Indonesia has recently opened a center at Universal's Portofino Bay Hotel *(see p141)*.

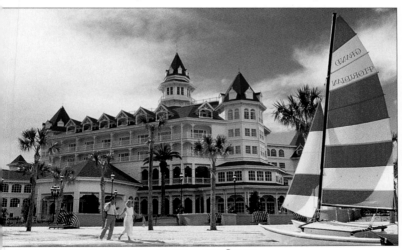

The luxurious Grand Floridian Resort & Spa at Walt Disney World® Resort

The Hyatt Regency Hotel, Orlando International Airport *(see p145)*

PLACES TO STAY AWAY FROM THE CROWDS

Hotels in Downtown Orlando and in smaller suburbs can offer high-end accommodations at much lower prices *(see pp141–5)*. Conveniently located inside the Orlando International Airport, Hyatt Regency is a good choice for travel-weary tourists and is only 16 miles (26 km) from Disney. Visitors using the Orlando-Sanford International Airport have a choice of several three- and four-star hotels in Sanford and Lake Mary. You can be far from the crowds at these hotels, and at the same time, within fairly easy reach of the theme parks. The attractive Park Plaza Hotel, in upscale Winter Park, has "garden suites" and bougainvillea-draped balconies. The Art Deco Westin Grand Bohemian Hotel in Downtown Orlando has 250 rooms as well as a AAA Four Diamond Award-winning restaurant. For lower room rates, try La Quinta Inn.

BED-AND-BREAKFASTS

Travel to the north and east of Orlando for cosy and affordable B&Bs. Old-world hospitality and homes with antique furnishings are on offer here. Thurston House in Downtown Orlando is a restored Queen Anne Victorian farmhouse with fruit trees, a wraparound porch to unwind on, and lovely flower gardens. The Courtyard at Lake Lucerne is a group of four historic buildings, built between 1883 and 1945; a quiet oasis in the heart of Downtown Orlando. This romantic getaway is popular with honeymooners. The PerriHouse Bed & Breakfast Inn is close to the Walt Disney World Resort and is surrounded by orange groves. All B&Bs offer short- and long-term stays, and guests often eat together in an informal atmosphere. The ambience and the personal touch of the hosts usually make up for the absence of the amenities offered by a full-service hotel.

CONDO RENTALS

Renting a condominium is a popular alternative to hotels and resorts. This is specially true for long-term stays or large family groups. One and two bedroom apartments tend to be near the theme parks; the larger homes are farther away.

Logo of La Quinta Inn *(see p144)*

Weekly apartments, townhouses, and full-size home rentals can cost the same as or less than a medium-rate hotel room. However, the in-house kitchens, private pools, and multiple bedrooms are very convenient and are good value for money. Most places require security deposits in advance, and also ask for cleaning fees. There is usually a minimum stay requirement too. If you wish to cancel your reservation, it is a good idea to notify the owners well in advance as the cancelation fees at most condos are fairly high.

A condo rental in Orlando, set amid lush green gardens

The hotels mentioned here are listed on pp138–45

An elegant dining area setting at an Orlando lodging

HOW TO RESERVE

Rooms at the Disney and the Universal resorts can be booked when you buy the theme park tickets. Tickets can be purchased either by phone or online. The closer it is to the busy season, the harder it might be to book a first-choice room, but rarely are resorts or larger hotels sold out. Online brokers such as **Priceline** and **Travelocity** can usually secure rooms, but many hotels hold back rooms for their telephone or website reservations. If a late check-in is expected, notify the hotel in advance. Many multi-day packages are also available from the theme parks as well as through travel agents.

PRICES & SEASONS

Room rates vary greatly, depending on the season and location. The busiest and most expensive periods are the holidays during November–April and summer vacation (June–August). Most hotels, even the high-priced chains, will often negotiate a lower rate if asked, but won't volunteer it. Be sure to ask for any special rates that might be available for senior citizens, students, frequent flyers, or corporate clients. Many resorts and non-park hotels offer packages that include theme park admissions and free shuttle services. Disney hotels will sometimes upgrade a room at no extra charge during "off-season," if asked.

HIDDEN EXTRAS

Room rates are generally quoted exclusive of both sales tax and the so-called resort tax. These add up to 11.5 percent in Orlando and 13 percent in Kissimmee. The cost of making a phone call from a hotel room can be exorbitant. Some hotels offer free local phone calls from rooms, but most will add a surcharge for local calls or when dialing toll-free numbers. Using the hotel's dial-up service for Internet access could also incur a per-minute charge. Many hotels charge for valet parking too.

TRAVELING WITH CHILDREN

Most hotels provide cribs, fold-away cots, and other facilities for children. The theme park resorts also offer baby-sitting services, child-friendly rooms, and fun-filled activities. Specially designed guided tours for children include the popular Hidden Mickey tours where kids search eagerly for the concealed Disney icon.

A deluxe children's suite; a popular choice at many resort hotels

Staying at the Theme Parks

When Walt Disney started buying untouched Florida wilderness in the late 1960s, he began a multi-billion dollar industry that would change the culture of sleepy citrus town Orlando forever. Currently, the area in and around the theme parks has several thousands of hotel, motel, and resort rooms – and many more are being created – for the never-ending stream of tourists flocking each year to Disney World, Universal Orlando, and SeaWorld. The descriptions on these pages highlight accommodations on theme park property or those located nearby.

Visitor enjoying the slide at Port Orleans Resort *(see p139)*

A giant replica of Woody at All-Star Movies Resort *(see p139)*

WALT DISNEY WORLD® RESORTS

Disney property has the largest collection of resorts in Orlando, with offerings to suit every pocket and taste *(see p133 & pp138–40)*.

The opening of Walt Disney World's Pop Century Resort in 2003 – with 2,880 rooms – was the largest single hotel opening in Disney's history. It joined the ranks of the 23 resort hotels directly owned by the parks. Dedicated to American fashions and fads, Pop Century features icons and relics from the 1950s to the 1990s, such as a larger-than-life Rubik's Cube and Sony Walkman, as well as giant bowling pins and yo-yos. All-Star Resorts, the triple-treat of movie, sports, and music-themed hotels, are the least expensive of all on-site lodgings.

The Animal Kingdom Lodge is advantageously located on the western edge of Disney's newest theme park. Most of its 1,293 rooms include balconies overlooking three savannas, and provide breathtaking views of more than 200 grazing animals and birds, including giraffes, zebra, ibis, and ostriches. Guest rooms include a Royal Suite, with a domed ceiling, a kitchen and a dining room, and sweeping porches. The resort is also host to two of the best restaurants on Disney property.

The two massive hotels that make up the Swan and Dolphin resorts offer almost 2,270 rooms, including 191 special suites themed to Italian, Egyptian, Japanese, and Southwest decor.

Disney's Port Orleans Resort echoes the majestic mansions and row houses of romantic Louisiana. The Beach Club Resort transports Nantucket Bay to Orlando with access to the 25-acre (10-ha) Crescent Lake facility, where canopy and paddleboats are available, as well as the Stormalong Bay water park for the kids.

HOTELS AT WALT DISNEY WORLD® RESORT

Downtown Disney hosts excellent hotels on its property *(see pp138–9)*. Those closest to most of the attractions include Best Western Lake Buena Vista, literally a brisk walk from the Downtown Disney shopping and entertainment area; Hilton, the only hotel to offer "Extra Magic Hour," which allows guests staying at the hotel to enter the Disney theme parks one hour prior to the general opening; Doubletree Guest

Rooms overlook wild animals grazing at Animal Kingdom Lodge *(see p138)*

The hotels mentioned here are listed on pp138–45

The family-friendly Nickelodeon Family Suites, Lake Buena Vista *(see p145)*

Suites, with on-site ticket sales and free shuttles to the parks; Holiday Inn, a 323-room hotel featuring a 14-story atrium; Hotel Royal Plaza, with tennis courts and spa; Wyndham Palace, featuring the award-winning Arthur's 27 restaurant and Disney character breakfasts; and last but not the least, Grosvenor Resort, a British-themed complex which offers special packages for meals and theme park admission. The 626-room Grosvenor is heavily steeped in Florida amenities, including Disney character meals for the kids and a huge Aquatic Center with heated swimming pools, a thermal spa, and beach volleyball. Each hotel has at least one full-service restaurant.

UNIVERSAL ORLANDO RESORTS & HOTELS

Hotels on Universal grounds are located along the perimeter of the two parks – the Islands of Adventure and Universal Studios Florida. Most of the hotels offer themed vacation packages in keeping with Universal's somewhat more adult image *(see p133 & pp140–41)*. The Royal Pacific takes its cue from a tropical island paradise, offering a lagoon-style swimming pool and sandy beach on which to relax, transportation by water taxi to the parks, and an orchid-draped courtyard. There are also five restaurants, including Emeril's Hawaiian-inspired Tchoup Chop. The Portofino Bay Hotel is a faithful recreation of a traditional seaside resort

in Italy, with cobble streets and outdoor cafés, bocce ball courts, and a full spa and fitness center. For those with rock star dreams, the Hard Rock Hotel features rock memorabilia in every room, an "exclusive" seventh-floor Club level with a lounge and music library, and an underwater audio system in the pool. The hotel's Graceland Suite, a tribute to Elvis, is of gigantic proportions.

All these three hotels are pet-friendly, with special rooms and a room-service menu for four-legged guests.

The Universal Express service, offered by all the hotels, allows guests access to all the park rides without having to wait in long lines. In addition, it also provides priority seating at the hotel restaurants, of which there are many to choose from.

HOTELS & MOTELS NEAR THE PARKS

Most places to stay form concentric rings around both Disney and Universal, diminishing in price the farther away they get from Main Street. But some of the most affordable hotels are just beyond the front door of the parks. The two AmeriSuites hotels, with rooms at less than a third of the price at the Hard Rock Hotel, are under a mile (1.6 km) from Universal. The Caribe Royale All-Suites Resort, virtually right outside Disney's doors, and with 1,200 rooms and 120 villas, manages to be less expensive than many of the resorts on Disney property.

Bargains can be found within sight of the parks, many offering amenities such as pools and restaurants. There are thousands of hotels in the area. Sand Lake Road, north of Interstate 4, has several miles of motels and hotels of all ranges, many offering free shuttles to the parks and concierge service for tickets to other attractions. To the south of I-4 is International Drive, a long stretch of commercial properties and outlet malls, with places to stay that range from seedy no-name motels to five-star resorts. To the north and east are the grand hotels of Downtown Orlando and smaller motel chains on Colonial Drive.

Portofino Bay Hotel *(see p141)*, a replica of an Italian seaside resort

Camping & Trailer Parks

Those with an outdoor spirit and the desire to sleep under the stars can find accommodations in Central Florida that range from a tent in the woods to modern, almost luxurious RV camps, complete with swimming pools and clubhouses. Visitors can choose from a wide range of campsites – on state land and private Kampgrounds of America (KOA) parks, and even right on Disney property. Depending on the season, pitching a tent can be fairly inexpensive or can cost as much as a good hotel. RV parks can help tourists on a tight budget save thousands of dollars. In fact, many regular visitors reserve special spots in these parks for years.

Campers picnicking at Disney's Fort Wilderness Resort & Campground

CAMPING

Offering the finest campsite amenities, Disney World stakes out 700 camping spaces at the **Fort Wilderness Resort & Campground** (see p73), with sites ranging from spartan to luxurious. This pet-friendly resort offers charcoal grills,

Boating in scenic heaven, Wekiwa Springs State Park

electric golf carts, cable TV hook-ups, and campfire singalongs. Prices here range from $40 to $80 per night; cabins cost $200 to $300.

Other camping sites also have cabins, priced from $30 to $70 depending on season, which can sleep four to eight people. Many of the Disney-centric campgrounds are located just off US Route 192 in Kissimmee.

Campsites are to be found all across Central Florida. The **East Lake Fish Camp** in Kissimmee combines outdoor living with Florida's fresh-water bounty, offering some of the best bass in the world.

Of all local campgrounds, **Wekiwa Springs State Park** is the most rustic, and most typical of authentic Florida. Open year-round, it is located on the Wekiva River, with 8,000 acres (3,237 ha) of wild scenery that has remained unchanged for centuries.

RV PARKS

RV camps are very popular with cross-country travelers, especially visitors from the far North. Most camps offer all the amenities of resort living, including pools and fitness centers, clubhouses and movie theaters, laundry facilities, cable television and electrical hook-ups, as well as the splendor of the great Florida outdoors. RV site rates vary and can range from $30 a night to almost $400 per month. Permanent spots are also available for those who choose to return every year.

Just 5 miles (8 km) from Disney is the largest RV and trailer park in the area, the **Encore RV Resort**. Located in Clermont, it is host to 467 sites with electrical, water, and sewage hook-ups, two heated pools, a fitness center with a Jacuzzi, shuffleboard courts, tennis courts, laundry, cable TV and telephone services, and social activities such as bingo and dances.

KOA Kissimmee/Orlando is Orlando's nearest KOA Campground. It is just 5 miles (8 km) from Disney, 6 miles (9.6 km) from SeaWorld, and 8 miles (13 km) from Universal. Patio sites with picnic tables, casual furniture, and Mexican chimineas are on offer here.

The **Tropical Palms Fun Resort** in Kissimmee offers campers access to swimming pools, private cottages with air conditioning and kitchens, watercraft rentals, picnic areas, and nearby restaurants.

Picturesque cabins at Orlando SW/ Fort Summit KOA Campground

DIRECTORY

RV & CAMPING CENTERS

Florida Association of RV Parks and Campgrounds
1340 Vickers Rd,
Tallahassee.
Tel (850) 562-7151.
www.floridacamping.com

Florida Department of Environmental Protection (State Parks)
3800 Commonwealth Blvd, Tallahassee.
Tel (850) 245-2157.
www.dep.state.fl.us/parks

KOA Campgrounds
Tel (406) 248-7444.
www.koa.com

Passport America
Tel (800) 283-7183.
www.passport-america.com

RV on the Go
2650 Holiday Trail,
Kissimmee.
Tel (800) 647-2567.
www.rvonthego.com

CAMPSITES

Canoe Creek Campground
4101 Canoe Creek Rd, St. Cloud.
Tel (407) 892-7010.

Cypress Cove Nudist Resort & Spa
4425 S Pleasant Hills Rd,
Kissimmee.
Tel (407) 933-5870.

East Lake Fish Camp
3705 Big Bass Rd,
Kissimmee.
Tel (407) 348-2040.

Elite Resorts Campground
2500 US Hwy 27 S,
Clermont.
Tel (352) 394-4051.

Orlando SW/Fort Summit KOA
Lake Buena Vista,
Orlando.
Tel (800) 424-1880.

Fort Wilderness Resort & Campground
4510 N Fort Wilderness Trail,
Lake Buena Vista,
Orlando.
Tel (407) 824-2900.

KOA Kissimmee/Orlando Campground
2644 Happy Camper Place,
Kissimmee.
Tel (407) 396-2400.

Orange Blossom RV Resort LLC
3800 W Orange Blossom Trail,
Apopka.
Tel (407) 886-3260.

Orange Grove Campground
2425 Old Vineland Rd,
Kissimmee.
Tel (407) 396-6655 .

Orlando Lake Whippoorwill KOA
12345 Narcoossee Rd,
Orlando.
Tel (407) 277-5075.

Orlando Winter Garden Campground
13905 W. Colonial Dr,
Winter Garden.
Tel (407) 656-1415.

Sanlan Ranch Campground
3929 US Hwy 98 S,
Lakeland.
Tel (800) 524-5044.

Southport Park Campground & Marina
2001 W Southport Rd,
Kissimmee.
Tel (407) 933-5822.

Stage Stop Campground
14400 W Colonial Dr,
Winter Garden.
Tel (407) 656-8000.

Tropical Palms Fun Resort
2650 Holiday Trail,
Kissimmee.
Tel (800) 647-2567;

(407) 396-4595.

Twelve Oaks RV Resort
6300 State Route 46,
W Sanford.
Tel (800) 633-9529.

Wekiwa Springs State Park
1800 Wekiwa Circle,
Apopka.
Tel (407) 884-2008.

RV PARKS

Aloha RV Park
4648 S Orange Blossom Trail,
Kissimmee.
Tel (407) 933-5730.

Encore RV Resort
9600 Hwy 192,
West Clermont.
Tel (888) 558-5777.

Fairview Mobile Court
4462 Edgewater Dr,
Orlando.
Tel (407) 293-8581.

Floridian RV Resort
5150 Boggy Creek Rd,
St. Cloud.
Tel (407) 892-5171.

Great Oak RV Resort
4440 Yowell Rd,
Kissimmee.
Tel (407) 396-9092.

Merry D RV Sanctuary
4261 Pleasant Hill Rd,
Kissimmee.
Tel (407) 870-0719.

Orange City RV
2300 E Graves Ave,
Orange City.
Tel (800) 545-7354.

Paradise Island RV Resort
32000 S US Hwy 27,
Haines City.
Tel (863) 439-1350.

Ponderosa RV Park
1983 Boggy Creek Rd,
Kissimmee.
Tel (407) 847-6002.

Sherwood Forest RV Park
5300 W Irlo Bronson Hwy,
Kissimmee.
Tel (407) 396-7431.

Southern Palms RV Resort
1 Avocado Lane,
Eustis.
Tel (352) 357-8882.

Sun Resort RV Park
3000 Clarcona Rd #99,
Apopka.
Tel (407) 889-3048.

Choosing a Hotel

The hotels in this guide have been selected across a wide price range for their good value, facilities, and location. These listings highlight some of the factors that may influence your choice. Hotels are listed by area, beginning with the Walt Disney World Resort. All entries are listed alphabetically within each price category.

PRICE CATEGORIES
Price categories for a standard double room per night in high season, including tax and service charges.

ⓢ under $100
ⓢⓢ $100–$150
ⓢⓢⓢ $150–$200
ⓢⓢⓢⓢ $200–$250
ⓢⓢⓢⓢⓢ over $250

WALT DISNEY WORLD® RESORT

ANIMAL KINGDOM Disney's All-Star Movies Resort   ⓢⓢ
1991 W. Buena Vista Dr., 32830 **Tel** *(407) 939-7000* **Fax** *(407) 939-7111* **Rooms** *1920*

Larger than life characters straight out of Disney's most popular movies tower over guests in every nook and cranny. Among these are favourites from *Toy Story, 101 Dalmatians, The Love Bug, Fantasia,* and *The Mighty Ducks.* Rooms are smaller than most but the price is right for those on a budget. **www.disneyworld.com**

ANIMAL KINGDOM Disney's All-Star Music Resort   ⓢⓢ
1801 W. Buena Vista Dr., 32830 **Tel** *(407) 939-6000* **Fax** *(407) 939-7222* **Rooms** *1920*

The theme is obvious from the walk-through jukebox and the variety of gigantic musical instruments that adorn the resort's many buildings. Calypso, country, and classical music can often be heard in the background. Rooms are small and basic, but the resort offers the benefits of staying at Disney on a budget. **www.disneyworld.com**

ANIMAL KINGDOM Disney's All-Star Sports Resort   ⓢⓢ
1701 W. Buena Vista Dr., 32830 **Tel** *(407) 939-5000* **Fax** *(407) 939-7333* **Rooms** *1920*

Sports fans will appreciate the oversized sporting equipment both inside and outside the buildings. There are reminders of baseball, basketball, football, tennis, and surfing everywhere. The amenities and rooms are basic, but this is one of only four budget-conscious Disney resorts. **www.disneyworld.com**

ANIMAL KINGDOM Disney's Pop Century Resort   ⓢⓢ
1050 Century Dr., 32830 **Tel** *(407) 938-4000* **Fax** *(407) 938-4040* **Rooms** *2,880*

One of Disney's four "value" resorts, this homage to pop culture is as popular with adults as children. Giant icons represent each of the decades from the 1950s to the 1980s, and others are planned. A giant Walkman, Rubik's cube, flower power daisies, and cell phone are just a sample of what adorns the grounds. **www.disneyworld.com**

ANIMAL KINGDOM Disney's Coronado Springs Resort   ⓢⓢⓢⓢ
1001 W. Buena Vista Blvd., 32830 **Tel** *(407) 939-1000* **Fax** *(407) 939-1001* **Rooms** *1921*

Themes of the American southwest and Mexico are apparent throughout the resort's three distinctive villages of Casitas, Ranchos, and Cabanas. Landscaped plazas and courtyards, an open market-style restaurant, colorful stucco architecture, and a five-story Mayan pyramid further enhance the experience. **www.disneyworld.com**

ANIMAL KINGDOM Disney's Animal Kingdom Lodge   ⓢⓢⓢⓢⓢ
2901 Osceola Pkwy., 32830 **Tel** *(407) 938-3000* **Fax** *(407) 938-4799* **Rooms** *1293*

A stay here feels as if you are on a thrilling African game reserve. The impressive glass wall in the lobby overlooks a vast savanna that allows for random sightings of birds, giraffe, and other wildlife. The authentic design, amazingly ornate chandeliers, and high suspension bridge all contribute to the stunning surroundings. **www.disneyworld.com**

DOWNTOWN DISNEY Grosvenor Resort   ⓢⓢ
1850 Hotel Plaza Blvd., 32830 **Tel** *(407) 828-4444* **Fax** *(407) 828-8192* **Rooms** *626*

An official Walt Disney World Resort hotel, the Grosvenor provides good value in a great location. The lobby features elegant colonial decor, while outside there are tennis courts. There is a continuous shuttle service to all the Disney theme parks, and guests can have breakfast with Disney characters three days a week. **www.grosvenorresort.com**

DOWNTOWN DISNEY Hotel Royal Plaza   ⓢⓢ
1905 Hotel Plaza Blvd., 32830 **Tel** *(407) 828-2828* **Fax** *(407) 827-3977* **Rooms** *394*

A beautiful interior, spacious well-appointed rooms with French doors separating the living and sleeping areas, and a location close to Disney set this resort apart. One of the oldest resorts around, it has recently been renovated and offers reasonable rates, exceptional service, and very pleasant decor. **www.royalplaza.com**

DOWNTOWN DISNEY Best Western Lake Buena Vista   ⓢⓢⓢ
2000 Hotel Plaza Blvd., 32830 **Tel** *(407) 828-2424* **Fax** *(407) 594-5276* **Rooms** *318*

Amidst the collection of "unofficial" Disney resorts along the beautiful tree-lined boulevard is the Best Western. Rooms have private balconies, many offering views of Disney, and there are lushly landscaped grounds. Downtown Disney, with its array of shops, restaurants, and entertainment venues, is close by. **www.orlandofunspots.com**

Key to symbols *see back cover flap*

DOWNTOWN DISNEY Buena Vista Palace Resort & Spa $$$

1900 Buena Vista Dr., 32830 **Tel** *(407) 827-2727* **Fax** *(407) 827-6034* **Rooms** *1,015*

Just a walk across the roadway to Downtown Disney, this upscale resort provides great views of Disney's evening fireworks from its upper floors and has one of the best restaurants in Orlando. Most of its recreational activities, including the pools, are on a small private inner island. **www.buenavistapalace.com**

DOWNTOWN DISNEY Doubletree Guest Suites $$$

2305 Hotel Plaza Blvd., 32830 **Tel** *(407) 934-1000* **Fax** *(407) 934-1015* **Rooms** *229*

This family-friendly resort boasts a pint-sized children's theater, bird aviary, and colorful murals which adorn the lobby. Rooms are large and offer the comforts and conveniences of home. Upon check-in, guests are given a sample of the famous Doubletree chocolate chip cookies. **www.doubletree.com**

DOWNTOWN DISNEY Disney's Port Orleans Resort; French Quarter $$$$

2201 Orleans Dr., 32830 **Tel** *(407) 934-5000* **Fax** *(407) 934-5353* **Rooms** *1008*

A Disney recreation of New Orleans' famous French Quarter, with intricate wrought iron railings, cobblestone walkways, and garden-style courtyards, this resort has a Mardi Gras atmosphere. Children will appreciate the giant sea serpent waterslide, alligator fountains, and extensive recreational activities. **www.disneyworld.com**

DOWNTOWN DISNEY Disney's Port Orleans Resort; Riverside $$$$

1251 Riverside Dr., 32830 **Tel** *(407) 934-6000* **Fax** *(407) 934-5777* **Rooms** *2048*

This antebellum, Southern-style resort has two distinctive areas alongside a picturesque Mississippi-style waterway. Magnolia Bend features elegant Dixie mansions set among gardens, while Alligator Bayou has Spanish moss draped from gigantic trees, a swimming hole, and rope swings to give rustic appeal. **www.disneyworld.com**

DOWNTOWN DISNEY Disney's Old Key West Resort $$$$$

1510 N. Cove Rd., 32830 **Tel** *(407) 827-7700* **Fax** *(407) 827-7710* **Rooms** *761*

Spread over several acres, this remarkable recreation of Key West is one of Disney's most popular resorts. Palm trees and pastel villas with picket fences are scattered throughout. The recreational facilities, guest services, and amenities are extensive, and the atmosphere is relaxing and welcoming. **www.disneyworld.com**

DOWNTOWN DISNEY Disney's Saratoga Springs Resort & Spa $$$$$

1960 Broadway, 32830 **Tel** *(407) 827-1100* **Fax** *(407) 827-4444* **Rooms** *840*

This luxurious resort features Victorian cottages in a village setting with sprawling grounds, gardens, hills, and gurgling springs. Relaxation and rejuvenation are the top activities here, with a full-service spa, skin therapy programs, and soothing body treatments on offer. **www.disneyworld.com**

DOWNTOWN DISNEY Hilton at the Walt Disney World Resort $$$$$

1751 Hotel Plaza Blvd., 32830 **Tel** *(407) 827-4000* **Fax** *(407) 827-3890* **Rooms** *814*

Recently renovated and popular with both families and business travelers, this resort has a nautical New England theme that is evident in the lobby area with its restaurants, shops, and small market. The decor in the rooms has a modern shaker motif. Two pools, landscaped grounds, and a great location add to the appeal. **www.hilton.com**

EPCOT Disney's Caribbean Beach Resort $$$$

900 Cayman Way, 32830 **Tel** *(407) 934-3400* **Fax** *(407) 934-3288* **Rooms** *2112*

Five distinctive "villages", with five different Caribbean islands as their theme, comprise this inviting resort. Playgrounds and a Spanish fortress-themed pool, sandy beaches, a pool in each village, and an abundance of recreational activities will keep everyone busy while allowing for a relaxed atmosphere. **www.disneyworld.com**

EPCOT Disney's Beach Club Resort $$$$$

1800 Epcot Resorts Blvd., 32830 **Tel** *(407) 934-7000* **Fax** *(407) 934-3450* **Rooms** *583*

Echoing the style of the New England beach cottages of the 1800s, this casually elegant resort features a lengthy list of recreational facilities and restaurants that it shares with its more refined neighbor, the Yacht Club Resort. White wicker furnishings help to create a comfortable yet upscale atmosphere. **www.disneyworld.com**

EPCOT Disney's Beach Club Villas $$$$$

1800 Epcot Resorts Blvd., 32830 **Tel** *(407) 934-7000* **Fax** *(407) 934-3450* **Rooms** *282*

This resort, whose seaside theme is evident in its brightly painted architecture, shares restaurants and recreational facilities with both the Beach Club and Yacht Club Resorts. Spacious rooms and the convenience of fully equipped kitchens make this the perfect choice for large families or groups. **www.disneyworld.com**

EPCOT Disney's Yacht Club Resort $$$$$

1700 Epcot Resorts Blvd., 32830 **Tel** *(407) 934-7000* **Fax** *(407) 934-3450* **Rooms** *630*

A short walk from Epcot, this upscale resort, styled and decorated to resemble a Cape Cod yacht club, shares a wide range of facilities with its more casual neighbor, the Beach Club Resort. An extensive sand-bottom lagoon pool area, sandy beach, shipwreck, and lighthouse complete the picture. **www.disneyworld.com**

EPCOT Walt Disney World Dolphin $$$$$

1500 Epcot Resorts Blvd., 32830 **Tel** *(407) 934-4000* **Fax** *(407) 934-4884* **Rooms** *1509*

Home to Tod English's BlueZoo restaurant, a must no matter where you stay, this whimsical, recently renovated resort is best known for the tremendous dolphins that sit atop its exterior. It is only a water taxi ride from Epcot, which adds to the already lengthy list of dining choices. A full service spa has recently been added. **www.swandolphin.com**

EPCOT Walt Disney World Swan
1200 Epcot Resorts Blvd., 32830 **Tel** *(407) 934-3000* **Fax** *(407) 934-4884* **Rooms** *756*

Like its neighbor, the Dolphin, this resort is both whimsical and recently renovated, with giant swans adorning its exterior. A covered walkway connects it to the Dolphin, with which it shares many facilities, including the sandy beach, playgrounds, and pool. The resort caters to business travelers and families alike. **www.swandolphin.com**

MAGIC KINGDOM Disney's Fort Wilderness Resort & Campground
4510 N. Fort Wilderness Tr., 32830 **Tel** *(407) 824-2900* **Fax** *(407) 824-3508* **Rooms** *784 campsites, 409 cabins*

For a more "back to nature" experience, campsites and cabins are scattered throughout a heavily wooded area. The cabins themselves are, however, full of creature comforts. Recreational activities are extensive and often unique to the resort, and also on offer is Disney's best, and most popular, dinner show. **www.disneyworld.com**

MAGIC KINGDOM Disney's Contemporary Resort
4600 N. World Drive, 32830 **Tel** *(407) 824-1000* **Fax** *(407) 824-3539* **Rooms** *1008*

The monorail passes right through the middle of this concrete resort, where the rooms have recently undergone a complete renovation. The decor is ultra chic and reflects retro-Asian flair. It is moments to the Magic Kingdom by rail or by foot, and upper-level rooms offer a great view of the park and the evening fireworks. **www.disneyworld.com**

MAGIC KINGDOM Disney's Grand Floridian Resort & Spa
4401 Grand Floridian Way, 32830 **Tel** *(407) 824-3000* **Fax** *(407) 824-3186* **Rooms** *867*

This opulent Victorian-style resort features a magnificent five-story lobby topped by an ornate stained-glass dome. High tea is served daily, and a band often plays 1940s music. The beautifully appointed rooms all offer views of the meticulously maintained grounds. The facilities, services, and amenities are extensive. **www.disneyworld.com**

MAGIC KINGDOM Disney's Polynesian Resort
1600 Seven Seas Dr., 32830 **Tel** *(407) 824-2000* **Fax** *(407) 824-3174* **Rooms** *847*

Lush tropical gardens and waterfalls, a white sand beach, and a lagoon swimming pool with a steaming volcano and torch-lit walkways create the illusion of an island paradise, located on the Magic Kingdom monorail. Recent renovations include new furnishings and decor in all the guestrooms. **www.disneyworld.com**

MAGIC KINGDOM Disney's Wilderness Lodge
901 W. Timberline Dr., 32830 **Tel** *(407) 824-3200* **Fax** *(407) 823-3232* **Rooms** *765*

The setting resembles that of the great national parks of the Northwest, with towering pines, a spewing geyser, and rough rocky terrain surrounding a spectacular pool. This rustic, though very upscale, lodge features a spectacular stories-high lobby with authentic twin totem poles. Artist Point restaurant is a must. **www.disneyworld.com**

MAGIC KINGDOM The Villas at Disney's Wilderness Lodge
901 W. Timberline Dr., 32830 **Tel** *(407) 824-3200* **Fax** *(407) 824-3232* **Rooms** *181*

Sharing all the facilities of Wilderness Lodge, the villas here are roomy enough for larger groups or families and have either kitchenettes or full kitchens. They also offer forest views and a cabin-style decor. The grand antler chandelier in the lobby is most impressive as are the decor and attention to detail throughout. **www.disneyworld.com**

OTHER THEME PARKS

SEAWORLD Hilton Garden Inn Orlando SeaWorld
6850 Westwood Blvd., 32821 **Tel** *(407) 354-1500* **Fax** *(407) 354-1528* **Rooms** *233*

Large rooms with conveniences such as a fridge and microwave make this a good choice for those seeking comfortable surroundings without too many extras. The pool is small but adequate, and a trolley service transports guests to International Drive's many restaurants and shops. **www.orlandoseaworld.gardeninn.com**

SEAWORLD Residence Inn SeaWorld International Center
11000 Westwood Blvd., 32821 **Tel** *(407) 313-3600* **Fax** *(407) 313-3611* **Rooms** *350*

Set back from International Drive, yet still close to its many offerings, this casual large-scale resort offers full kitchens in every one-, two-, or three-bedroom suite; free high-speed Internet access; and a complimentary hot breakfast buffet. Palm trees are scattered around the large pool and recreational areas. **www.residenceinnseaworld.com**

SEAWORLD Renaissance Orlando Resort at SeaWorld
6677 Sea Harbor Dr., 32821 **Tel** *(407) 351-5555* **Fax** *(407) 351-9991* **Rooms** *778*

Recent renovations have made this upscale resort even more impressive than before. In the ten-story glass-topped lobby, the ornate aviary and cascading waterfalls ensure that guests take notice of the beautiful surroundings. Rooms are impeccably decorated, combining function and beauty. **www.renaissanceseaworld.com**

UNIVERSAL ORLANDO Hard Rock Hotel
5800 Universal Blvd., 32819 **Tel** *(407) 503-2000* **Fax** *(407) 503-2010* **Rooms** *750*

Mission-style architecture, an impressive collection of musical memorabilia, and an underwater sound system built into the impressive pool make this the hippest of Universal's luxury resorts. The perks of staying on-site if you are heading for the Universal parks are well worth investigating. **www.universalorlando.com**

Key to price guide *see p138* **Key to symbols** *see back cover flap*

UNIVERSAL ORLANDO Portofino Bay Hotel 🛏️🍴🏊👥📺 ⑤⑤⑤⑤⑤
5601 Universal Blvd., 32819 **Tel** *(877) 917-2682, (407) 503-1000* **Fax** *(407) 503-1,010* **Rooms** *650*

The charm and ambience of the Italian seaside village of Portofino have been meticulously re-created at this lavish resort. Luxurious surroundings await guests both inside and out. There are five restaurants, extensive recreational facilities, a full-service spa, and a water taxi to transport guests to Universal's parks. **www.universalorlando.com**

UNIVERSAL ORLANDO Universal's Royal Pacific Resort 🛏️🍴🏊👥📺 ⑤⑤⑤⑤⑤
6300 Hollywood Way, 32819 **Tel** *(407) 503-3000* **Fax** *(407) 503-3010* **Rooms** *1,000*

Guests at this resort are stranded on a breathtaking Pacific island paradise, with a lagoon-style pool and play area, Emeril's Tchop Chop restaurant (a must for adults), and superior service. The densely landscaped grounds are worth a tour even if you do not choose to stay here. **www.universalorlando.com**

ORLANDO & CENTRAL FLORIDA

CAPE CANAVERAL Radisson Resort at the Port 🛏️🍴🏊👥📺 ⑤⑤⑤
8701 Astronaut Blvd.., 32920 **Tel** *(321) 784-0000* **Fax** *(321) 784-3737* **Rooms** *284*

While not directly on the beach, the resort is not too far away. The suites feature French doors, some have whirlpools, and all have kitchen facilities. Standard rooms are more basic but still pleasant. The tropically landscaped pool area is inviting, and the view of the port and its cruise ships unique. **www.radisson.com/capecanaveralfl**

CAPE CANAVERAL Residence Inn Port Canaveral 🛏️🍴🏊👥📺 ⑤⑤⑤
8959 Astronaut Blvd., 32920 **Tel** *(321) 323-1100* **Fax** *(321) 323-1029* **Rooms** *150*

New in 2006, this home away from home provides spacious suites with one, two, or three bedrooms and a fully-equipped kitchen; landscaped grounds; and beautiful beachside surroundings. Kennedy Space Center is a short drive away and the best surfing on the east coast is right outside your door. **www.marriott.com**

CAPE CANAVERAL Ron Jon Cape Caribe Resort 🛏️🍴🏊👥📺 ⑤⑤⑤⑤
1000 Shorewood Dr., 32920 **Tel** *(321) 799-4900* **Fax** *(321) 784-3949* **Rooms** *206*

Even with pristine beaches a short walk away, guests will find the extensive waterpark with pools, river, waterslide, and fountains a fun way to cool off. Mini golf, tennis, basketball, a children's play center, and a movie theater are available on-site. The comfortable villas can accommodate up to 12. **www.ronjonresort.com**

CELEBRATION Celebration Hotel 🛏️🍴🏊👥📺 ⑤⑤⑤⑤⑤
700 Bloom Street, 34747 **Tel** *(407) 566-6000* **Fax** *(407) 566-6001* **Rooms** *115*

In a picture-perfect town, this three-story wooden-framed hotel is straight out of 1920s Florida. The beautiful rooms offer great views of the artificial lake. The atmosphere is romantic, the restaurant elegant, and the entire experience unique. Smart boutiques and restaurants line nearby Market Street. **www.celebrationhotel.com**

COCOA BEACH Comfort Inn & Suites Hotel & Convention Center 🛏️🏊👥📺 ⑤
3901 N. Atlantic Ave., 32931 **Tel** *(321) 783-2221* **Fax** *(321) 783-0461* **Rooms** *170*

Close to the beach and a short drive to top attractions such as the Kennedy Space Center, this is a casual and friendly hotel. The large pool area is lined with palm trees and plenty of lounge chairs, perfect for soaking up the Florida sunshine. Accommodation ranges from standard rooms to multi-room suites. **www.comfortinncocoabeach.com**

COCOA BEACH Holiday Inn Express & Suites 🛏️🏊👥📺 ⑤⑤
5575 N. Atlantic Ave., 32931 **Tel** *(321) 868-2525* **Fax** *(321) 868-3602* **Rooms** *60*

A wide variety of accommodation, including family suites, kidsuites, and standard rooms, is available here. So, too, is a rather unique pool, which is open to the outdoors yet protected by a roof, making it easy to swim, relax, and enjoy the Florida sunshine without worrying too much about getting sunburnt. **www.hiexpress.com**

COCOA BEACH La Quinta Inn Cocoa Beach 🛏️🍴🏊👥📺 ⑤⑤
1275 N. Atlantic Ave., 32931 **Tel** *(321) 783-2252* **Fax** *(321) 783-4486* **Rooms** *127*

Good-sized rooms provide plenty of space to relax at La Quinta. A mini fridge, free high-speed Internet access, and a 100 per cent satisfaction guarantee are all included in the very reasonable rates. Several restaurants are within walking distance, as are two major surfing retailers for those in need of swim or surf gear. **www.lq.com**

COCOA BEACH Holiday Inn Cocoa Beach Oceanfront Resort 🛏️🍴🏊👥📺 ⑤⑤⑤
1300 N. Atlantic Ave., 32931 **Tel** *(321) 783-2271* **Fax** *(321) 783-8569* **Rooms** *501*

In this ideal place for families, the accommodation includes newly renovated kidsuites and oceanfront suites. There is an extensive array of recreational activities scattered throughout the tropically landscaped grounds, as well as direct access to the beach and a pirate-themed pool and play area. **www.hicocoabeach-oceanfront.felcor.com**

CYPRESS GARDENS/ WINTER HAVEN Best Western Admiral's Inn 🛏️🍴🏊👥📺 ⑤⑤
5665 Cypress Gardens Blvd., 33884 **Tel** *(863) 324-5950* **Fax** *(863) 324-2376* **Rooms** *156*

The attractions of Cypress Gardens Adventure Park are just steps away. The rooms, while not particularly lavish, are comfortable, and there is a mini-golf course, as well as a pool. After eating in one of the two restaurants, guests can dance the night away in the hotel lounge. **www.bestwesternadmiralsinn.com**

DAYTONA BEACH Bahama House $$$$
2001 S. Atlantic Ave., 32118 **Tel** *(386) 248-2001* **Fax** *(386) 248-0991* **Rooms** *95*

Located right on the beach, this friendly Bahamas-themed hotel offers seven large room layouts to choose from. The decor features bleached-wood furnishings, and most rooms have kitchen facilities. Some have Jacuzzis. Planned recreational activities include scavenger hunts, pool games, and movies. **www.daytonabahamahouse.com**

DOWNTOWN ORLANDO The Courtyard at Lake Lucerne $$
211 N. Lucerne Circle East, 32801 **Tel** *(407) 648-5188* **Fax** *(407) 246-1368* **Rooms** *29*

Four historic homes, including the oldest in Orlando, are meticulously maintained. Each is decorated in period with authentic antiques, and both the 19th-century Victorian and 1940s Art Deco styles are represented. Winding walkways and a beautifully landscaped central courtyard add to the ambience. **www.orlandohistoricinn.com**

DOWNTOWN ORLANDO The Veranda $$
115 N. Summerlin Ave., 32801 **Tel** *(407) 849-0321* **Fax** *(407) 849-1875* **Rooms** *12*

A complex of five historic buildings, this B&B is located in fashionable Thornton Park. Some of Orlando's hottest and hippest restaurants, and the lovely Lake Eola, are all located here as well. The grounds are beautifully landscaped and the attractive central courtyard is the perfect place to sit and relax. **www.theverandabandb.com**

DOWNTOWN ORLANDO Thurston House B&B $$$
851 Lake Ave., 32751 **Tel** *(407) 539-1911* **Fax** *(407) 539-0365* **Rooms** *4*

Built in 1885 and restored in 1991, this period Queen Ann-style Victorian farmhouse sits on a beautiful lakefront. The inn's four rooms are quaint yet elegant and each feature a queen bed; reading area; modern amenities such as a TV, VCR, and CD player; and complimentary high-speed Internet access. **www.thurstonhouse.com**

DOWNTOWN ORLANDO EO Inn & Urban Spa $$$$
227 N. Eola Dr., 32801 **Tel** *(407) 481-8485* **Fax** *(407) 481-8495* **Rooms** *17*

Upscale, chic, and luxurious, the Urban Spa features smart rooms as well as a day spa. The inn also plays host to the trendy Panera Café. Views of Lake Eola are stunning. Downtown Orlando is once again becoming a hot spot for adults seeking to escape the family atmosphere near the theme parks. **www.eoinn.com**

DOWNTOWN ORLANDO The Westin Grand Bohemian $$$$$
325 South Orange Ave., 32801 **Tel** *(407) 313-9000* **Fax** *(407) 313-9001* **Rooms** *250*

In the heart of downtown Orlando, this hotel pays tribute to the arts. Decadently luxurious, it showcases classic and contemporary artwork from local and internationally renowned artists. Catering mainly to business people, the Bohemian also attracts art aficionados who love the museum-like ambience here. **www.grandbohemianhotel.co**

INTERNATIONAL DRIVE Comfort Suites Orlando $
9350 Turkey Lake Rd., 32819 **Tel** *(407) 351-5050* **Fax** *(407) 363-7953* **Rooms** *214*

Just off the beaten track, yet not too far from the area's many attractions, this hotel offers peaceful surroundings and large rooms with a half-wall between the bed and living area. A large tropically landscaped courtyard with palm trees and stone pathways winds around the hotel pool. **www.comfortsuitesorlando.com**

INTERNATIONAL DRIVE Fairfield Inn & Suites International Cove $
7495 Canada Ave., 32819 **Tel** *(407) 351-7000* **Fax** *(407) 351-0052* **Rooms** *200*

Located on a quieter street just off International Drive, the Fairfield Inn & Suites is only steps away from all the action. Featuring large rooms and suites, the inn also offers a daily complimentary breakfast and free high-speed wireless access to the Internet. **www.marriott.com/mcosl**

INTERNATIONAL DRIVE Howard Johnson Plaza Hotel & Suites $
9956 Hawaiian Ct., 32819 **Tel** *(407) 351-5100* **Fax** *(407) 352-7188* **Rooms** *223*

Adjacent to the Orlando Orange County Convention Center and a short walk away from numerous restaurants, this casual hotel features standard rooms and one-bedroom suites with kitchen facilities. SeaWorld is minutes away by trolley, and it is a 10- to 15-minute drive to Disney and Universal. **www.orlandohowardjohnson.com**

INTERNATIONAL DRIVE La Quinta Inn $
5825 International Dr., 32819 **Tel** *(407) 351-4100* **Fax** *(407) 996-4599* **Rooms** *117*

The interior decor at this recently renovated western-themed hotel features warm colors, lots of wood, and wrought iron lanterns. Wet 'n' Wild is nearby, or there is the hotel pool for a more relaxing experience. The reasonable rates make it a good choice for those who are budget-conscious. **www.lq.com**

INTERNATIONAL DRIVE Sleep Inn Convention Center $
6301 Westwood Blvd., 32821 **Tel** *(407) 313-4100* **Fax** *(407) 313-4101* **Rooms** *94*

While the hotel is basic, the lengthy list of amenities makes it worth considering. Rates include free high-speed Internet access, a complimentary breakfast buffet, and a shuttle service to all of the area's theme parks, including Disney. The International Drive Trolley also stops nearby. **www.orlandosleepinn.com**

INTERNATIONAL DRIVE Best Western Movieland $$
6233 International Dr., 32819 **Tel** *(407) 351-3900* **Fax** *(407) 352-5597* **Rooms** *254*

Within splashing distance of Wet 'n' Wild, minutes from Universal Orlando, and a walk to many of the area's numerous shops, restaurants, and smaller attractions, this is a friendly hotel that provides comfortable surroundings and oversized rooms. Services include a free shuttle to Universal and SeaWorld. **www.bestwesternmovieland.co**

Key to price guide *see p138* **Key to symbols** *see back cover flap*

INTERNATIONAL DRIVE Best Western Plaza International

8738 International Dr., 32819 **Tel** *(407) 345-8195* **Fax** *(407) 352-8196* **Rooms** *672*

Ideally located on International Drive, with its plethora of restaurants and shops, this is the largest Best Western in the world and is a tempting choice for anyone heading to Orlando. The rooms range from standards to suites, and the list of amenities and guest services is long given the hotel's reasonable rates. **www.bestwesternplaza.com**

INTERNATIONAL DRIVE Holiday Inn Hotel & Suites at Universal

5905 Kirkman Rd., 32819 **Tel** *(407) 351-3333* **Fax** *(407) 351-6404* **Rooms** *256*

This popular chain offers comfortable rooms and suites, casual on-site dining, and a free shuttle to many nearby attractions. Recreational facilities include an outdoor pool, a toddler pool, and a games room. The atmosphere is friendly and welcoming, and the decor is bright and cheerful. **www.hiuniversal.com**

INTERNATIONAL DRIVE La Quinta Inn & Suites Convention Center

8504 Universal Blvd., 32819 **Tel** *(407) 345-1365* **Fax** *(407) 345-5586* **Rooms** *184*

Located on a quieter street, though only a short walk to the many restaurants and shops of International Drive, this is a reasonably priced hotel with large rooms and suites that include additional conveniences such as a fridge and microwave. The decor is pleasant and the atmosphere friendly. **www.lq.com**

INTERNATIONAL DRIVE The Enclave

6165 Carrier Dr., 32819 **Tel** *(407) 351-1155* **Fax** *(407) 351-2001* **Rooms** *321*

With a prime location just off International Drive, this hotel provides stunning views from private balconies and terraces. Both the buildings and landscaped grounds, with two outdoor pools, are appealing. The large comfortable rooms and suites, some designed especially for children, have fully equipped kitchens. **www.enclavesuites.com**

INTERNATIONAL DRIVE Wyndham Orlando Resort

8001 International Dr., 32819 **Tel** *(407) 351-2420* **Fax** *(407) 352-8759* **Rooms** *1059*

Spread out over several blocks along International Drive, this resort has some of the prettiest grounds in the area. The fountains, steps, and statues are reminiscent of a grand Southern plantation. The rooms are large and comfortable, and there is also a handful of child-friendly suites. **www.wyndham.com**

INTERNATIONAL DRIVE Doubletree Castle Hotel

8629 International Dr., 32819 **Tel** *(407) 345-1511* **Fax** *(407) 248-8181* **Rooms** *216*

In the style of a medieval fairytale castle, this popular hotel features fanciful surroundings, gargoyles in the lobby, and a large pool. Suites are standard and fabulous chocolate chip cookies await guests at the check-in desk. Many restaurants and shops are within walking distance or a short trolley ride. **www.doubletreecastle.com**

INTERNATIONAL DRIVE Doubletree Hotel Orlando

5780 Major Blvd., 32819 **Tel** *(407) 351-1000* **Fax** *(407) 363-0106* **Rooms** *742*

There is no mistaking this hotel as its two golden buildings shine brightly in the Florida sunlight. The resort offers a free scheduled shuttle to nearby attractions, including Universal, Wet 'n' Wild, and SeaWorld, each only minutes away. Rooms are spacious and feature a tropical decor. **www.hiltonhotel.com**

INTERNATIONAL DRIVE Sheraton Studio City

5905 International Dr., 32819 **Tel** *(407) 351-2100* **Fax** *(407) 345-5249* **Rooms** *302*

This round hotel stands out among the others lining the busy thoroughfare. The Art Deco-style here pays tribute to Hollywood movies, with spotlights reminiscent of a Hollywood movie premiere and glamorous touches throughout. Rates include large rooms and numerous amenities. **www.sheratonstudiocity.com**

INTERNATIONAL DRIVE Embassy Suites International Dr. South

8978 International Dr., 32819 **Tel** *(407) 352-1400* **Fax** *(407) 363-1120* **Rooms** *244*

Ornate iron railings adorn the interior balconies, while the inner courtyard is landscaped with lush vegetation. Each room features separate sleeping and living areas and a kitchenette. Free breakfasts and evening receptions are offered too, though several restaurants are nearby. **www.embassysuites.com**

INTERNATIONAL DRIVE JW Marriott Orlando Grande Lakes

4040 Central Florida Pkwy., 32837 **Tel** *(407) 206-2300* **Fax** *(407) 206-2301* **Rooms** *1000*

Sharing with the Ritz Carlton its spectacular and meticulously kept grounds as well as a long list of amenities, this luxurious property is one of the finest around. A beautifully landscaped river feature, fine dining, spa treatments, and an exclusive golf club with a caddie concierge are all available here. **www.grandelakes.com**

INTERNATIONAL DRIVE Peabody Orlando

9801 International Dr., 32819 **Tel** *(407) 352-4000* **Fax** *(407) 354-1424* **Rooms** *891*

Renowned for its superior service, this luxurious and upscale resort offers fine living and fine dining can be experienced at Dux (*see p154*), one of the few starred restaurants in Orlando. Room decor is subtle and quite tasteful, and the furnishings, in particular the beds, are amazingly comfortable. **www.peabodyorlando.com**

KISSIMMEE Amerihost Resort

7491 W. Irlo Bronson Memorial Hwy., 32819 **Tel** *(407) 396-6000* **Fax** *(407) 396-7393* **Rooms** *442*

A large indoor pool, casual eateries, and plenty of places to relax can all be found in this resort's large inner courtyard. The rooms are spacious and comfortable. Children will appreciate the activities and in-room video games on offer. Reasonable rates add to the appeal. **www.amerihostresortorlando.com**

KISSIMMEE Holiday Inn Nikki Bird

7300 W. Irlo Bronson Memorial Hwy., 34747 **Tel** *(407) 396-7300* **Fax** *(407) 396-7555* **Rooms** *530*

The shiny silver diner here immediately catches the eye of anyone entering the hotel. This resort features more recreational facilities and activities than to be expected from the prices. There is a supervised kids' program, Camp Nikki, and kidsuites that are sure to be a hit with families. **www.orlando-nikkibird.holiday-inn.com**

KISSIMMEE Oak Plantation

4090 Enchanted Oaks Cir., 34741 **Tel** *(407) 847-8200* **Fax** *(407) 847-7948* **Rooms** *332*

This park-like gated community provides quiet, peaceful surroundings. There are magnificent oak trees lining the roadways and walkways throughout the grounds. The self-catering apartment-style accommodation has a homely feel and there are abundant recreational facilities. **www.oakplantationresort.com**

KISSIMMEE The Inn at Summer Bay

9400 US Hwy. 192, 34714 **Tel** *(863) 420-8282 (reservations: 1-888-742-1100)* **Fax** *(352) 241-2268* **Rooms** *95*

Given the rather basic accommodation, the bonus of this inn is that it shares facilities with the entire collection of Summer Bay vacation homes and villas. Guest services and amenities are extensive and very family-friendly. There are pools and playgrounds, tennis and basketball courts, scheduled activities, and more. **www.sumerbayresort.com**

KISSIMMEE Best Western Lakeside

7769 West Irlo Bronson Memorial Hwy., 34747 **Tel** *(407) 396-2222* **Fax** *(407) 396-1399* **Rooms** *651*

Close to Walt Disney World as well as the many attractions and restaurants that line the busy thoroughfare of US Highway 192, this casual family-friendly resort features a wide variety of amenities and recreational activities. They include a general store, several eateries, a pool, and a mini-golf course. **www.bestwesternlakeside.com**

KISSIMMEE Comfort Suites Maingate Resort West

7888 W. Irlo Bronson Memorial Hwy., 34746 **Tel** *(407) 390-9888* **Fax** *(407) 390-0981* **Rooms** *150*

Large rooms that can accommodate up to six, a free continental breakfast, and a location that is hard to beat are all on offer here. So, too, is free scheduled transportation to Universal, Wet 'n' Wild, SeaWorld, and Disney. The resort has a modern look that is attractive and inviting. **www.comfortsuiteskissimmee.com**

KISSIMMEE La Quinta Inn & Suites

3484 Polynesian Isle Blvd., 34746 **Tel** *(407) 997-1700* **Fax** *(407) 997-1701* **Rooms** *132*

Often overlooked as it is not on the main thoroughfare, this casual hotel has plenty to offer, including large comfortable rooms, suites for larger families, and a pool. Free high-speed Internet access and a complimentary Continental breakfast are added perks. The Mediterranean-style lobby is inviting. **www.lqinn.com**

KISSIMMEE Radisson Resort Worldgate

3011 Maingate La., 34747 **Tel** *(407) 396-1400* **Fax** *(407) 396-1171* **Rooms** *426*

As well as beautifully decorated and well-appointed rooms, this reasonably priced resort offers a long list of guest services. Palm trees are scattered throughout the pool area in the central courtyard, giving it a tropical atmosphere. On-site dining is available, but numerous restaurants are only minutes away. **www.worldgateresort.com**

KISSIMMEE Seralago Hotel & Suites Main Gate East

5678 W. Irlo Bronson Memorial Hwy., 34746 **Tel** *(407) 396-4488* **Fax** *(407) 396-8915* **Rooms** *614*

Inviting and family-friendly, this hotel has plenty to offer, including kidsuites, a variety of casual restaurants, and a wide array of recreational activities. The atmosphere and service are both upbeat and friendly. Gatorland is a 15-minute drive away, while Disney is just down the road. **www.seralagohotel.com**

KISSIMMEE Radisson Resort Orlando Celebration

2900 Parkway Blvd., 34747 **Tel** *(407) 396-7000* **Fax** *(407) 396-0097* **Rooms** *718*

Beautiful surroundings are the signature of this popular and budget-minded resort. A lavishly landscaped pool features waterfalls, a waterslide, whirlpools, and a children's pool, while the on-site dining options include a casual 1950s-style diner and a full service Mediterranean-style restaurant. **www.radisson.com/orlando-celebration**

KISSIMMEE Acadia Estates All Star Vacation Homes

7822 West Irlo Bronson Memorial Hwy., 34747 **Tel** *(407) 997-0733* **Fax** *(407) 997-1370* **Rooms** *37 homes*

This quiet, upscale, and gated neighborhood features some very distinctive vacation homes. Each has a secluded patio with a private pool and hot tub, and between four and seven bedrooms. Some include a gameroom, and all are beautifully decorated. Numerous guest services are also available. **www.allstarvacationhomes.com**

LAKE BUENA VISTA Fairfield Inn Orlando at the Marriott Village

8623 Vineland Ave., 32821 **Tel** *(407) 938-9001* **Fax** *(407) 938-9002* **Rooms** *388*

Three separate Marriott-brand hotels are situated together in a village-style setting here to offer guests a wide range of room types and services to choose from. A pool is located in the large central courtyard. Also on offer are a free buffet breakfast and wireless high-speed Internet access. **www.marriott.com**

LAKE BUENA VISTA Holiday Inn Sunspree Resort

13351 State Rd.535, 32821 **Tel** *(407) 239-4500* **Fax** *(407) 239-8462* **Rooms** *507*

This family-friendly resort features kidsuites with separate sleeping and play areas, plus kitchenettes. In the play area children have their own TV, video game system, and pint-sized furnishings. A mini-theater plays child-friendly movies and a supervised activity center provides parents with some time for themselves. **www.kidsuites.com**

Key to price guide *see p138* **Key to symbols** *see back cover flap*

LAKE BUENA VISTA Perrihouse B&B Inn

⬛🚶 ⑤⑤

10417 Vista Oaks Ct., 32836 **Tel** *(407) 876-4830* **Fax** *(407) 909-1294* **Rooms** *8*

Located on a 16-acre (6-ha) nature preserve adjacent to Walt Disney World, this small and secluded country inn is ideal for those who want a peaceful and eco-friendly experience while being only 5 minutes away from the Disney attractions. Bird-watching is one of the resort's main activities. **www.perrihouse.com**

LAKE BUENA VISTA Springhill Suites Orlando at the Marriott Village

🖼⬛🚶🏨 ⑤⑤

8623 Vineland Ave., 32821 **Tel** *(407) 938-9001* **Fax** *(407) 938-9002* **Rooms** *400*

Another of the Marriott Village hotels that has large comfortable rooms with kitchen facilities and other conveniences to ensure a comfortable stay. Also on offer are a shared pool, courtyard, and casual eateries in a village-like setting. Additional restaurants are within walking distance. **www.marriott.com/mcolx**

LAKE BUENA VISTA Palomino Suites

🖼⬛🚶🏨 ⑤⑤⑤

8200 Palm Pky., 32836 **Tel** *(407) 465-8200* **Fax** *(407) 465-0200* **Rooms** *123*

Palm Parkway is a quiet tree-lined roadway filled with newer somewhat upscale, though casual, hotels. Many a restaurant is nearby, as is Downtown Disney. Spacious suites with kitchens, complimentary breakfast, and evening receptions are standard here. The surroundings are pleasant though not over the top. **www.palominosuites.com**

LAKE BUENA VISTA Sheraton Safari Hotel

🖼🍴⬛🚶🏨 ⑤⑤⑤

12205 Apopka-Vineland Rd., 32836 **Tel** *(407) 239-0444* **Fax** *(407) 239-4566* **Rooms** *489*

A wild safari theme ensures that guests' adventures do not end at the theme parks. A giant python resides in the hotel pool, but he is friendly and allows people to slide down him into the pool. Jungle-like landscaping adds to the ambience. The numerous amenities and services ensure guest satisfaction. **www.sheratonsafari.com**

LAKE BUENA VISTA Caribe Royale Orlando

🖼🍴⬛🚶🏨 ⑤⑤⑤⑤

8101 World Center Dr., 32821 **Tel** *(407) 238-8000* **Fax** *(407) 238-8400* **Rooms** *1,338*

Spread out over 45 acres (18 ha) of beautifully landscaped grounds filled with towering palm trees, this resort features large suites and multi-room villas to accommodate any size of family. The list of guest services, amenities, and recreational activities is extensive, and it is minutes from Disney. **www.cariberoyale.com**

LAKE BUENA VISTA Gaylord Palms Resort & Convention Center

🖼🍴⬛🚶🏨 ⑤⑤⑤⑤

6000 West Osceola Pkwy., 34746 **Tel** *(407) 586-0000* **Fax** *(407) 586-1999* **Rooms** *1,406*

A spectacular recreation of St. Marco, the oldest Spanish castle in America, is among the attractions of this visually stunning upscale resort. Several Florida themes, including St. Augustine and the Everglades, are reflected in the decor of the luxurious bedrooms. Recreational facilities, amenities, and service are top-notch. **www.gaylordhotels.com**

LAKE BUENA VISTA Staybridge Suites LBV

🖼⬛🚶🏨 ⑤⑤⑤

8751 Suiteside Dr., 32836 **Tel** *(407) 238-0777* **Fax** *(407) 238-2640* **Rooms** *150*

Particularly large and uniquely designed rooms, plus a central location and a grocery delivery service, make this the perfect choice for families and groups. The central courtyard is lined with palm trees overlooking the large pool and sundeck. There is a second location on International Drive. **www.sborlando.com**

LAKE BUENA VISTA Hyatt Regency Grand Cypress

🖼🍴⬛🚶🏨 ⑤⑤⑤⑤

One Grand Cypress Blvd., 32836 **Tel** *(407) 239-1234* **Fax** *(407) 239-3800* **Rooms** *750*

Waterfalls, caves, grottoes, and rope bridges surround the pool at this upscale resort. There is plenty on offer for guests of every age, including a sandy beach and crystal-blue lake, an equestrian center, golf, tennis, an array of children's activities, and award-winning fine dining at La Coquina. **www.hyattgrandcypress.com**

LAKE BUENA VISTA Nickelodeon Family Suites by Holiday Inn

🖼🍴⬛🚶🏨 ⑤⑤⑤⑤

14500 Continental Gateway, 32821 **Tel** *(407) 387-5437* **Fax** *(407) 387-1490* **Rooms** *777*

This child-friendly Nickelodeon-themed resort now sports two waterpark play areas filled with flumes, waterslides, fountains, and more. Entertainment is top priority here. Suites with special separate bedrooms for the children, living areas, and kitchenettes are standard. **www.nickhotel.com**

LAKE BUENA VISTA Orlando World Center Marriott

🖼🍴⬛🚶🏨 ⑤⑤⑤⑤

8701 World Center Dr., 32821 **Tel** *(407) 239-4200* **Fax** *(407) 238-8777* **Rooms** *2,000*

An array of restaurants, a premier golf club, a spectacularly landscaped pool and play area, and beautifully decorated spacious rooms are all combined with exceptional service. This resort caters to both families and business travelers alike – a combination that is rare and difficult to find. **www.marriottworldcenter.com**

MOUNT DORA The Lakeside Inn

🍴⬛🚶 ⑤⑤⑤

100 N. Alexander St., 32757 **Tel** *(352) 383-4101* **Fax** *(352) 735-2642* **Rooms** *88*

Built in 1863 and refurbished a century later, this resort is ideal for a period of peaceful solitude. The inn is extremely popular with bird-watchers, anglers, and antique hunters. Children, while welcome, will not find the inn as captivating as adults invariably do. **www.lakeside-inn.com**

ORLANDO INTERNATIONAL AIRPORT Hyatt Regency

🖼🍴⬛🚶🏨 ⑤⑤⑤⑤⑤

9300 Airport Blvd., 32827 **Tel** *(407) 825-1234* **Fax** *(407) 859-9652* **Rooms** *446*

The convenience of not having to leave the airport can save time, money, and stress for many a business traveler. First-rate amenities are at the guests' disposal at this upscale hotel, as are the many shops and restaurants now located at the Orlando International Airport. **www.orlandoairport.hyatt.com**

WHERE TO EAT

A food lover's paradise, the joy of Florida is in the rich and abundant fresh produce it has to offer. From juicy tropical fruits to mouthwatering seafood, every restaurant is overflowing with Florida's natural bounty. Catering to every palate and budget, the region's restaurants range from small cafés to trendy din-

Stone crab claws

ers to five-star resorts. A vast immigrant population and the constant flow of tourists contributes to a wide variety of ever-changing food choices. See the listings on pages 148–55. Intimate suppers by candlelight, and themed dinners ensure that the dining experience is as much about entertainment as sustenance.

Mexican food at its best – Chili's Grill & Bar, I-Drive *(see p153)*

TYPES OF RESTAURANTS

Orlando is a multi-cultural city offering a wide range of cuisines. The large number of Thai and Vietnamese residents guarantees a bounty of high-quality Asian restaurants. Mexican and Cuban eateries are also plentiful and, since this is the South, barbecue is never far away. African, Irish, Lebanese, Pakistani, Polish, and Indian – foods from all over the world are joyfully served to cater to all tastebuds. Almost every regional American cuisine is represented, from Maine to New Orleans, while a breed of innovative chefs has combined Florida's finest local produce with zesty Caribbean flavors to create what is called New Florida or "Floribbean" cuisine. Sushi is available in every supermarket, and every street corner has a pizza joint. "Natural" supermarkets, Whole Foods, and Chamberlain's offer organic meals.

Restaurants of every size and shape serve seafood. In

one Florida institution, the "raw bar," you can enjoy deliciously fresh raw oysters or clams and steamed shrimp.

RESERVATIONS

Reservations are usually not required at smaller restaurants. But it would be a good idea to make advance reservations at larger places in upscale areas such as Sand Lake Road, International Drive, and the theme parks, particularly on weekends. Guests staying at the Disney World and Universal resorts get preferred seating at the attraction-owned restaurants.

DINING ON A BUDGET

There are several ways to reduce your food budget. Most restaurants offer huge and inexpensive breakfasts. Bargain meals are plentiful away from the hotels and theme parks, particularly at the large number of Indian, Vietnamese, and Thai eateries.

Several seafood and Chinese all-you-can-eat buffets can be found along I-Drive. Southern barbecue is also affordable. Check online for discount coupons, which can cut a bill by 25 percent or more.

Some restaurants will cook your own fish for a reduced price. In addition, many state parks have barbecues where you can grill your catch or any other food that you care to bring along. Delis and supermarkets are good for picnic provisions.

EATING OUT LATE

Most restaurants close at 10pm since Floridians prefer to eat early – usually between 7 and 9pm. Some restaurants, however, do stay open until 11pm. The Globe, at 25 Wall Street Plaza in Downtown Orlando, serves food until 2am. Diners on East Colonial Drive such as Denny's (No. 3162), and the 5 & Diner (No. 12286), plus the B-Line at 9801 International Drive, are

The highly acclaimed Emeril's Restaurant *(see p151)* **at Universal Orlando**

Ran Getsu of Tokyo *(see p153)*, an exclusive Japanese restaurant near the Sand Lake Road, I-Drive area

open 24 hours. Mexican food lovers can drive north on State Road 436 to Beto's at No. 103, near the junction with US 17-92.

CELEBRITY DINING

The new word in Orlando dining is "celebrity." Names that would generally be found attached to big-city restaurants or appearing on the Food Network are popping up all over Central Florida. Emeril Lagasse, who set up Emeril's at Universal and the Tchoup Chop at the Royal Pacific Resort, is now joined by Todd English, who operates Olives in New York and now bluezoo at Disney's Dolphin Hotel *(see p139)*. Norman Van Aken founded Norman's at the Ritz-Carlton (4012 Central Florida Parkway), and innovative chef Melissa Kelly has set up Primo at the JW Marriott. Wolfgang Puck and Roy Yamaguchi own signature restaurants, and a trio of French superstars – Paul Bocuse, Gaston Lenotre, and Roger Verge – run Les Chefs de France at Epcot.

DINING DISTRICTS

Restaurants emerge in groups in Orlando. The Sand Lake Road "Restaurant Row," near the theme parks, is home to corporate-owned, high-end eateries such as Seasons 52, Bonefish Grill, Roys, and Timpano Italian Chophouse, as well as stand-alone destinations Essence of India, Anaelle & Hugo, and Vines. To the west, Bistro 1501 at the Orlando Marriott Hotel

offers fine dining in Lake Mary. The ViMi district of Colonial Drive is home to scores of Vietnamese, Thai, and Chinese restaurants. Old favorites such as Little Saigon and Shin Jung are next to the newcomers Lemongrass Bistro and Pho Hoa. Thornton Park in downtown is host to HUE, Napasorn Thai, the Japanese eatery Ichiban, lunchtime favorite Dexters, and upscale Arthur's 27 and Harvey's Bistro. Nearby College Park draws diners with Jade Bistro, K Restaurant, Babbo Wine Bar, Edgewater Grill with a taste of the Mediterranean, and the hip tapas eatery Taste.

THEME PARK DINING

Some of the finest dining in Orlando can be found at the parks, including the AAA Five-Diamond Award winner, Victoria & Albert's, at the Grand Floridian Resort & Spa, and the award-winning Palm

at Universal's Hard Rock Hotel. You can be fairly certain that anything consumed, from hot dogs to haute cuisine, at any of the theme parks will be on the expensive side. However, the food is generally worth it.

The parks are full to the brim with themed restaurants. The Coral Reef Restaurant at Epcot has an 8-ft (2.5-m) high glass wall panorama of the 5.7 million gallon (21.5 million liter) Living Seas aquarium. Delfino Riviera at Universal's Portofino Bay Hotel transports diners to a full-scale replica of Italy's Portofino harbor. Also at Universal, CityWalk treats sports-loving guests to NBA City for basketball-themed goodies, and racing meals at the NASCAR Café. Disney's Rainforest Café features hourly thunderstorms amid animatronic gorillas. The parks are also home to the Hard Rock Café, House of Blues, and Planet Hollywood.

Chef's table at Victoria & Albert's *(see p150)*, Grand Floridian Resort & Spa

Choosing a Restaurant

The restaurants in this guide have been selected for their good value, exceptional food, or interesting location. These listings highlight some of the factors that may influence your choice, such as whether you can opt to eat outdoors or if the venue offers live music. Entries are alphabetical within each price category.

PRICE CATEGORIES
Price categories include a three-course meal for one, a glass of house wine, and all unavoidable extra charges including service and tax.

$ under $30
$$ $30–$40
$$$ $40–$50
$$$$ $50–$65
$$$$$ over $65

WALT DISNEY WORLD® RESORT

ANIMAL KINGDOM Boma – Flavors of Africa $$

Disney's Animal Kingdom Lodge, Bay Lake, 32830 **Tel** *407-939-3463*

Tables laden with spicy and unusual African dishes invite exploration at the overwhelming dinner and breakfast buffets at this Disney-themed resort. Dishes are flavored with delicious combinations of tamarind, cumin, coriander, cinnamon, hot chillies, cilantro, papaya, and other uncommon tastes.

ANIMAL KINGDOM Jiko – The Cooking Place $$$$

Disney's Animal Kingdom Lodge, Bay Lake, 32830 **Tel** *407-939-3463*

Pan-African splendor surrounds you in this gorgeous restaurant overlooking a large stretch of savanna where wild animals roam. Traditional foods from across the continent include a tasty, slow-cooked Moroccan stew and flatbread with yogurt and onions baked in open jiko ovens.

DISNEY-MGM STUDIOS Hollywood Brown Derby $$$

Lake Buena Vista, 32830 **Tel** *407-560-5376*

Re-creating the fabled Brown Derby of 1930s Hollywood, the Art Deco interior here echoes the retro menu, which includes a world-famous Cobb salad. Seafood and steaks in fusion style and acclaimed desserts (try the grapefruit cake) round off the offerings. This restaurant is known for serving up the best-mixed drinks in the park.

DISNEY-MGM STUDIOS Sci-Fi Dine-In Theater $$$

Lake Buena Vista, 32830 **Tel** *407-560-3359*

The theme is drive-in movies and the menu offers appropriate options, with burgers, fries, pasta, ribs, and outrageous milkshakes. The food is expensive for what it is, but the experience of sitting in a replica 1950s car and watching old sci-fi movies is nostalgic for old-timers and provides fun for children too.

DOWNTOWN DISNEY Dakshin $$

12541 Suite Road 535, 32830 **Tel** *407-827-9080*

A South Indian haven for lovers of seafood and vegetarian wonders, Dakshin's offerings include lobster curry, delicacies from Goa and Mangalore, and a separate dinner menu featuring delicious Indian crêpes. The weekend brunch is worth a visit. Attentive service can guide the unfamiliar diner through the varied menu.

DOWNTOWN DISNEY Olivia's Café $$

Disney Old Key West **Tel** *407-939-3463*

Diners will think they are in old Key West at this café serving conch-style meals. Check out the Florida paella, conch chowder, and mojo chicken. Floridians feel that Olivia's does Key West pretty good justice with its focus on local flavors. A fun menu and good staff help make it enjoyable for children as well.

DOWNTOWN DISNEY Planet Hollywood Orlando $$

1506 E Buena Vista Drive, 32830 **Tel** *407-827-7827*

Located within a purple neon globe, this new institution in Orlando has large video screens and masses of movie memorabilia. The fare is mainstream, with meaty burgers and tasty pizzas. Children will particularly enjoy eating here, but adults may find the dining room too loud for conversation.

DOWNTOWN DISNEY Wolfgang Puck Café $$

1482 E. Buena Vista Drive, 32830 **Tel** *407-938-9653*

Located within Downtown Disney, this is actually several restaurants in one – from a casual, California-influenced express café to fine dining – all powered by the chef's vision and taste. It is an imaginative concept, catering to many different tastes good for the whole family. The fire-roasted pizzas, pastas, and grilled foods are tasty.

DOWNTOWN DISNEY Fulton's Crab House $$$$

Downtown Disney Market Place **Tel** *407-939-3463*

Located in a replica of a riverboat dating from the end of the 19th century, this steak and seafood eatery is a treat for adults and children alike. As well as a grand staircase and hand-painted ceiling murals, there are beautiful artifacts reflecting the nautical theme. A children's menu is available.

Key to symbols *see back cover flap*

DOWNTOWN DISNEY The Outback

1900 Buena Vista Drive, 32830 **Tel** *407-827-3430*

An indoor waterfall creates a soothing atmosphere at this Down Under chain bistro. Feast on jumbo stuffed shrimp and steaks. Portions are massive, sides are good, and try to save room for the decadent desserts. This is more of a family or group destination, where the din can get in the way of romance.

EPCOT Cape May Café

Disney's Beach Club Resort **Tel** *407-939-3463*

The buffet breakfast proceedings here are conducted by Admiral Goofy. At dinner, a bell announces the start of the clam bake buffet, where tables are laden with a great array of food from which to choose. Good entertainment is provided for the whole family at every meal every day.

EPCOT Gulliver's Grill

Walt Disney World Swan Hotel **Tel** *407-934-1609*

Try the tastes of Brobdingnag, the legendary land of giants, at this lovely plant-filled restaurant that serves well-prepared American cuisine. Good service adds to the enjoyment of the food from the decent but unremarkable menu, which includes a buffet. The restaurant is also obviously and famously family-friendly.

EPCOT Les Chefs de France

Epcot World Showcase, Walt Disney World, 32830 **Tel** *407-939-3463*

Haute cuisine does not get much higher than that served in a restaurant created by Bocuse, Lenotre, and Verge, three masters of French cooking. From appetizers to classics such as duck *à l'orange*, every dish is a definition of the art. Epcot admission is necessary for anyone wishing to dine here.

EPCOT Shula's

Walt Disney World Dolphin Hotel **Tel** *407-934-1609*

This is one of the resort's finest steakhouses. They also have a fine selection of seafood, and the desserts are spectacular. It is one local eatery where the emphasis is on food and not entertainment, and it shows in each and every dish. Kids are welcome but they will find it tame compared to other resort restaurants.

EPCOT Yachtsman Steakhouse

Disney Yacht Club Resort, 32830 **Tel** *407-939-3463*

This eatery is open all day for hearty favorites, including fish, steak, and pasta, all to be enjoyed in themed nautical surroundings. The scrumptious desserts that are available at the very good dinner buffet are not to be missed. Dining here is likely to be more enjoyable for adults unaccompanied by kids.

EPCOT Flying Fish Café

Disney's Boardwalk, Lake Buena Vista, 32830 **Tel** *407-939-3463*

This restaurant is another good reason to visit the free Disney Boardwalk area, aside from the view of nightly fireworks. The service is superb – the staff seem to anticipate your every need while serving creative American seafood cuisine. The daily specials change according to what is in season.

FORT WILDERNESS Whispering Canyon Café

Disney Wilderness Lodge **Tel** *407-939-3463*

Snap on your six-guns and settle in for an all-you-can-eat campfire buffet in a Wild West setting. The café is also open for frontier-style breakfasts. Families with children will find this particularly appealing. The food is decent and entertainment value quite high. Stop in for a unique local experience.

FORT WILDERNESS Artist Point

Disney's Wilderness Lodge, Lake Buena Vista, 32830 **Tel** *407-939-3463*

From the size of the plate to the size of the portions, everything here is big. The innovative, Northwestern-themed menu offers exotic items such as sautéed elk sausage, and the service and setting are spectacular. The restaurant has more appeal for adult diners, but children are certainly welcome.

MAGIC KINGDOM Chef Mickey's

Disney's Contemporary Resort **Tel** *407-939-3463*

Very much a family-oriented place, Mickey's offers breakfast and dinner buffets. Diners can enjoy the antics of their favorite Disney characters as they eat dishes from a mixed, unassuming menu that is available throughout the day. The service is quite good and children are especially welcome.

MAGIC KINGDOM Bongo's Cuban Café

2426 Viscount Row, 32809 **Tel** *407-828-0999*

An unpretentious restaurant – a great Disney antidote – that welcomes families. The food can range dramatically from seafood pltters to shrips sautéed in sauce. Spanish or Neo-Spanish dishes dominate the menu. The bustling, fast-paced energetic environment can detract from conversation at times.

MAGIC KINGDOM Ohana

Disney's Polynesian Resort **Tel** *407-939-3463*

This buzzing, open-plan dining room is the setting for Polynesian-style cuisine. Set-price dinners include meat and shellfish roasted over a fire pit and served on 3-ft (1-m) long skewers. Terrific evening entertainment livens up the dining experience for everyone, whether part of a visiting couple or family.

MAGIC KINGDOM Cinderella's Royal Table $$$

Cinderella's Castle, 32830   **Tel** *407-939-3463*

Prime rib and chicken for adults and Disney characters for the kids – this is the traditional Disney breakfast experience taken to the extreme. Little girls love to get a glimpse of Cinderella during their meal. Advance reservations – sometimes as much as three to four months in advance – are mandatory.

MAGIC KINGDOM Magic Kingdom: California Grill $$$$

Disney's Contemporary Resort   **Tel** *407-939-3463*

This stylish restaurant, with good views and an open-plan kitchen, serves creative West Coast fare such as smoked salmon pizza, and pork and polenta. It is not too trendy for children to find menu items that appeal to them and is a good spot for those who would rather not eat red meat.

MAGIC KINGDOM Citrico's at the Grand Floridian $$$$

Disney's Grand Floridian Resort & Spa, Lake Buena Vista, 32830   **Tel** *407-939-3463*

This delightful eatery offers international fare, with a focus on slow-roasted meats. Influenced by French cuisine, everything from breads to desserts is exquisite – even the view of the dramatic action in the open kitchen. Requiring formal attire, it is expensive but worth it. It is closed on Mondays and Tuesdays.

MAGIC KINGDOM Disney's Spirit of Aloha Dinner Show $$$$

Disney's Polynesian Resort, Lake Buena Vista, 32830   **Tel** *407-939-3463*

Tropical appetizers and "Island" ribs are the highlights of the menu in this Polynesian-style diner. The food is served to the accompaniment of the traditional music and dances of Tahiti, Samoa, Tonga, New Zealand, and Hawaii. Dining here is enormous fun for both children and adults who like the hula.

MAGIC KINGDOM Narcoossee's $$$$

Disney's Grand Floridian Resort   **Tel** *407-824-1400*

This restaurant in an octagonal chalet alongside the Seven Seas Lagoon serves delicious meat and fish dishes with fresh local vegetables. The food here is fresh and consistent and the pace not as rushed as elsewhere in the Disney area. Ask about daily specials and for local fish highlights.

MAGIC KINGDOM Victoria & Albert's $$$$$

Disney's Grand Floridian Resort   **Tel** *407-824-1089*

Reservations are a must at this lavish restaurant. The six-course fixed-price menu is superlative, and diners are waited on by a butler and a maid. Ask for the chef's table, the most exclusive one in the house. One of the most delightfully decadent dining experiences in the area, and not one for children.

OTHER THEME PARKS

SEAWORLD Sharks Underwater Grill $$

7007 SeaWorld Drive, 32837   **Tel** *407-370-1573*

Take the opportunity to enjoy Caribbean and Florida-style seafood inches away from more than 50 sharks at SeaWorld – a setting that is ideal for children. The menu is upscale and the food is as fresh as getting it directly from the tank – but don't worry, they don't. Admission to SeaWorld is required.

SEAWORLD Atlantis $$$$

6677 Sea Harbor Drive, 32837   **Tel** *407-351-5555*

Located in the Renaissance Orlando Resort *(see p140)*, Atlantis serves up dishes from a Mediterranean seafood menu to the accompaniment of live harp music. Crystal chandeliers and European-quality service complete the picture in what is almost a theme park of its own. Chargrilled steaks are available for those not enamored of fish.

SEAWORLD Primo $$$$$

4040 Central Florida Parkway, 32837   **Tel** *407-393-4444*

Organic cuisine is served up at this restaurant located in the enormous JW Marriott Orlando *(see p143)*. From free-range lamb to homemade sausages, care is taken with every ingredient and the result is deliciously successful. Prices are very high, but for anyone looking for a very special meal, Primo is the place to be.

UNIVERSAL ORLANDO NASCAR Café $

6000 Universal Boulevard, 32819   **Tel** *407-224-7223*

Race-car lovers and motorheads will be fascinated by the racing cars and racing memorabilia featured here, as well as the food, which includes steaks, chops, and other barbecued meats. There are also around 40 televisions featuring highlights of great car races. Open until late, this restaurant provides fun for the whole family.

UNIVERSAL ORLANDO Hard Rock Café Orlando $$

6050 Universal Boulevard, 32819   **Tel** *407-351-7625*

This massive restaurant in CityWalk overflows with pop memorabilia. The sundaes are great, and the live music in the concert hall (Fridays and Saturdays) makes this an extremely popular hangout. The Hard Rock Café is not an environment for intimate conversation as it has a tendency to be boisterous.

Key to price guide *see p148*   **Key to symbols** *see back cover flap*

UNIVERSAL ORLANDO Latin Quarter 🚹 ♿ 🚃 🎵 $$

6000 Universal Boulevard, 32819 **Tel** *407-224-2800*

Spice up meal times with the culture, cuisine, music, and dance of 21 Latin nations. This popular eatery in upscale CityWalk serves a huge variety of Latin American dishes, as well as seafood and steaks. It is open for lunch and dinner daily, and usually stays open for late-night revelry until 2am.

UNIVERSAL ORLANDO Jimmy Buffett's Margaritaville 🚹 ♿ 🎵 $$$

6000 Universal Boulevard, 32819 **Tel** *407-224-2155*

Soak up the Key West flavor and Jimmy Buffett tunes at Margaritaville in the very heart of glitzy CityWalk. There is more appeal in the colorful atmosphere than in the food at this noisy and crowded spot, but the ocean of margarita varieties will easily satisfy your drink-and-be-merry craving.

UNIVERSAL ORLANDO Emeril's Restaurant Orlando 🚹 ♿ $$$$$

6000 Universal Boulevard, 32819 **Tel** *407-224-2424*

Savor the casual, contemporary atmosphere, the warm and spicy colors, and first-class service in this CityWalk restaurant that has become an institution. Highlighting the "Bam!" cuisine of Emeril Lagasse, the menu offers flawlessly prepared items such as the andouille-crusted Texas redfish.

UNIVERSAL ORLANDO Palm Restaurant 🚹 ♿ 🚃 $$$$$

5800 Universal Boulevard, 32819 **Tel** *407-503-7256*

The first Palm opened in New York circa 1926, and this Orlando branch within the Hard Rock Hotel *(see p140)* features fine, uncomplicated dishes, including enormous steaks. In contrast to most Universal eateries, free valet parking is provided right at the door.

ORLANDO & CENTRAL FLORIDA

COCOA BEACH The Mango Tree Restaurant 🚹 ♿ 🎵 $$$$

118 N. Atlantic Avenue, 32931 **Tel** *321-799-0513*   **Map** *F3*

This gourmet restaurant serves local dishes, with seafood as its specialty. Situated just yards from the Atlantic Ocean, there is a tropical garden with waterfowl, Japanese carp, and lush foliage to help create a mood and atmosphere that is ideal for couples in search of a romantic evening.

DAYTONA BEACH Aunt Catfish 🚹 ♿ 🚃 $$

4009 Halifax Drive, 32127 **Tel** *386-767-4768*

This eatery – popular with travelers and local residents alike – is located on the Intracoastal Waterway. With seafood featuring strongly on the menu, it is especially renowned for its fried catfish and other Southern-style dishes such as crab cakes and clam strips. On Sunday it is open for a popular and varied brunch.

DAYTONA BEACH Down the Hatch 🚹 ♿ 🎵 🚃 $$

4894 Front Street, Ponce Inlet, 32127 **Tel** *386-761-4831*

Family-oriented and serving fresh fish and a few meat dishes, this restaurant is located on the waterfront, so diners can watch the boats unload their catch at the end of the day. A very casual and friendly environment, with live music from Wednesday through to Sunday, helps to make it popular with local residents.

DOWNTOWN ORLANDO Johnny's Fillin' Station ♿ 🎵 $

2631 S. Ferncreek, 32806 **Tel** *407-894-6900*   **Map** *F2*

Local critics claim that Johnny's serves the best burgers in Orlando. American food and atmosphere at their purest are on offer at this great family destination that will thrill the kids. The atmosphere is friendly and the staff helpful and upbeat. But there is not much variety on the menu for those who are not particularly meat-inclined.

DOWNTOWN ORLANDO Little Saigon ♿ 🎵 $

1106 E. Colonial Drive, 32803 **Tel** *407-423-8539*   **Map** *F2*

This highly praised restaurant serves the best Vietnamese cuisine in the area. Casual, comfortable, affordable, and authentic are all words used to describe this small, family-friendly place that serves up sizable portions. The staff are happy to describe dishes and guide diners through the menu.

DOWNTOWN ORLANDO Babbo Wine Bar & Café 🚹 ♿ 🚃 $$

1710 Edgewater Drive, 32804 **Tel** *407-649-9770*

A throwback to restaurants in Naples, this café features dishes straight from the trattorias of Southern Italy, such as savory baked gnocchi and tortellini alla Campagnola. The select, individual pizzas are hand-tossed, crispy, and delicious. The wine bar serves over 100 wines, around half of them by the glass.

DOWNTOWN ORLANDO Dexters of Thornton Park 🚹 ♿ 🚃 $$

808 E. Washington Street, 32801 **Tel** *407-648-2777*

Spacious, light, and airy, with seating at the bar or on barstools at elevated tables. Dexters has a casual ambience and is popular with the urban-professional set. Sandwiches and pastas – small and large portions – are staples, while wines can be ordered both by the bottle and "on tap".

DOWNTOWN ORLANDO Edgewater Grill $$
2306 Edgewater Drive, 32804 **Tel** *407-425-1801*

The main street of College Park is the setting for this modern Mediterranean bistro. Lots of root vegetables, tomatoes, and beans are served as accompaniments to thick cuts of meat, grilled seafood, and roasted chicken. The high-quality cooking fills plates and amply satisfies appetites.

DOWNTOWN ORLANDO Il Pescatore $$
651 N. Primrose Drive, 32803 **Tel** *407-896-6763*

A simple setting is provided for food that is truly Italian through and through. Traditional house specialties like *trippa del pescatore* (tripe in tomato sauce) make this spot unique in its authenticity. Choosing between the various pasta sauces is pleasingly difficult. This restaurant is closed on Sundays and Mondays.

DOWNTOWN ORLANDO Jade Bistro $$
2425 Edgewater Drive, 32804 **Tel** *407-422-7968*

Veteran sushi chefs join seasoned restaurant owners for a truly delightful combination. The pan-Oriental cuisine here is excellent and often exceeds expectations. Although not entirely Japanese, Chinese, or Thai, it still manages to exce in all these areas. Some small children may find the food too adventurous.

DOWNTOWN ORLANDO Napasorn Thai $$
56 E. Pine Street, 32801 **Tel** *407-245-8088*

The young yet experienced Napasorn owners wander slightly from traditional Thai food, but serve up well-prepared dishes. The basil duck stands out in particular. The reasonably good sushi bar also helps to make it a most enjoyable destination, though be warned that young children may find the cuisine too experimental.

DOWNTOWN ORLANDO Fishbones $$$
6707 Sand Lake Road, 32819 **Tel** *407-352-0135*

Fresh selections from the sea are made daily, and diners have the chance to mix various tasty sauces with their selection. Others might opt for the rack of lamb or prime rib at this particularly family-friendly restaurant. It is always worth asking about the catch of the day and local fish and seafood.

DOWNTOWN ORLANDO Gargi's $$$
1414 N. Orange Avenue, 32801 **Tel** *407-894-7907*

A local favorite for more than two decades, the new location here on Lake Ivanhoe provides diners with spectacular sunset views of Downtown Orlando. Enjoy a romantic evening with offerings of old-world service and classic traditional Italian food. Take the wine suggestions as gospel.

DOWNTOWN ORLANDO Harvey's Bistro $$$
390 N. Orange Avenue, 32801 **Tel** *407-246-6560*

The reputation here for reasonably priced, beautifully presented dishes, served in a lively but elegant atmosphere, is well-earned. Harvey's continues to be one of downtown's best options for indulging in American bistro cuisine and is a suitable place for special events or family occasions.

DOWNTOWN ORLANDO Pebbles Restaurant $$$
12551 State Road 535, 32836 **Tel** *407-827-1111*   **Map** *F2*

This popular casual restaurant located on the outskirts of the metro area is favored by locals for its friendly atmosphere and eclectic menu. The good, locally-influenced cuisine includes a variety of tasty dishes such as mussels Chardonnay and lobster penne pasta with artichoke hearts.

DOWNTOWN ORLANDO Christini's Ristorante $$$$
7600 Dr. Phillips Boulevard, 32819 **Tel** *407-345-8770*

This fairly formal restaurant is ideal for a romantic evening. Excellent service, a scenic dining room, and a solid wine list add to the enjoyment of the regional Italian dishes on offer here. The menu varies according to what ingredients are in season, and it is always worth asking about the specials of the day.

DOWNTOWN ORLANDO Hemingway's $$$$
1 Grand Cypress Boulevard, 32836 **Tel** *407-239-3854*

Drawing on the Key West theme intrinsic to the restaurant's name, Hemingway's has a lovely, romantic dining room as well as a deck overlooking a waterfall. Beer-battered coconut shrimp and blackened swordfish with Cajun tartar sauce are among the highlights of the interesting menu.

DOWNTOWN ORLANDO Hue $$$$
629 E. Central Boulevard, 32801 **Tel** *407-849-1800*

With decor that has a distinctively big-city look, with large windows and high ceilings, the Hue serves up progressive American cuisine with style. The menu, which changes daily, features dishes such as wood-grilled filet mignon, tamari roasted duck breast, and oven-roasted Chilean sea bass.

DOWNTOWN ORLANDO K Restaurant & Wine Bar $$$$
2401 Edgewater Drive, 32804 **Tel** *407-872-2332*

The former Café Allegre reaches a grand level of food and service, creating dishes that are both simple and elegantly delicious. From salads to starters to the main course, everything hits the right note, surpassing the restaurant's already-sterling reputation. It is closed on Sundays and Mondays.

Key to price guide *see p148* **Key to symbols** *see back cover flap*

DOWNTOWN ORLANDO The Boheme

🚶♿🎵 $$$$$

325 S. Orange Avenue, 32801 **Tel** *407-581-4700*

Map *F2*

One of only two Grand Bosenderfer pianos in the world is the centerpiece of this otherwise contemporary setting. Diners can not go wrong with the menu, which features lavishly prepared seafood, game, and pasta. Among the dishes that are highly coveted is the asparagus crusted diver scallops.

DOWNTOWN ORLANDO O'Boys Barb-Q

♿ $

924 W. Colonial Drive, 32804 **Tel** *407-425-6269*

Map *F2*

This local favorite combines simple decor with stunning slow-smoked barbecue cuisine. All-you-can-eat specials feature in the evenings. The sauce is terrific, the side dishes good, and the portions sizable – whether or not there is a buffet on offer. Great fun for all the family, with just a touch of old Florida rustic charm.

DOWNTOWN ORLANDO Le Coq au Vin

♿ $$$

4800 S. Orange Avenue, 32806 **Tel** *407-851-6980*

Map *F2*

Welcoming surroundings and consistently fine rustic French cuisine are the draw to Le Coq au Vin, which is considered to be one of the best French restaurants in the region. The romantic environment is perfect for special occasions. Younger children could, however, become bored with the pace and cuisine.

INTERNATIONAL DRIVE Bahama Breeze

🚶♿🎵🍴 $$

8849 International Drive, 32819 **Tel** *407-248-2499*

A menu laden with tastes of the tropics gives diners the chance to indulge their tropical fancy at this eatery. Drinkers might want to sample the delicious *bahamarita*. The light-hearted fun environment helps make it amenable to the whole family, and there are good mingling opportunities for those who are unaccompanied.

INTERNATIONAL DRIVE Cedar's Restaurant

🚶♿🎵 $$

7732 W. Sand Lake Road, 32819 **Tel** *407-351-6000*

Cedar's spin on traditional Lebanese food has a lightness of texture and flavor that is both refreshing and inviting. Use the puffy, hot pitas to scoop up *baba ghanoush*, a smooth roasted eggplant and garlic puree with a wonderfully smoky taste. The lunch buffet is a bargain that is well known to locals.

INTERNATIONAL DRIVE Chili's Grill & Bar

🚶♿ $$

7021 International Drive, 32819 **Tel** *407-352-7618*

Signature dishes at this casual dining family restaurant include the famous double-basted baby back ribs and enormous burgers. There are also a number of tasty Mexican offerings such as tacos and sizzling fajitas. Outstanding margaritas are available from the full bar.

INTERNATIONAL DRIVE Bergamo's Italian Restaurant

🚶♿🎵 $$$

8445 International Drive, 32819 **Tel** *407-352-3805*

This trattoria offers excellent Italian cuisine served by operatic waiters. Try the *osso bucco* (a veal and tomato stew) with risotto, or any of the pasta dishes. Family-friendly, it provides entertainment fairly frequently. The talented singing waiters are pretty good with their non-performance work as well.

INTERNATIONAL DRIVE Ran Getsu of Tokyo

🚶♿ $$$

8400 International Drive, 32819 **Tel** *407-345-0044*

This upscale two-tiered restaurant has an extensive offering of authentic Japanese fare and fabulously fresh sushi. Floor-to-ceiling windows overlook a landscaped Japanese garden and koi ponds. The signature dish here is *sukiyaki*, pan-fried thinly sliced beef, tofu, and fresh vegetables.

INTERNATIONAL DRIVE Season's 52

🚶♿🍴 $$$

7700 W. Sand Lake Road, 32819 **Tel** *407-354-5212*

The concept here is of fresh seasonal foods. So, be aware that a favorite dish made with pears from Oregon might not be available the next time you go, but you can be sure that something equally impressive will be. The satisfying and occasionally unusual combinations of regional and global ingredients make the food enjoyable.

INTERNATIONAL DRIVE Bonefish Grill

🚶♿ $$$$

7830 W. Sand Lake Road, 32819 **Tel** *407-355-7707*

Moderately priced seafood and a pleasant atmosphere are on offer here. The bar is also popular, and appetizers such as the saucy shrimp and the mussels Josephine are superb, perhaps better than the multiple-choice fish entrées. The seafood offerings change according to what is available on the day.

INTERNATIONAL DRIVE Everglades

♿🎵 $$$$

9840 International Drive, 32819 **Tel** *407-996-9840*

Much better than the average upscale hotel restaurant, Everglades serves creative gourmet dishes inspired by seasonal Florida cuisine. The gator chowder is a colorful touch of Old Florida. Its consistency makes Everglades one of the more popular local restaurants, and there is every chance that kids will enjoy the menu oddities.

INTERNATIONAL DRIVE The Butcher Shop Steakhouse

♿ $$$$

8445 International Drive, 32819 **Tel** *407-363-9727*

Some of the biggest and best steaks along International Drive are on offer here. Diners can even cook their own at the grill for a touch of dinner theater if that is what they fancy doing. The alternative is to sit back and enjoy the good service from staff who deliver cooked-to-order dishes of top quality and consistency.

INTERNATIONAL DRIVE Dux

9801 International Drive, 32819 **Tel** *407-345-4550*

This elegant, formal restaurant in the Peabody Hotel (*see p143*) is named after the resident aquatic fowl that stroll about freely. The menu changes weekly, but is consistently impressive and always includes a vegetarian main course as well as a meat and fish option. This is definitely a destination for special occasions.

INTERNATIONAL DRIVE Roy's Restaurant

7760 W. Sand Lake Road, 32819 **Tel** *407-352-4844*

This upscale restaurant, founded by celebrity chef Roy Yamaguchi, provides a curious fusion of Pacific Rim cuisines, with an emphasis on Hawaiian ingredients. Among typical dishes is the shutome swordfish in a Thai curry sauce. Both the menu and wine list offer a wide variety of selection.

INTERNATIONAL DRIVE Ruth's Chris Steak House

7501 W. Sand Lake Road, 32819 **Tel** *407-226-3900*

Within a gentlemen's club ambience, both the menu and service are delivered with excellence. This New Orleans-based chain serves only aged meats from corn-fed Hereford cows, seared on a 1,800 degree grill – the meat is so tender that a knife is not necessary. This is a restaurant for expense accounts and special occasions.

INTERNATIONAL DRIVE Timpano Italian Chophouse

7488 W. Sand Lake Road, 32819 **Tel** *407-248-0429*

The experience of big-city dining with the allure of 1950s New York nightclubs is re-created here. The result is extraordinary quality and impeccable service. The veal *saltimbocca* – thin cutlets served with prosciutto ham and provolone in a subtle garlic and sage sauce – is particularly brilliant.

KISSIMMEE Fred Marion's

5770 W Irlo Bronson Memorial Highway, 34746 **Tel** *407-397-9444*

Good dining for all the family is offered at this no-frills restaurant, 30 minutes from Disney World. Great ribs, steaks, and seafood all feature on the menu. Marion's sauce is terrific, the sides are sizable and tasty, and the barbecued meat is moist and tender. There are also delicious desserts.

KISSIMMEE Pacino's Italian Ristorante

5795 W Highway 192, 34746 **Tel** *407-396-8022*

Charbroiled food is the focus of this comfortable and friendly-family restaurant, which also provides a free delivery service to nearby hotels. Steaks tend to be the most favored items on the menu, but Pacino's does a good job of offering a mix of entrées for broad appeal. The service is good too.

KISSIMMEE Phoenician Restaurant

2920 Vineland Road, 34746 **Tel** *407-397-2230*

This is a Turkish delight sheltered in a strip mall off the busy US Highway 192. The tabbouli and hummus are made fresh daily, the shish kabob is sizzling hot, and the coffee is bracingly strong. There is authentic couscous for non-meat-eaters, and a great pastry shop next door. Young children may struggle with the menu.

KISSIMMEE Magic Mining Steaks & Seafood Company

7736 W. Highway 192, 34747 **Tel** *407-396-1950*

Ribs, steaks, chicken, more ribs, and anything that will fit on a grill are what is on offer here. Kids will adore the Gold Mine decor with its styrofoam rock walls, full-scale electric train that runs through the restaurant, and video game "depot." After the meal, parents can enjoy the two 18-hole golf courses on the roof.

MAITLAND Bucca de Beppo

1351 S. Orlando Avenue, 32751 **Tel** *407-622-7663*

Think big, big, and bigger at this fun, family-style restaurant with foot-long lasagnes, sandwiches that last a week, and pizzas as big as the table. A good place for those who like to take food home with them; the doggie bags have handles. Reservations for this locals' favorite are highly recommended.

MAITLAND Enzian Theater

1300 S. Orlando Avenue, 32751 **Tel** *407-629-1088*

Nachos and hummus with avant-garde films, pasta and salads with thrillers, tiramisu and ice cream with musicals. The premier film and dinner destination all rolled into one, the Enzian shows first-run indie movies with a small but varied menu of dinner and snack items to enjoy while watching the show.

SANFORD Da Vinci

107 S. Magnolia Avenue, 32771 **Tel** *407-323-1388*

A slightly funky and as yet undiscovered restaurant nestled in downtown Sanford, where ongoing renovation is still very much in evidence. Yet, diners continue to find their way here. Alongside traditional dishes are interesting Mediterranean-inspired creations that make it well worth the trip.

WINTER PARK Brooklyn Pizza

1881 W. Fairbanks Avenue, 32789 **Tel** *407-622-7499*

Most in the area – and in the know – consider this to be the best place in town for New York-style pizza. Trading on a family tradition going back over 40 years, Brooklyn Pizza delivers the kind of handmade, authentic pies you had as a child, along with sandwiches, baked dinners, and a few other items.

Key to price guide *see p148* **Key to symbols** *see back cover flap*

WINTER PARK Briar Patch $$
252 N. Park Avenue, 32789 **Tel** *407-628-8651*

A perennial favorite on Park Avenue for locals and visitors alike, the front porch coziness and creative menu items keep old fans coming back to the Briar Patch for more. There are long lines at breakfast and weekend lunchtimes – and many who are more then willing to wait. Dining here is fun for the whole family.

WINTER PARK Fiddler's Green $$
544 W. Fairbanks Avenue, 32789 **Tel** *407-645-2050*

One of the largest selections of draft ales, lagers, and stouts in the area is available at this pub, which also serves traditional Irish fare and ambitious offerings such as grilled salmon with champagne sauce. It is all proof that a focus on flavor, presentation, and service can spell "gourmet" for Irish cuisine.

WINTER PARK Thai Place $$
501 N. Orlando Avenue, 32789 **Tel** *407-644-8232*

With dark walls and glittery artwork, this is one of the best Thai restaurants around. The food is always as good as you remember it – which is good indeed. The fragrant *tom kha gai*, a salad with peanut dressing, and choice of seafood, chicken, beef, or pork in a variety of sauces are all excellent.

WINTER PARK Allegria Wine Bar & Café $$
115 E. Lyman Avenue, 32789 **Tel** *407-628-1641*

Allegria offers a joyous Italian experience just off Park Avenue. Savor the house antipasto (cheese, polenta, and sausage in a red pepper sauce) over a glass of wine to start off with. The *pollo Rosario* – chicken topped with sundried tomatoes, shrimp, and pink garlic-vodka sauce – is superb.

WINTER PARK Limoncello Ristorante $$$
702 Orange Avenue, 32789 **Tel** *407-539-0900*

A chef from Sorrento and an owner from Rome are responsible for the divijne food served here. Handmade pasta dishes like gnocchi Porto Cervo, deeply satisfying seafood dishes, and impeccable service make this restaurant a winner and ensure a memorable experience. Limoncello is recommended for special or romantic occasions.

WINTER PARK Sakura Japanese Restaurant $$$
525 S. Park Avenue, 32789 **Tel** *407-740-8018*

A modest spot where elements of Japanese cuisine – notably artistic presentation – and the setting in which it is served come together gracefully. Sushi, sashimi, and service that is restrained but casual and friendly round off a good, reasonably priced dining experience. Not ideal for young children.

WINTER PARK The Cheesecake Factory $$$
520 N. Orlando Avenue, 32789 **Tel** *407-644-4220*

Huge, towering interiors, with portions that are almost as large, are typical of this popular chain. More than 30 varieties of mouthwatering cheesecake complement the meal, though you can pick up a piece at the take-out counter for later too. Salads and sandwiches are huge. It is wonderful from beginning to end.

WINTER PARK Café de France $$$$
526 Park Avenue S, 32789 **Tel** *407-647-1869*

This cozy French bistro serves lighter meals such as crêpes at lunchtime; at dinner, try the rack of lamb or the daily special. A terrific little corner of France in an unlikely location, it can serve as both a great romantic getaway and a special occasion family restaurant. Worth the trip from the central theme park areas.

WINTER PARK Chef Justin's Park Plaza Gardens $$$$
319 Park Avenue S, 32789 **Tel** *407-645-2475*

An airy courtyard in a plant-filled atrium provides the setting at this elegant restaurant. The consistently delicious and award-winning American cuisine is served with panache. Good service and a pleasant setting add to the pleasures of the regionally-inspired menu. Children may enjoy it, but it is more adult-oriented.

WINTER PARK East of Paris $$$$
358 N. Park Avenue, 32789 **Tel** *407-644-2880*

With decor best described as European chic with an Asian twist, and comfortable seating both inside and out, East of Paris serves up classical-style French cooking influenced by Asian herbs and spices. Dishes such as teriyaki salmon or seared ahi tuna are typical, as are decadent desserts such as hot chocolate soufflé with pistachio ice cream.

WINTER PARK Luma on Park $$$$
290 S. Park Avenue, 32789 **Tel** *407-599-4111*

Contemporary American cuisine is served up in cozy surroundings embellished by rich wood and stylish leather trimmings. From the open kitchen appear beautifully presented dishes such as Gulf red snapper, wood-grilled lamb, and Blue Hill Bay mussels with fennel and orange. It is the ideal place for a relaxing meal.

WINTER PARK Fleming's Steak House $$$$$
933 N. Orlando Avenue, 32789 **Tel** *407-699-9463*

Fleming's is an upscale steakhouse that places great emphasis on the wine. It also offers aged, hand-cut beef in huge, thick-as-a-brick servings and family-style sides, giant seafood entrées, and enormous and highly coveted desserts. Well worth a visit on a special or romantic occasion.

SHOPPING IN CENTRAL FLORIDA

Shopping is one of the major forms of entertainment for visitors to Central Florida. Indoor malls with more than 100,000 sq ft (9,300 sq m) of shopping compete with discount outlet centers, traditional department stores and chain outlets sit side-by-side with unique local shops, and rows of antiques stores are within miles of boutique clothing stores and art galleries. Almost any national retailer can be found on International Drive or in Florida Mall, the state's largest shopping center, while

A typical Florida souvenir

specialty shops sell a wide selection of items, such as antiques, electronics, and sports equipment. Prices range from bargain basement cheap to haute-couture expensive. The theme parks have combined shopping, dining, and entertainment in two massive spending belts running right through their properties, where restaurants and circuses sell souvenirs and souvenir stores offer free magic shows. For listings of malls and factory outlets, see pages 158–9. Shopping districts are described on pages 160–61.

Shops and boutiques along the Park Avenue strip, Winter Park

SALES TAX

Sales tax on clothing is 6 percent in Orange County (Orlando) and 7 percent in Osceola County (Kissimmee), where Walt Disney World is actually situated, so park souvenirs are at the higher rate.

SHOPPING SEASONS

Although actual weather seasons don't vary very much in Central Florida, fashion seasons still turn four times a year. This has led to massive sales in late spring and early fall on clothing and household items.

BOUTIQUE SHOPPING CENTERS

Sitting on the grounds of the first outdoor shopping center in the area, **Winter Park Village** is home to a wide

variety of sleek boutique shops that cater to the latest styles. Fashion can be found at the Ann Taylor Loft store, career-wear at Camille La Vie, and fine men's clothing at Jos. A. Bank. Many young hipsters

New Metropolis, an upmarket furniture store in Winter Park

have filled their homes from New Metropolis, the "Urban Chic" furniture store, while their well-off parents were buying fine linens at Angela Neel. The center offers not only clothing, home furnishings, and jewelry stores, but also several fine restaurants, a large Borders bookstore, and, uniquely, condominium lofts above some of the shops.

The Mall at Millenia might also be called a boutique, as it is the only place in Orlando to shop for Jimmy Choo shoes, Max Azria handbags, Betsey Johnson clothing, and Giorgio's of Palm Beach accessories.

DEPARTMENT STORES

Department stores are still a way of life in Orlando, even with a wealth of smaller specialty shops in malls and neighborhoods. Regional chains such as **Dillard's**, **Bealls**, and **Macy's** dominate the department store scene in Central Florida, offering not only shopping mall outlets but stand-alone stores and discount outlets as well. The Bealls outlets in particular dominate the retail shopping segment, offering discounts on overstock and discontinued goods from the larger stores, and special outlet-only goods and merchandise.

But with the advent of upscale giant malls such as the Mall at Millenia and

An outlet of the exclusive and upscale Saks Fifth Avenue, Orlando

the Florida Mall, national chains are developing a larger presence. Fans of big-city favorites Bloomingdales, Macy's, Nordstrom, Saks Fifth Avenue, and Neiman Marcus can find outlets alongside the more traditional and budget-conscious JC Penney, Sears, and Lord & Taylor in the big malls. For essentials, you need look no further than the no-frills supermarkets such as Target, K-Mart, and Wal-Mart, which can be found anywhere.

Photographic equipment available at a bargain price

SHOPPING FOR BARGAINS

Discount stores and factory outlets carry all kinds of general merchandise, with electronic equipment, household goods and clothing being the biggest draw. Inexpensive designer clothes, sometimes out of season, turn up at local outlets of the TJMaxx, Marshalls, and **Stein Mart** chains at substantial savings over retail. Consignment clothing outlets such as **Deja Vu** and **Orlando Vintage Clothing Co** have deals on pre-owned clothes from modern times back to the 1920s. Shops in the outlet malls have big savings on electronics such as discontinued or factory-second cameras, video equipment, and portable stereos. Then there are the late spring and the fall clearance sales that turn even the high-priced department stores into bargain basements.

DIRECTORY

Bealls
8205 S John Young Parkway,
Orlando, FL 32819.
Tel (407) 370-9557.
Osceola Square Mall,
4081 W Vine St,
Kissimmee, FL 34741.
Tel (407) 847-4301.

Deja Vu
1825 N Orange Ave,
Orlando, FL 32804.
Tel (407) 898-3609.

Dillard's
3403 E Colonial Dr,
Orlando, FL 32803.
Tel (407) 896-1211.

Macy's
3505 E Colonial Dr,
Orlando, FL 32803.
Tel (407) 896-5300.

Orlando Vintage Clothing Co
2117 W Fairbanks Ave,
Winter Park, FL 32789.
Tel (407) 599-7225.

Stein Mart
7506 Dr. Phillips Blvd,
Orlando, FL 32819.
Tel (407) 363-5770.
2530 E Colonial Dr,
Orlando, FL 32803.
Tel (407) 895-2581.

Winter Park Village
510 N Orlando Ave,
Winter Park, FL 32789.
www.shopwinterparkvillage.com

One of Florida's many factory outlets, advertising its bargain prices

Shopping Malls

Shopping malls are a quintessential feature of the shopping scene in Florida, where the indoor, air-conditioned mall was invented. They provide all kinds of facilities from movies to restaurants, some even offering personal shoppers and child-minding services. Most malls are conveniently located, often visible from the highway, and in Central Florida range from the Seminole Towne Center on the banks of the St. Johns River to the enormous Florida Mall near the attractions.

Each mall has its own style, some designed as outdoor pavilions, others fully enclosed for all-weather shopping. The discount outlet malls tend to attract large crowds of out-of-town shoppers on the weekends, while the upscale centers fill up during sales. The local Sunday *Orlando Sentinel (see p191)* is a source of sale flyers for the malls. Hotels offer discount cards for most stores, and malls themselves have frequent-shopper programs.

The amazing interior of the Mall at Millenia

The huge food court at the Florida Mall

THE FLORIDA MALL

Sprawling over an area of 200,000 sq ft (18,580 sq m) the Florida Mall is the largest shopping location in Central Florida. It is anchored by the big names of the US

shopping industry – Dillard's, JC Penney, Macy's, Saks Fifth Avenue, Sears, Nordstrom, and Lord & Taylor department stores. With more than 250 specialty stores, it's difficult to imagine a category this shopping oasis doesn't cover. Check with guest services for a free discount coupon book.

The Florida Mall is so popular that many local hotels run shuttles to it. It is particularly favored by teens, having an enormous food court and several clothing stores aimed at the younger generation.

For visitors exhausted after hours of shopping, the Florida Mall Hotel has an entrance right on the main Mall concourse. Other hotels in the vicinity include the Howard Johnson, Archway Inn, and the Best Western Florida Mall.

THE MALL AT MILLENIA

Upscale and beyond, the luxury Mall at Millenia offers valet parking, a full service concierge and personal shopper service, and a foreign currency exchange. With its own exit on Interstate 4, the Millenia has Bloomingdales, Macy's, and Neiman Marcus department stores, along with flagship stores from Louis Vuitton, Gucci, Tiffany, Chanel, Apple Computer, Lancel, Tommy Bahama, Burberry, Cartier, St-John, and Cole Haan. Also featured are California Pizza Kitchen, McCormick & Schmick, Brio Tuscan Grille, P.F. Chang's China Bistro, Cheesecake Factory, and Panera Bread.

The atypical food court has more full-service restaurants than many Orlando

The dazzling façade of the Mall at Millenia, one of Orlando's swankiest malls

neighborhoods. Dramatic architectural highlights and dancing fountains add to the glitz of many stores unique to the Orlando area, such as Bang & Olufsen, Japanese Weekend Maternity, Metropolitan Museum of Art Store, and home furnishings specialist Z Gallerie.

DISCOUNT SHOPPING MALLS

One of the most popular malls, the giant **Prime Factory Outlet World** draws as many people as Universal Orlando on a good day. With 170 stores and 700,000 sq ft (6,500 sq m) of outlet shopping, the largest discount center in the country takes up two fully enclosed malls and four strip centers, requiring its own shuttle buses to cover it all.

Factory seconds and overruns cover the spectrum of shopping, from 15 different shoe stores to camera and electronic equipment, from vitamins to bibles, and jewelry to music. Cooks can find discounts on professional knives, while souvenir hunters head for the Universal Studios outlet. Designer labels, such as Geoffrey Beane and Tommy Hilfiger, are all available, along with Mikasa and Pfaltzgraff dishware.

Within walking distance from Prime Factory Outlet World is **Prime Designer Outlet Centre**, which has around 45 stores. These include the **Lenox Factory Outlet**, where you can buy

Orlando Premium Outlets, which stocks designer brands

discounted china and crystal, and **Off 5th-Saks Fifth Avenue Outlet**, with trendy yet affordable apparel.

Orlando Premium Outlets, near SeaWorld, caters to the upscale shopper, offering deep discounts on Coach, Burberry, DKNY, Fendi, Nike, Giorgio Armani, and Versace. More than 100 designer brands end up here, from shoes and handbags to apparel and jewelry, as well as a vast selection of housewares and home furnishings.

On the low end of the bargain scale are flea markets, dealing in a mixture of new discount merchandise and recycled bargains. The largest example is **Flea World**, located between Orlando and Sanford. More than 1,700 vendors man booths of antiques, clothing, used books, jewelry, and several more odd assortments of items than can be listed.

The Nike Factory Store at Prime Factory Outlet World, Orlando

Shopping Districts

Retail stores congregate along the high-traffic areas of Orlando, alongside Disney and Universal, and near the large hotels. Aside from the shopping area following the village green of Winter Park, districts tend to be outside of central areas, Downtown Orlando having little shopping of its own. But follow the traffic, and on roads heading southwest to the theme parks and farther west toward the Coast, shopping becomes a journey of discovery. Here, antiques stores and art galleries stand cheek-by-jowl with souvenir stands, and hand-painted furniture is as easily obtainable as a pair of sunglasses.

The Mercado shopping center at International Drive

ORLANDO SHOPPING DISTRICTS

North Orange is a high-traffic strip heading directly out of downtown toward Winter Park. Antiques stores sell tiny knickknacks, huge, almost mall-sized stores hawk fine furniture, and several stores cater to home improvement via decorative stone and tile. One of the last great bastions of vinyl and used CDs is **Rock & Roll Heaven**. **Flo's Attic** is the rambling two-story home of fine – and not so fine – furniture, while comic book fans looking to redecorate can visit **Boom-Art** for furniture in a pop art style.

A few blocks away from North Orange Street is Mills Avenue, affectionately known as Rainbow Row. This area has more antiques malls, a smattering of art galleries, and several gay-friendly stores. In a small strip mall northeast of Downtown Orlando, **Park Ave CDs** is a mainstay of new music from smooth jazz to the outer reaches of rock.

The **Orlando International Airport** (see p192) has become a major shopping stop, with two Disney Store outlets alongside a Universal Studios store, two wet-looking shops from SeaWorld, and the Warner Brothers Studio Store in the main concourse.

Tile with flamingos

International Drive rewards shoppers by having row upon row of stores catering to every taste. There are brand-name shops and designer outlet stores, many of which target clothing, shoe, and home decor bargain hunters. Tommy Hilfiger and Armani hold sway at **Pointe Orlando**, an open-air shopping complex replete with palm trees and fountains. The complex also offers several shaded spots where tired shoppers can rest awhile.

Also on International Drive is **The Mercado** shopping center, a quirky place, with marionettes at Puppets Unlimited and spy cameras at Spy USA. It has some good restaurants and a food court.

WINTER PARK SHOPPING DISTRICTS

Upscale Park Avenue in Winter Park caters to the well-to-do, on a 10-block strip of shops, restaurants, art galleries, and even a museum or two. **Bari Men's** features fine suits, **Nicole Miller** and **Talbots** handle upscale women's clothing, and Banana Republic and The Gap take care of everyone else. Stores such as Williams-Sonoma and Caswell-Massey supply kitchen and makeup tables, while **Restoration Hardware** and Pottery Barn fill the home.

Winter Park offers contemporary work from 150 local artists in the Scott Laurent Gallery (see pp162–3), while

A wide variety of shops lined up at Orlando International Airport

Visitors crowding a street at Downtown Disney's West Side

Timothy's Gallery handles art furniture and home decor. The exemplary gift shop at the **Charles Hosmer Morse Museum of American Art** offers reproductions and apparel based on the museum's collection of Louis Comfort Tiffany artworks.

An expansive outdoor shopping plaza, Winter Park Village (see pp156–7) offers an all-round experience, with its many – and varied – clothing shops, home decor and furniture stores, jewelry outlets, a bookstore, fine dining, and a state-of-the-art movie theater.

SHOPPING AT THE THEME PARKS

Souvenirs are not the only expensive things visitors can buy at the theme parks. **Universal CityWalk** (see pp98–9) is a center for music and funky dining, but shopping also rules, with a San Francisco-style rambling hill that houses establishments such as the Art Deco jewelry store Silver, and Glow!, which sells only stuff that glows in the dark. The

Souvenirs from Universal Studio

Universal Studios store sells movie memorabilia, while All Star Collectibles offers autographed sports photos and merchandise. After dinner, wander through Cigarz At Citywalk for, yes, cigars, or pick up a realistic – but fake – diamond ring at Elegant Illusions.

Downtown Disney's West Side (see pp74–5) is the home of $3,000 sunglasses at Celebrity Eyeworks and a $30,000 guitar at the Guitar Gallery. West Side's Virgin Megastore is the largest CD outlet in the city of Orlando. Autograph hunters flock to Starabilia's for framed signatures of the stars. There are also gift shops attached to the House of Blues, Planet Hollywood, and Cirque du Soleil in West Side.

Downtown Disney's Marketplace (see p75), right next door, is home to the LEGO Imagination Center, with giant Lego dinosaurs towering outside. Disney toys abound in stores at the Marketplace, from the Hasbro Once Upon A Toy store to the World of Disney superstore.

DIRECTORY

ORLANDO

Boom-Art
1821 N Orange Ave,
Orlando, FL 32804.
Tel (407) 281-0246.

Flo's Attic
1800 N Orange Ave,
Orlando, FL 32804.
Tel (407) 895-1800.

The Mercado
8445 S International Dr,
Orlando, FL 32819.
Tel (407) 345-9337.
www.themercado.com

Orlando International Airport
One Airport Blvd,
Orlando, FL 32827.
Tel (407) 825-2001.

Park Ave CDs
2916 Corrine Dr,
Orlando, FL 32803.
Tel (407) 629-5293.
www.parkavecds.com

Pointe Orlando
9101 International Dr,
Orlando, FL 32819.
Tel (407) 248-2838.
www.pointeorlando.com

Rock & Roll Heaven
1814 N Orange Ave,
Orlando, FL 32804.
Tel (407) 896-1952.

WINTER PARK

Bari Men's
309 Park Ave N,
Winter Park, FL 32789.
Tel (407) 539-7044.

Charles Hosmer Morse Museum of American Art
445 Park Ave N,
Winter Park, FL 32789.
Tel (407) 645-5311.
www.morsemuseum.org

Nicole Miller
312 Park Ave S,
Winter Park, FL 32789.
Tel (407) 628-0400.
www.nicolemiller.com

Restoration Hardware
400 Park Ave S,
Winter Park, FL 32789.
Tel (407) 622-1050.
www.restorationhardware.com

Talbots
180 Park Ave N,
Winter Park, FL 32789.
Tel (407) 629-6444.
www.talbots.com

THEME PARKS

Downtown Disney's Marketplace
10,000 Lake Buena Vista Blvd,
Lake Buena Vista,
FL 32831.
Tel (407) 824-4321.

Downtown Disney's West Side
Buena Vista Dr,
Lake Buena Vista,
FL 32830.
Tel (407) 828-3058.

Universal CityWalk
1000 Universal Studios Plaza, Orlando,
FL 33612.
Tel (407) 224-2691.

Specialty Shops

While bargains on clothing is the big retail draw, Central Florida holds its own on more eclectic shopping as well. Indoor and outdoor antiques malls are widespread and popular, cheap electronics hold sway in outlet centers, and Florida's fresh produce can be found in neighborhood farmers' markets almost every day of the week. Work by local artists fills galleries and restaurants alike, and the tourist trade hungers for theme park souvenirs. Orlando's temperate climate means that outdoor sports are a year-round undertaking, which makes sports items a big shopping draw.

Antique Row on Orange Avenue, Orlando

ANTIQUES

The Mecca of antiques in Central Florida is a one-hour drive away from a town called Mount Dora (*see p114*). The picturesque village on a chain of lakes has the largest collection of antiques dealers and stores in Southern USA. The most dramatic shopping experience is at **Renninger's Antique Center**, with more than 180 shop sites in a 40,000 sq ft (3,716 sq m) air-conditioned building. Open on weekends, the collection of furniture, dolls, silver, and jewelry is difficult to surpass. Dealers here specialize in Art Deco items, World's Fair collectibles, Mission and Arts & Crafts furniture, and art pottery. The area also hosts one of the largest antiques fairs in the US (*see p27*). This extravagant

event takes place four times a year. There are 20 more antiques shops on the streets of Mount Dora, including **Uncle Al's Time Capsule** for collectible books and souvenirs, and **Village Antique Mall** offers a huge range of antique furniture and lighting. The North Orange and Mills Avenue areas, in Downtown Orlando, are antiques strips worth exploring. **A & T Antiques** takes on mainly English furniture while **Iron Gate Antiques** handles new and restored iron furniture. **Webb's Antique Mall** in Winter Garden is full of antiques dealers.

ART GALLERIES

A growing local arts community means an increasing supply of items for the **Scott Laurent Gallery** in Winter Park, which specializes in local work. **Creative Spirits Art Gallery** displays work from an Orlando artists' guild, while **Millenia Gallery of Fine Art** offers paintings by renowned artists of years past as well as contemporary pieces. Nearby, **Grand Bohemian Gallery** offers the work of artists from all over the world. Most downtown restaurants have paintings by new artists for sale.

(see p114). (see p27).

FARMERS' MARKETS

From Friday to Sunday, the **Osceola Flea and Farmers' Market**, starting at 8am, sells locally-grown produce; and every Wednesday at 5:30am there's the **Volusia County Farmers' Market**. At **Top Produce**, which is open every day including Sunday, you can find farm-grown vegetables, herbs, and flowers. Saturday is a fresh treasure-trove for shopping in **Winter Park Farmers' Market**. Sunday means greens from 9am at the **Downtown Orlando Farmers' Market** and the **Celebration Sunday Farmers' Market**.

GIFTS & SOUVENIRS

A popular gift for Florida's visitors are fresh citrus fruits, including the varieties grown in Central Florida such as pink, red, and white grapefruit, Hamlin and Valencia oranges, and tangerines. Not the giant fruit producer it once was, Orlando still has some groves where one can buy fruit or have it shipped directly. Disney and the theme parks have turned merchandising into a fine art, and shopping for souvenirs is a major activity. From concession stands within the parks to shopping arcades, such as Universal's CityWalk and Disney's West Side, from the authorized **SeaWorld Stores** at Orlando International Airport to the Universal clearance store at Belz Factory Outlets, it's hard to escape branded gifts. Shops all along International Drive sell

The bounty at Winter Park Farmers' Market

discounted Disney clothing and merchandise. Local museums have stores, such as the **Orlando Science Center Store**, with gifts geared toward current exhibits.

ELECTRONICS OUTLETS

Because of the large influx of foreign tourists, many electronics shops along International Drive and in the outlet malls carry camcorders and video equipment suited for international customers. Sony, Panasonic, Bose, and others have factory outlet shops for bargains on overruns and reconditioned goods. Bang & Olufsen, Sound Advice, and Absolute Sound offer premium equipment not found in the chain outlets.

Ron Jon Surf Shop, one of the best-known sports retailers

SPORTS EQUIPMENT

While an hour from either coast and any ocean, several retailers in Orlando sell scuba equipment and surfboards. The largest of these is **Ron Jon Surf Shop**, a 40-year tradition in Cocoa Beach that opened an outlet in Orlando in 2003 – it features a huge collection of surfboards and swimwear. **Jet Ski Orlando** handles the power water sports toys, while **Play It Again Sports** recycles used golf, tennis, and exercise equipment.

DIRECTORY

ANTIQUES

A & T Antiques
1620 N Orange Ave, Orlando, FL 32804.
Tel (407) 896-9831.

Iron Gate Antiques
1722 N Mills Ave, Orlando, FL 32803.
Tel (407) 896-0181.

Renninger's Antique Center
20651 US Hwy 441, Mt Dora, FL 32757.
Tel (352) 383-8393.

Uncle Al's Time Capsule
140 E 4th Ave, Mount Dora, FL 32757.
Tel (352) 383-1958.
www.sign-here.co

Village Antique Mall
405 Highland St, Mount Dora, FL 32757.
Tel (352) 385-0257.

Webb's Antique Mall
13373 W Colonial Dr (State Rd 50), Winter Garden, FL 34787.
Tel (407) 877-5921.
www. webbantique malls.com

ART GALLERIES

Creative Spirits Art Gallery
820 Humphries Ave, Orlando, FL 32803.
Tel (407) 898-8343.

Grand Bohemian Gallery
325 S Orange Ave, Orlando, FL 32801.
Tel (407) 581-4801.

Millenia Gallery of Fine Art
4190 Millenia Blvd, Orlando, FL 32839.
Tel (407) 226-8701
www.milleniafineart.com

Scott Laurent Gallery
348 Park Ave N, Winter Park, FL 32789.
Tel (407) 629-1488.

Timothy's Gallery
236 Park Ave N, Winter Park, FL 32789.
Tel (407) 629-0707.

FARMERS' MARKETS

Downtown Orlando Farmers' Market
9am–2pm Sun.
Central Blvd & Osceola at Lake Eola Pk, Orlando, FL 32801. *Tel (321) 689-2798.*

Celebration Sunday Farmers' Market
Oct–Jun: 9am–3pm.
Market St, Celebration, FL 34747.
Tel (407) 892-1135;
(407) 566-1234.

Osceola Flea and Farmers' Market
8am–5pm Fri–Sun.
2801 East Hwy 192, Kissimmee, FL 34744.
Tel (407) 846-2811.
www.fleaamerica.com

Top Produce
8am–7pm Mon–Sat, 9am–6pm Sun.
2225 South Goldenrod Rd, Orlando, FL 32822.
Tel (407) 306-8811.

Volusia County Farmers' Market
5:30–11am Wed.
3090 E New York Ave, Deland, FL 32724.
Tel (386) 734-1614.

Winter Park Farmers' Market
7am–1pm Sat.
New England & New York Aves.
Winter Park, FL 32789.
Tel (407) 599-3358.

GIFTS & SOUVENIRS

Hollieanna Groves
PO Box 940067, 540 S Orlando Ave, Maitland, FL 32794. *Tel (407) 644-8803.*
www.hollieanna.com

Orlando Science Center Store
777 E Princeton St, Orlando, FL 32803.
Tel (407) 514-2245.

SeaWorld Store
Orlando International Airport, West Hall, One Airport Blvd, Orlando, FL 32827. *Tel (407) 825-2642; (407) 825-2632.*

SPORTS EQUIPMENT

Jet Ski Orlando
6801 S Orange Ave, Orlando, FL 32809.
Tel (407) 859-3006.
www.jetskiorlando.com

Play It Again Sports
2823 S Orange Ave, Orlando, FL 32806.
Tel (407) 872-3351.

Ron Jon Surf Shop
5160 International Dr, Orlando, FL 32819.
Tel (407) 481-2555.

ENTERTAINMENT IN CENTRAL FLORIDA

Theme parks are just one of the many forms of entertainment available to tourists in Central Florida. This region is home to a wide and varied assortment of theater, dance, and music venues, as well as popular nightspots and bars. The classics are well represented in Orlando by the Philharmonic Orchestra, the Orlando Opera, and the several classical music festivals held each year. A thriving Shakespearean company caters to theater patrons, presenting world-class stage productions.

Advertisement for the Florida Film Festival

The annual Florida Film Festival brings independent movie-making closer to home, and offers a launch pad to student filmmakers from local universities who get the opportunity to screen their films alongside professionals. Local theaters such as Enzian regularly showcase an array of art films. Apart from the cultural activities, Orlando also offers nighttime entertainment with nightclubs and dinner shows in Downtown Disney *(see pp74–5)*, Universal CityWalk *(see pp98–9),* and Downtown Orlando.

Scene from a performance in progress, Orlando Opera

SOURCES OF INFORMATION

The two most popular and reliable sources for current and new entertainment listings are the calendar sections of the *Orlando Sentinel*, which is included in Friday's edition of the daily paper, and the free *Orlando Weekly*, which is available on Thursdays. Both can be accessed online as well. You can also check the websites of MSN's City Guide as well as Digital City Orlando *(see p189 & p191)* for any additional information.

THEATER

Orlando has a surprisingly rich theater community, and a wide variety of offerings. The not-to-miss event is the **Orlando International Fringe Festival** *(see p25),* which takes place in May

each year. The festival brings more than 60 companies from around the world together for an exciting ten days of almost continuous theatrical activities. A wide range of productions as well as plays of every imaginable kind are showcased here.

Actors dressed in character, Orlando-UCF Shakespeare Festival

The **Bob Carr Performing Arts Center** hosts a Broadway series of touring shows with productions such as *The Producers* and *Les Miserables*. With actors constantly drawn to Orlando for work at the theme parks, the local theater has a large pool of talent that organizes shows at the Mad Cow Theatre *(see p109)* and the award-winning **Theatre Downtown**. The **Starlight Theater** serves a dinner with a choice of four entrées along with performances of Broadway musicals.

The University of Central Florida, Rollins College, and Valencia Community College all have their own individual and unique theater programs. The colleges have full seasons of productions that are open to the public.

At one time only a seasonal theater, the famous Orlando-UCF Shakespeare Festival *(see p107)* now produces the classics throughout the year. The theater has a state-of-the-art center with three indoor stages, but the late spring performances are generally held at the 900-seat outdoor Lake Eola Amphitheater, located in Downtown Orlando.

CLASSICAL MUSIC & DANCE

Orlando's public radio station, WMFE (90.7 FM), broadcasts classical music almost continuously. Broadcasting more than two dozen

◁ **A dazzling display of fireworks at the Wishes™ Nighttime Spectacular, Magic Kingdom®**

ncers from the Orlando Ballet performing on stage

rformances a year on the
dio, the highly gifted
lando Philharmonic
chestra also performs more
an 100 times each season.
ey also provide the accom-
niment to **Orlando Ballet**,
e of the oldest and most
nowned professional dance
mpanies in the Southern
ited States. The Central
orida Ballet, a popular
nce company in Orlando,
so gives several perfor-
ances through the year. The
lando Opera stages great
rdi, Puccini, and Mozart
citals, plus performances
less well-known pieces.
Classical music festivals, such
the **Festival of Orchestras**
ncert series, features five or
ore internationally acclaim-
l symphony orchestras each
ar, including the National
rchestra of France and the
w York Philharmonic. The
llins College **Winter Park**
ch Festival offers perfor-
ances from the famous Bach
stival Choir and Orchestra.

DINNER SHOWS

Dinner theater is a popular
concept in Central Florida.
You can partake of an appe-
tizing dinner while watching
an entertaining show. Take a
short trip into the
Middle Ages as
jousting knights
fill the arena in
front of you at the
**Medieval Times
Dinner &
Tournament**
show *(see p170)*.
**Pirates Dinner
Adventure** is a
Broadway-style
show alive with
swashbuckling
stunts and songs.
**Arabian Nights
Dinner Attraction** is a show
that combines magnificent
Arabian stallions with gypsy
stunt riders and a Wild West
show. The newest attraction
in Orlando, **Dolly Parton's
Dixie Stampede Dinner &
Show**, is a country hoedown

featuring animal races and
Civil War rivalries with lots of
music and dancing.
Disney is also home to two
dinner shows with large-scale
extravaganzas: Hoop-Dee-
Doo Musical Revue at the Fort
Wilderness Resort, with a
country buffet and Western
entertainment, and Disney's
Spirit of Aloha *(see p75)*, an
evening of hula, fire dancing,
and a luau feast at the popular
Polynesian Resort.

NIGHTCLUBS & BARS

While clubs and bars
are found everywhere, from
the theme parks to the coast,
the hub of nighttime
entertainment is Downtown
Orlando. **The Social** is the
ideal destination for everything from rock music to the

Neon sign of
Southern Nights

weekly Phat-n-
Jazzy show. Most
clubs have DJs
and places such
as **The Club at
Firestone** are
perennial hot
spots with nights
of Latin, hip-hop,
and dance music.
**Central Station
Bar** and **Sky 60**, a
rooftop bar with
small booths and
a great view of
the Orlando
skyline, are more intimate
downtown clubs for dancing.
Clubs such as **Parliament
House and Southern Nights**
form an east-west bracket of
downtown for gay nightlife.
The fun usually ends at 2am
when bars stop serving liquor.

exciting chariot race at the central arena, Arabian Nights Dinner Attraction show

The colorful and illuminated exterior of CityJazz®, CityWalk

LIVE MUSIC AT THE THEME PARKS

Universal's CityWalk and Disney's Pleasure Island are two exciting hot spots for adults. **CityJazz®** presents both the Down Beat Hall of Fame jazz museum and live music from top jazz talents. Nearby, **Bob Marley – A Tribute to Freedom** plays reggae music. Both **Hard Rock Live®** at CityWalk and **House of Blues** at Disney's West Side are enormous world-class venues, featuring famous bands from around the globe.

The **Raglan Road Irish Pub and Restaurant** at Pleasure Island features live music. Disney also stages the Epcot Flower & Garden Festival from April to June (see p24), with a Flower Power concert of stars from the 1960s. Held annually, the Blues Festival at Pleasure Island features live performances on several stages, and

Universal celebrates Mardi Gras in spring with concerts by stars such as Cyndi Lauper and the Black Eyed Peas.

LIVE MUSIC AWAY FROM THE PARKS

The eclectic nature of Orlando's music scene is reflected at **Will's Pub**, which offers musical acts from heavy metal and punk to soft rock. The Orange Avenue strip in Downtown Orlando offers hip-hop and avant-garde rock in underground clubs such as Tanqueray's. The hip **Ballard & Corum** offers great live music and **Kate O'Brien's** features popular live bands. April brings music lovers to downtown's Florida Music Festival.

The **Copper Rocket** in Maitland is a local favorite for folk and rock bands. Winter Park's **East of Paris** offers everything, including jazz and great vocalists and trios. R Bistro hosts pop and jazz bands, while singers at the popular **Red Fox Lounge** croon love songs. For something different, the waiters at **Bergamo's** sing arias, opera, and Broadway hits, while **Scruffy Murphy's Irish Pub** showcases Irish folk music performers.

CHILDREN'S ENTERTAINMENT

Apart from Mickey Mouse and the theme parks, there is plenty to entertain kids. The **DisneyQuest** (see p75) indoor interactive video arcade lets guests design and ride their own thrill ride.

Live concert performance, Hard Rock Live®, CityWalk

Children learn how to draw Disney characters and can record CDs at the Radio Disney Song Maker.

The popular Gatorland (see p119), features 110 acre (44 ha) of live alligators, cro odiles, and scenes from Old Florida. A highlight of the pa is the Gator Jumparoo where the reptiles leap into the air be fed by the trainers.

WonderWorks (see p110), set in an "upside-down" buil ing on International Drive, ha interactive science exhibits such as virtual roller coaster and a simulated earthquake.

CRUISES & BOAT TRIPS

With thousands of lakes, rivers, springs, and swamps, Florida's waters are a prime source of entertainment. One of the oldest continuing attractions is the Winter Park Scenic Boat Tour (see p113), one-hour cruise through thre lakes interconnected by 12 miles (19 km) of canals, whic takes you past mansions and the sights of natural, unspoile Florida. Other boat tours in th area navigate beautiful Lake Tohopekaliga in Kissimmee, up the north-flowing St. John River on the Beresford Lady paddle wheeler, or along the vast Intracoastal Waterway that separates Daytona from the Florida mainland. Trips an authentic Florida airboat guide sightseers along ancie swampland, and dayboats ca be hired out of Port Canaver for fishing trips.

A family enjoying the day out on relaxing boating trip

DIRECTORY

THEATER

Annie Russell Theatre
Rollins College, 1000 Holt Ave, Winter Park.
Tel (407) 646-2501.
www.rollins.edu/theatre/annie.html

Bob Carr Performing Arts Center
401 Livingston St, Orlando.
Tel (407) 849-2020.
www.orlandocentroplex.com/bobcarr.shtml

Orlando International Fringe Festival
398 W Amelia St, Orlando.
Tel (407) 648-0077.
www.orlandofringe.org

Starlight Theater
3376 Edgewater Dr, Orlando.
Tel (407) 843-6275.
www.starlightorlando.com

Theatre Downtown
2113 N Orange Ave, Orlando.
Tel (407) 841-0083.
www.theatredowntown.net

UCF Conservatory Theatre
4000 Central Florida Blvd, Orlando.
Tel (407) 823-1500.
www.cas.ucf.edu/theatre

CLASSICAL MUSIC & DANCE

Festival of Orchestras
1353 Palmetto Ave, Suite 100, Winter Park.
Tel (407) 539-0245.
www.festivaloforchestras.com

Orlando Ballet
1111 N Orange Ave, Orlando.
Tel (407) 426-1739.
www.orlandoballet.org

Orlando Opera
1111 N Orange Ave, Orlando.
Tel (407) 426-1717.
www.orlandoopera.org

Orlando Philharmonic
812 E Rollins St, Suite 300, Orlando.
Tel (407) 896-6700.
www.orlandophil.org

Winter Park Bach Festival
1000 Holt Ave, Winter Park.
Tel (407) 646-2182.
www.bachfestivalflorida.org

DINNER SHOWS

Arabian Nights Dinner Attraction
3081 Arabian Nights Blvd, Kissimmee
Tel (407) 239-9223.
www.arabian-nights.com

Bergamo's
8445 International Dr (in Mercado Mediterranean Village), Orlando.
Tel (407) 352-3805.

Dolly Parton's Dixie Stampede Dinner & Show
8251 Vineland Ave, Orlando.
Tel (407) 238-4455.
www.dixiestampede.com

Medieval Times Dinner & Tournament
4510 W Irlo Bronson Hwy, Kissimmee.
Tel (407) 396-1518.
www.medievaltimes.com

Pirates Dinner Adventure
6400 Carrier Dr, Orlando.
Tel (407) 248-0590.
www.piratesdinneradventure.com

NIGHTCLUBS & BARS

Central Station Bar
100 E Central Ave, Orlando.
Tel (407) 426-8336.

The Club at Firestone
578 N Orange Ave, Orlando.
Tel (407) 872-0066.

Parliament House
410 N Orange Blossom Trail, Orlando.
Tel (407) 425-7571.
www.parliamenthouse.com

Sky 60
64 N Orange Ave, Orlando.
Tel (407) 246-1599.

The Social
54 N Orange Ave, Orlando.
Tel (407) 246-1419.
www.orlandosocial.com

Southern Nights
375 S Bumby Ave, Orlando
Tel (407) 898-0424.
www.southernnights.com

LIVE MUSIC

Ballard & Corum
535 W New England Ave, Winter Park.
Tel (407) 539-1711.

Bob Marley – A Tribute to Freedom
1000 Universal Studios Plaza, Orlando.
Tel (407) 224-2690.

CityJazz®
6000 Universal Blvd, Orlando.
Tel (407) 224-2189 .

The Copper Rocket
106 Lake Ave, Maitland.
Tel (407) 645-0069.

East of Paris
358 N Park Ave, Winter Park.
Tel (407) 644-2880.

Hard Rock Live®
6050 Universal Blvd, Orlando.
Tel (407) 351-5483.
www.hardrock.com

House of Blues
1490 E Buena Vista Dr, Lake Buena Vista, Orlando.
Tel (407) 934-2583.
www.hob.com

Kate O'Brien's
42 W Central Blvd, Orlando.
Tel (407) 649-7646.
www.kateobriens.net

Raglan Road Irish Pub and Restaurant
3180 Buena Vista Dr, Lake Buena Vista, Orlando.
Tel (407) 938-0300.

Red Fox Lounge
Best Western Mt. Vernon Hotel, 110 S Orlando Ave, Winter Park.
Tel (407) 647-1166.

Scruffy Murphy's Irish Pub
25 S Magnolia Ave, Orlando.
Tel (407) 648-5460.

Will's Pub
1850 N Mills Ave, Orlando.
Tel (407) 898-5070.

CHILDREN'S ENTERTAINMENT

Central Florida Zoological Park
3755 NW Hwy 17-92 Sanford.
Tel (407) 323-4450.
www.centralfloridazoo.org

DisneyQuest
1486 E Buena Vista Dr, Lake Buena Vista, Orlando
Tel (407) 828-4600.
www.disneyquest.com

CRUISES & BOAT TRIPS

All Orlando Day Tours & Excursions
119 N Kirkman Rd, Orlando.
Tel (888) 609-5665.
www.allorlandotours.com

Beresford Lady Boat Tours
244 S Woodland Blvd, DeLand.
Tel (888) 740-7523.
www.beresfordlady.net

Rivership Romance
433 N Palmetto Ave, Sanford.
Tel (407) 321-5091.
www.rivershipromance.com

WEDDINGS IN CENTRAL FLORIDA

Apart from its fame as an immensely popular vacation spot, Central Florida is now widely recognized as one of the most sought-after wedding and honeymoon destinations. The region's picture-perfect weather is ideal for wedding ceremonies that range from simple, inexpensive backyard affairs to theme park extravaganzas that cost thousands of dollars. Themed weddings are extremely popular and organizers can create anything a couple desires. Private gardens, cruise ships,

Bridal bouquet

the Grand Staircase of *Titanic*, Cinderella's Castle, and several attractions from Rivership Romance to SeaWorld and Walt Disney World are available as wedding locations to fulfil every fantasy – many a bride with a flowing train has been seen sporting Mickey Mouse ears. Orlando is also famous for its unusual weddings. Couples exchange vows while golfing, fishing, and even in a hot-air balloon. Many local planners offer ceremony and honeymoon packages to suit all budgets.

Wedding ceremony in progress at Disney's Wedding Pavilion

INDOOR SPECTACULARS

Life-size replicas of certain rooms on the *Titanic* might seem an unusual place for a wedding, but **Titanic – The Experience** *(see p110)* offers just that. The stately surroundings of the ship are a compelling and romantic draw. The wedding package includes a ceremony on the Grand Staircase, photos in the parlor suite, and a tour of the exhibit.

The **Medieval Times Dinner & Tournament** show allows couples to wed against a backdrop of 11th-century England. Arabian stallions, knights, and fair damsels form a part of the wedding party.

TITANIC
THE EXPERIENCE
Logo of Titanic –
The Experience

The marble halls of Orlando Museum of Art *(see p107)* provide an elegant backdrop for a wedding or a reception. The ceremony is conducted amid a prestigious collection of American artworks.

The Art Deco **Westin Grand Bohemian Hotel** offers a Bohemian-themed wedding with a stay at the upscale hotel. The ceremony is conducted at their rooftop garden. Located at the Universe Shrine Church, the Mary Queen Roman Catholic Chapel can seat a wedding party of up to 2,000 people. The chapel has exquisite stained-glass windows and presents a charming venue for a wedding.

The plush, impressive Grand Ballroom at the **Florida Mall Hotel** holds up to 600 people. It is located within the Florida Mall and gives couples the opportunity to get married at the largest shopping center in Central Florida.

Couples can choose from a wide and exciting range of themed weddings at the **Royal Wedding Chapel**. Midnight services, Hawaiian ceremonies, pirate, gangster, and ghost-themed haunted weddings, and even a ceremony officiated by an Elvis impersonator – all these and many more options are available. It's hard to imagine a theme that organizers at the chapel won't attempt.

For a more intimate and exclusive gathering, **The Veranda** at Thornton Park is an ideal location. The B&B features a romantic courtyard hidden behind its five historic buildings, and has 12 rooms including a Bridal Suite with a king four-poster bed.

THEME PARKS

Call it romantic, child-like, or corny, a **Walt Disney World® Resort** wedding is always special. With more than 2,000 couples taking the plunge every year, Disney wedding packages start at around $3,000, while the custom wedding arrangements begin at about $7,500. For those not on a budget, a Disney wedding with 100 guests can cost up to $50,000.

bride arriving in Cinderella's glass coach

Weddings at Magic Kingdom are private and expensive events that are held after the park closes. The bride arrives in Cinderella's glass coach and couples exchange vows in the scenic Rose Garden by Cinderella's Castle. Adding to the revelry are costumed footmen and trumpeters. Animal Kingdom offers a safari-themed affair, while a bride at the Disney-MGM Studios is driven around in a limousine and can leave her handprints in front of Mann's Chinese Theater. Celebrants at Epcot can choose the country pavilion they want to get married in. Disney's Wedding Pavilion, a Victorian chapel surrounded by palm trees, can accommodate 300 guests and as many as 12 weddings in a day. Details such as food,

flowers, photography, entertainment, and the honeymoon hotel are all taken care of by Disney planners.

Weddings are also held at the Grand Floridian Resort & Spa and Disney's Polynesian Resort *(see p140)*. Of course, Disney characters are very willing to attend. **SeaWorld** *(see pp82–5)* not only has space, it also provides guests for your wedding. Ceremonies take place among dolphins, penguins, and a ring-bearing sea lion. The gardens at Ports of Call com-plex can entertain 750 guests.

OUTDOOR EXTRAVAGANZAS

Located near Downtown Orlando, **Harry P. Leu Gardens** *(see p108)* is a lush 50 acres (20 ha) of horticultural splendor. It offers several garden settings for weddings amid rose and camellia collections. The Rose Garden, the Edinburgh Floral Clock, and the Butterfly Garden here are very popular wedding venues. **Kraft Azalea Gardens** is a quiet spot on the banks of Lake Maitland in Winter Park. The garden has flowering trees from January to March and

provides a very romantic and beautiful setting for weddings and receptions. The secluded nature of the gardens lends an intimate quality to the event.

Wedding ceremonies at **Albin Polasek Museum & Sculpture Gardens** *(see pp112–3)* in Winter Park are performed on expansive grounds with Polasek's sculptures looking on. Couples can also get married in the garden's romantic chapel.

The **Rivership Romance**, a 100-ft (30-m) steel steamer ship, lives up to its name, creating a magical experience for couples who choose to get married aboard the ship. A party of up to 200 people can be accommodated on the ship and the package includes a cruise along the St. Johns River and an elaborate dinner, as well as dancing.

Offering 36 holes on two courses, the **Mission Inn Golf & Tennis Resort** combines sport and nuptials. Champagne breakfasts, bridal luncheons, and bachelor party golf outings are all available around the distinctive Spanish architecture. There's a 1930s yacht, *La Reina*, for cruises on Lake Harris. **Historic Bok Sanctuary** *(see p121)* is one of the highest points in Florida and is a National Historic Landmark. Couples can exchange vows in a romantic setting of palm trees, flowering plants, and a 57-bell carillon.

Albin Polasek Museum & Sculpture Gardens

the romantic setting of Disney's Wedding Pavilion, a Victorian chapel surrounded by palm trees and a lake

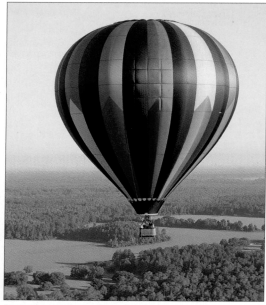

Orange Blossom Balloons, offering hot-air balloon weddings

THE UNUSUAL

Couples looking for a wedding ceremony that is out of the ordinary have a range of options to choose from. Companies such as **Orange Blossom Balloons** and **Blue Water Balloons** offer hot-air balloon weddings. The package includes transportation to the flight site, a ground-based ceremony that is followed by a one-hour balloon flight for two, and a congratulatory champagne toast at touchdown.

Brevard Zoo in Melbourne offers the use of its Serengeti Pavilion, Flamingo Pond, and Australian Aviary for weddings and receptions. As part of the event, zoo staff can conduct train rides through the park, and sometimes guide guests through a Native Florida Wetlands area by kayak. Biker couples get a slice of hog heaven at **Orlando Harley-Davidson**®. The bride and the groom, dressed in biker wedding garb, take a ride on prized Harley bikes, with the processional also following on Harleys. Those in search of even more speed can exchange vows at the

Daytona International Speedway. The ceremony is performed in the winner's circle and includes a victory lap. At **Fantasy of Flight**, high-flying and airplane-loving couples will find not only a hangar full of vintage aircraft in mint condition and World War II aircraft exhibits, but also facilities to accommodate between 50 and 3,000 guests for a wedding party.

WEDDING PACKAGES

Rather than leave for the honeymoon after the wedding, those getting married in Central Florida can choose from a wide range of wedding and vacation combination packages offered by most of the resorts and hotels.

The Westin Grand Bohemian in Downtown Orlando has three packages – ranging from a simple ceremony with live classical music to a three-course dinner for the couple and ten guests – all including a one-night stay in the Art Deco-inspired hotel. Prices range from $1,600 to more than $3,000.

Disney weddings are highly organized affairs, and offer

the celebrating couple man choices. Disney's Dream Maker plan includes admission to all four Walt Disney World theme parks, a horse drawn carriage ride with champagne, dinner at one of Disney's restaurants, a sp treatment, admission to Cirq du Soleil *(see p75)*, and a three night stay at a Disney resort. Disney's ultimate pac age includes the private use Magic Kingdom for as many 400 guests, and a complime tary room for the honeymoo night. The cost for this kind package starts at $42,000.

The **Wonderland Inn B & E** in Kissimmee is an excellent spot for a smaller, cosier wedding. The ceremony can be held in their garden gazeb under spreading oak trees. The package includes a chan pagne toast and wedding cake along with accommoda tions at the inn.

WEDDING DETAILS

There are entire books filled with lists of wedding planners, caterers, tuxedo rentals, coordinators, flower arrangers, and photographer Invitations can be ordered from local print shops and office supply stores such as Kinkos. There's a wide varie of flower suppliers, from budget dealers such as 1-800 Flowers to boutique florists. Wedding gowns are a hot business, and stand-alone haute couture shops and stores in the high-end shopping malls supply designer dresses. Wedding planners usually take care of all these details.

LEGALITIES

Marriage licenses are available at any court-house in Florida, and some weddin organizers can obtain the license for you by mail. No blood test or waiting period is required for out-of-state residents. Florida residents, however, are required to undergo a three-day waiting period. If previously married, the date of divorce or date of spouse's death must be supplied.

DIRECTORY

FLORIDA COUNTY CLERK'S OFFICES

Clerk of the Court, Orange County
425 N Orange Ave, Suite 355, Orlando.
Tel (407) 836-2067.

Clerk of Circuit Court, Osceola County
2 Courthouse Square, Suite 2000, Kissimmee.
Tel (407) 343-3530.

WEDDING PLANNERS

A Beautiful Wedding
6288 Indian Meadow, Orlando.
Tel (407) 876-6433.
www.orlandowedding
locations.com

Carolyn Allen's Bridals & Formals
5410 Central Florida Parkway, Orlando.
Tel (407) 238-2722.
www.carolynallen.com

Central Florida Wedding Locations
6288 Indian Meadow, Orlando.
Tel (407) 876-6433.
www.orlandowedding
locations.com

Just Marry! Just Celebrate!
222 W Comstock Ave, Suite 202, Winter Park.
Tel (407) 629-2747.
www.justmarry.com

Orlando Wedding Group
140 N Orlando Ave, Orlando.
Tel (407) 884-1809.
www.orlandowedding
group.com

WEDDING SITES

Albin Polasek Museum & Sculpture Gardens
633 Osceola Ave, Winter Park.
Tel (407) 647-6294.
www.polasek.org

Blue Water Balloons
566 Buckminster Circle, Orlando.
Tel (407) 894-5040.
www.bluewaterballoons.
com

Brevard Zoo
8225 N Wickham Rd, Melbourne.
Tel (321) 254-9453.
www.brevardzoo.org

Daytona International Speedway
1801 W International Speedway Blvd, Daytona Beach.
Tel (386) 253-7223.
www.daytonainternation
speedway.com

Fantasy of Flight
1400 Broadway Blvd SE Polk City.
Tel (863) 984-3500.
www.fantasyofflight.
com

Florida Mall Hotel
1500 Sand Lake Rd, Orlando.
Tel (407) 859-1500.
www.thefloridamall.com

Harry P. Leu Gardens
1920 N Forest Ave, Orlando.
Tel (407) 246-2620.
www.leugardens.org

Historic Bok Sanctuary
1151 Tower Blvd, Lake Wales.
Tel (863) 676-1408.
www.boksanctuary.
org

Kraft Azalea Gardens
Alabama Dr. off Palmer Ave, Winter Park.
Tel (407) 599-3334.
www.cityofwinterpark.
org

Medieval Times Dinner & Tournament
4510 W Irlo Bronson Hwy, Kissimmee.
Tel (407) 396-1518.
www.medievaltimes.com

Mission Inn Golf & Tennis Resort
10400 County Rd 48, Howey-In-The-Hills.
Tel (800) 874-9053.
www.missioninnresort.
com

Orange Blossom Balloons
PO Box 22908, Lake Buena Vista, Orlando.
Tel (407) 239-7677.
www.
orangeblossomballoons.com

Orlando Harley Davidson®
3770, 37th Street, Orlando.
Tel (877) 740-3770,
www.orlandoharley.com/
wedding

Rivership Romance
433 N Palmetto Ave, Sanford.
Tel (407) 321-5091.
www.rivershipromance.
com

Royal Wedding Chapel
7044 International Dr, Orlando.
Tel (407) 903-1933.
www.royalchapel.com

Titanic – The Experience
8445 International Dr, Orlando.
Tel (407) 248-1166.
www.titanicthe
experience.com

The Veranda
115 N Summerlin Ave, Orlando.
Tel (407) 849-0321.

Victorian Wedding Chapel
821 N Main St, Kissimmee.
Tel (407) 847-6775.
www.flwedusa.com

Westin Grand Bohemian Hotel
325 S Orange Ave, Orlando.
Tel (407) 313-9000.
www.grandbohemian
hotel.com

Wonderland Inn B & B
3601 S Orange Blossom Trail, Kissimmee.
Tel (407) 847-2477.
www.wonderlandinn.
com

THEME PARK WEDDINGS

SeaWorld Orlando
Tel (407) 363-2273.

Walt Disney World® Resort
Tel (321) 939-4610.
www.disneyweddings.
com

SPORTS IN CENTRAL FLORIDA

The average temperature of Central Florida is 72°F (22°C). That alone should be enough incentive to think of the Sunshine State as a good sports-oriented vacation destination. The Great Outdoors in Central Florida means fishing, hiking, golf, and more golf. The region's miles of protected land can be explored on foot, bicycle, or boat. Central Florida is the spring training ground for several

Golfers in Orlando

Major League teams and of course, home of Orlando Magic basketball. Then there's car racing, with NASCAR and the Daytona 500 an hour's drive away from Orlando. Indoor sports, water sports, and the odd horse-back ride are available year round. Disney adds to the mix, not only with their Wide World of Sports athletic complex, but even sports hotel, the All-Star Sports Resort

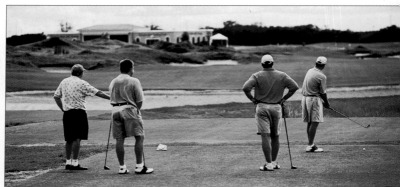

Tiger Woods in action at a tournament at Bay Hill Golf Club

SOURCES OF INFORMATION

Located in Tallahassee, the **Florida Sports Foundation** is the clearing house for state-wide sporting events. The **Department of Environmental Protection** can provide information on outdoor activities. Spectator sports

are listed in the sports section of the *Orlando Sentinel (see p191)*. You can also contact local tourist offices for information about specific areas. Further sources of information are given in individual sections.

GOLF

If golf is your passion, you may already know that Tiger Woods, Arnold Palmer, and 50 or so other PGA Tour players live in the Orlando area. There are over 130 courses within a 45-minute drive of downtown, and Orlando is home to six golf-instruction academies. The tourist comes first, and most of the best courses (several designed by Palmer and Jack Nicklaus) are open to the public.

In Walt Disney World, the **Palm & Magnolia Golf Clubs** challenge even seasoned pros, and host the PGA's Walt Disney World/Oldsmobile

Classic and the LPGA's Healthsouth Clinic. The Bay Hill Invitational is held every March at Palmer's **Bay Hill Golf Club & Lodge**, considered one of the fiercest courses in the country, while Nicklaus chips in with the **Grand Cypress Resort**'s 18-hole New Course, inspired by the Old Course at St. Andrews, Scotland. Other top-range courses include **The Oaks, Timacuan, Falcon's Fire Golf Club, Winter Pines Golf Course**, and **Dubsdread Golf Course**, all situated not more than a five-minute drive away from Downtown Orlando.

Combining vacation and golf is easy at resorts such as **Grande Pines Golf Club, Mission Inn Golf & Tennis Resort, Grenelefe Golf & Tennis Resort**, and the **Ventura Country Club. Kissimmee Bay Country Club** was nominated as one of America's best courses by *Golf Digest*.

A game in progress at Falcon's Fire Golf Club in Kissimmee

◁ **A newly wedded couple against the romantic backdrop of Cinderella's Castle**

TENNIS

Orlando serves up more than 800 tennis courts for visitors to raise a racquet everywhere, from public courts and clubs to resorts and apartment complexes. Walt Disney World has over 30 of the finest tennis courts in Central Florida, and most of the larger and not-so-large hotels have lit courts. The city of Orlando runs several public facilities, including the **Orlando Tennis Center** with 16 indoor courts and four outdoor lighted racquetball courts. On the West Coast, **Bollettieri Sports Academy** is the tennis school that produced Andre Agassi and Monica Seles. About a 90-minute drive from Orlando, it is the largest tennis training operation in the world. Many hotels have courts, and

Tennis court at Disney's Grand Floridian Resort & Spa

several resorts offer vacation packages that include tennis lessons. Contact the **United States Tennis Association (Florida Section)** for information on coaching, clubs, and competitions.

DRIVING SCHOOLS

Central Florida is the home of the Daytona 500 and numerous other NASCAR, Indy, truck, motorcycle, and dirt bike races. The **FinishLine Racing School** offers a three-day program at the New Smyrna Speedway. The program is unique in the racing school industry in that it covers both aspects of race car involvement – stock and NASCAR driving. Drivetech teaches hands-on stock car racing at the USA International Speedway in Lakeland.

Racing fans can enjoy the thrill of the auto-racing experience at two Richard Petty Driving Experience centers *(see p73)* and Test Track *(see p46)* at FutureWorld in Epcot, which offers a 65-mph (104-km/h) simulation on a mile-long electric-car track.

DIRECTORY

SOURCES OF INFORMATION

Department of Environmental Protection
3319 Maguire Blvd, Orlando, FL 32803.
Tel (407) 894-7555.

Florida Sports Foundation
2930 Kerry Forest Parkway, Tallahassee, FL 32309.
Tel (850) 488-8347.
www.flasports.co

GOLF

Bay Hill Golf Club & Lodge
9000 Bay Hill Blvd, Orlando, FL 32819.
Tel (407) 876-2429.
www.bayhill.com

Disney's Palm & Magnolia Golf Clubs
1950 W Magnolia Palm Dr, Lake Buena Vista, FL 32830.
Tel (407) 939-4653.

Dubsdread Golf Course
549 W Par St, Orlando, FL 32804.
Tel (407) 246-2551.
www.historical dubsdread.com

Falcon's Fire Golf Club
3200 Seralago Blvd, Kissimmee, FL 34746.
Tel (407) 397-2777.
www.falconsfire.com

Grand Cypress Resort
1 N Jacaranda, Orlando, FL 32836.
Tel (407) 239-4700.
www.grandcypress. com

Grande Pines Golf Club
6351 International Golf Club Rd, Orlando, FL 32821.
Tel (407) 239-6909.
www.grandpinesgolf club.com

Grenelefe Golf & Tennis Resort
3200 State Rd 546, Haines City, FL 33844.
Tel (863) 422-7511.

Kissimmee Bay Country Club
2801 Kissimmee Bay Circle, Kissimmee, FL 34744.
Tel (407) 348-4653.

Mission Inn Golf & Tennis Resort
10400 County Rd 48, Howey-in-the-Hills, FL 34737.
Tel (352) 324-3101.
www.missioninn resort. com

The Oaks
1500 Oaks Blvd, Kissimmee, FL 34746.
Tel (407) 933-4055.
www.kissimmeeoaks golf.com

Timacuan
550 Timacuan Blvd, Lake Mary, FL 32746.
Tel (407) 321-0010.
www.golftimacuan.com

Ventura Country Club
3201 Woodgate Blvd, Orlando, FL 32822.
Tel (407) 277-2640.

Winter Pines Golf Course
950 S Ranger Blvd, Winter Park, FL 32792.
Tel (407) 671-3172.

TENNIS

Bollettieri Tennis Academy
5500 34th St, W Bradenton, FL 34210.
Tel (800) 872-6425.
www.imgacademies.com

Orlando Tennis Center
649 W Livingston St, Orlando, FL 32801.
Tel (407) 246-2161.
www.cityoforlando.net/ recreation

United States Tennis Association (Florida Section)
1280 SW 36th Ave, Pompano Beach, FL 33069.
Tel (914) 696-7000.

DRIVING SCHOOLS

FinishLine Racing School
3113 S Ridgewood Ave, Edgewater, FL 32141.
Tel (386) 427-8522.
www.finishlineracing.com

Spectator Sports

Those who prefer sports action from the stands can shout out while watching a home game of Orlando Magic basketball at the TD Waterhouse Center. Also in residence are the Arena Football League Orlando Predators and the Orlando Seals hockey team. The University of Central Florida Golden Knights football team plays at the Florida Citrus Bowl, where the famed New Year's Day championship is decided, along with the Florida Classic game pitting Bethune-Cookman and Florida A&M.

Unique to Florida is *jai-alai*, a fast-paced game brought to America by Cuban immigrants. Visitors can watch the game at Orlando-Seminole Jai Alai, a place where you can also wager on horseracing.

An Orlando Predators game in progress

A basketball player making a move at a game, Orlando

DISNEY'S WIDE WORLD OF SPORTS®

A jewel in Disney's crown, Wide World of Sports is a world-class training and exhibition center for sports worldwide. It is the spring training home of the Atlanta Braves and the Tampa Bay Buccaneers and the permanent home of the Amateur Athletic Union, which holds more than 30 championship events a year. It also hosts the Pop Warner Super Bowl. There are almost too many pro and amateur events to list: USA Wrestling National Championships, the USA Judo Championships, and the US Men's Clay Court Championships are but a few.

The emphasis at DWWS is on baseball, with football or soccer taking a back seat. Baseball season runs from March to October, with basketball and football in the spring and summer respectively, and golf and track and field events being held throughout the season.

Visitors can buy tickets to games, or take tours of the complex, which boasts four Major League-sized fields, two Little League fields, six NBA-sized basketball courts, an 11-court tennis complex, six beach-like volleyball courts, complete track and field facilities, and the interactive football "playground" called the NFL Experience. The new Hess Sports Fields include four multi-sport fields for soccer, football, lacrosse, and other sports, as well as four new diamonds for baseball and softball. Naturally, there are several sports-related Disney shops. The excellent All Star Café restaurant rounds out the experience.

BASEBALL

Since World War I, Florida's warm climate has made it a favorite spring training site for Major League baseball teams. Each team returns to the same town every year, pumping millions of dollars into local economy and bringing much prestige. The towns identify strongly with their visitors.

In Central Florida, the training season is from mid-February through March. The Houston Astros spring-train at the **Osceola County Sports Stadium**, which is also home to the Kissimmee Cobras and the Senior Little League World Series. The Atlanta Braves work out the kinks at the expansive Disney's Wide World of Sports complex, accom-

The gigantic Disney's Wide World of Sports® complex

modating as many as 9,500 fans in the only double-decked baseball stadium set up for spring training in Florida; at 100-ft (30.5-m) high, this is also the tallest baseball stadium in the state. The AA Orlando Rays play a 70-game schedule at the stadium.

RODEOS

Every February and October since the 1920s, bull riders and cowboys from all over the country have been competing for big purses and top national rankings in Kissimmee's **Silver Spurs Rodeo**, which is billed as the largest in the Eastern United States. Echoing the time when Florida was one of the top cattle producers in the country, the event features competition in bull- and bronco-riding, steer-wrestling, and barrel-racing. There is year-round cowboy entertainment with the **Kissimmee Sports Arena & Rodeo**'s Friday night events, where riders and ropers from all over the Southeastern US compete for cash prizes for bareback riding, barrel-racing, and bull-riding.

AUTO RACING

World speed records were made and then broken on the hard, flat sand of Daytona Beach in the 1920s. Since then, Central Florida has been the center of American car racing. **Daytona International**

Bronco-riding at Silver Spurs Rodeo, Kissimmee

Speedway *(see p118)* is the home of NASCAR, the epitome of speed. In addition to 10 major weekends of racing activity, including the world-famous Daytona 500, the Speedweeks in February, and the motorcycle racing events in March and October, the speedway showcases 190-mph (305-km/h) stock cars, super-fast motorcycles, and souped-up, 125-mph (200-km/h) go-karts.

Logo of Silver Spurs Rodeo

Located just south of Daytona, **New Smyrna Speedway** offers various stock car racing events almost year-round, from the World Series of Asphalt in February to the Florida Governors Cup in November. Stock cars also roar west of Orlando at the USA International Speedway in Lakeland.

DIRECTORY

Daytona International Speedway
1801 W International Speedway Blvd, Daytona Beach, FL 32120.
Tel (386) 253-7223.
www.daytonainternational speedway.com

Disney's Wide World of Sports
800 Victory Way, Lake Buena Vista, FL 32830.
Tel (407) 828-3267.
www.disneyworldsports.com

Florida Citrus Bowl
1610 W Church St, Orlando, FL 32801.
Tel (407) 849-2020.

Kissimmee Sports Arena & Rodeo
1010 Suhls Lane, Kissimmee, FL 34741.
Tel (407) 933-0020.
www.ksarodeo.com

New Smyrna Speedway
State Rd 44, New Smyrna Beach, FL 32170.
Tel (386) 427-4129.
www.newsmyrnaspeedway. org

Orlando-Seminole Jai Alai
6405 S US Hwy 17-92, Fern Park, FL 32730
Tel (407) 339-6221.
www.orlandojaialai.com

Osceola County Sports Stadium
631 Heritage Parkway, Kissimmee, FL 34744.
Tel (321) 697-3200.
www.floridakiss.com/ sports/stadium.html

Silver Spurs Rodeo
1875 Silver Spur Lane, Kissimmee, FL. 34744.
Tel (407) 677-6336.
www.silverspursrodeo.com

TD Waterhouse Center
600 W Amelia St, Orlando, FL 32801.
www *(407) 849-2000.*
www.orlandocentroplex.com

Race cars whizzing by at the internationally renowned Daytona 500

The Great Outdoors

Central Florida is a land of thousands of lakes and crystal-clear spring-fed rivers, punctuated by forests, as well as some of the most temperate climate in the country. A pristine beach is never more than a comfortable drive from any spot in the area; it's entirely possible to catch a sunrise surfing in Daytona, canoe down the St. Johns River, ride at a dude ranch, para- or hang-glide, bike a 20-mile (32-km) marathon, and still catch a glorious sunset in Melbourne Beach. With lush state parks and nature sanctuaries dotting the region, Central Florida is also a major ecotourism center, as well as prime hunting and fishing territory. Central Florida, in other words, is just as much fun for an active vacationer as it is for the theme-park lover.

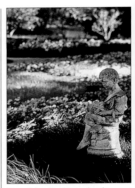

Harry P. Leu Gardens, a lovely, serene park in bustling Orlando

A family enjoying a leisurely cycle ride in an Orlando park

BIKING & BIKE TRAILS

Lake County, the only area that can be said to have hills, is the home of bicycling in Central Florida, with nine triathlons from May through October, and an annual 100-mile (160-km) Bicycle Festival in October. Clermont is the center of competition biking, including triathlons for kids over 7 and adults over 70.

Central Florida's "rails-to-trails" network affords hikers more than 220 miles (350 km) of reclaimed rail corridors for hiking. The 41-mile (66-km) stretch from Claremont is particularly impressive, running right through the Withlacoochee State Forest and paralleling the river of the same name.

Orange County alone has 22 miles (35 km) of trails, including 5 miles (8 km) across **Wekiwa Springs State Park**. The West Orange Trail extends 22 miles (35 km) along the borders of Lake Apopka and connects Oakland, Winter Garden, Ocoee, and Apopka. The trail features running routes, equestrian walkways, and paved paths for cyclists and skaters. The Cross-Florida Trail runs through the Little Big Econlockhatchee Forest, crossing Central Florida from the Gulf of Mexico to the St. Johns River, a 110-mile (177-km) corridor offering off-road biking opportunities as well as paddling along the Ocklawaha and Withlacoochee Rivers. The 12-mile (19-km) Rock Springs Run from the Wekiva River Basin to the Ocala National Forest is a designated mountain-biking trail.

PARKS & NATURE WALKS

The city of Orlando alone has 4,000 acres (1,618 ha) of parks, including the **Harry P. Leu Gardens** with the largest camellia collection and formal rose garden in Southern United States

A group of youngsters cycling along a scenic country trail near Orlando

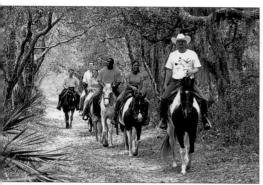

Nature viewing the cowboy way in Central Florida

(see p108). Several nature preserves flourish within the city limits; these include the 7-acre (3-ha) Delaney Park, near Downtown Orlando, and the beautifully wild Dickson Azalea Park, to the southeast of downtown, surrounded by native ferns, palms, and oaks. Located in Apopka, a short distance from Orlando, **Kelly Park** features Rock Springs, naturally fed and bubbling into a meandering stream. Wekiwa Springs State Park, also in Apopka, is another oasis with beautiful waters and acres of land. **Blue Spring State Park** is a restful spot that wintering manatee call home from December through February *(see p114)*.

HORSEBACK RIDING

Dozens of riding academies and stables offer trails and lessons to tourists, and two "dude ranches" give a taste of Florida's cowboy past. Located on 750 acres (300 ha) in Kissimmee, **Horse World Riding Stables** offers trail rides and Western riding lessons. The Crescent J Cattle Drive re-creates 19th-century Florida for a three-day drive on horseback, complete with whip-cracking lessons and driving a herd. **Westgate River Ranch** provides not only day-long excursions into Wild Florida, but fishing, riverboat tours, and a rodeo.

HANG- & PARA-GLIDING

Several outfitters in Central Florida offer courses in hang- and para-gliding, as well as rides. For hang- and para-gliding lessons, **Quest Air Soaring Center** takes you on flights of up to 60 miles (96 km). In Sebastian, **Freefall Adventures, Florida** offers excellent training. Facilities include over 600 acres (243 ha) of open landing area and the scenery is beautiful – it's just 10 minutes from the beach. The largest glider teaching school in Florida, **Seminole-Lake Gliderport**, in Clermont, offers introductory sailplane rides for one or two people and sailplane rental. While at **Central Florida**

Fountain in Harry P. Leu Garden

Flyers, you can learn to hang-glide and skydive, take a hot-air balloon ride in the morning, and glide or jump in the afternoon.

SURFING & OTHER WATER SPORTS

An hour's drive from Downtown Orlando, the Space Coast offers 72 miles (115 km) of Atlantic shore and white sand beaches. The Easter Surfing Festival is one of the major stops along the professional surfing circuit. Most of the hotels on the beach at Daytona offer windsurfer rentals, and two large windsurfing schools operate within minutes of Downtown Orlando. To the east, area residents head for New Smyrna Beach, Cocoa Beach, Sebastian Inlet, and the pristine stretches of the Canaveral National Seashore. Located on the western coast, Clearwater is the prime spot for surfing.

Swimming is as natural as breathing to most residents of Florida. Many hotels have pools, but the real joy of Florida is the chance to swim in the ocean or in the lakes, springs, and rivers that abound throughout the state. The full range of water sports, from windsurfing to jet skiing, is offered at the region's resorts; waterskiing can also be enjoyed on freshwater lakes and inland waterways.

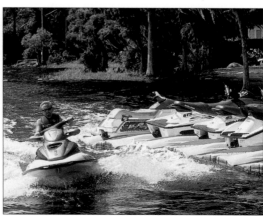

Jet skiers at a Buena Vista water sports complex

A couple enjoying brisk canoeing on an Orlando waterway

CANOEING

With more than 2,000 lakes and several connected chains, Orlando is prime boating territory. There are 17 miles (27 km) of natural springs leading from the clear, limpid waters of Wekiva Springs to the St. Johns River, with plenty of camping opportunities for the hardy and riverside restaurants and bars for the casual.

The Harris Chain of Lakes can take you, from the opposite end of the St. Johns, all the way to the Atlantic Ocean. The Econlockhatchee River runs through Orange and Seminole counties, affording ample opportunities to see undisturbed wilderness minutes from developed Florida. Blue Spring State Park's wonderfully clear water is as good for snorkeling and scuba diving as it is for boats. Many inland waterways are suitable for small boats. Houseboats can be rented from several marinas in Sanford on the St. Johns River, for example.

ECOTOURISM

With more species of plants and animals than any other state, Florida is a natural paradise, ranked 11th in the world for ecotourism. Just north of the Kennedy Space Center, the Merritt Island National Wildlife Refuge and the Canaveral National Seashore *(see p123)* is the largest wildlife preserve on the Eastern Seaboard, with more than 310 species of birds, best seen in winter. The Space Coast holds more than 220 sq miles (570 sq km) of protected wildlife refuges and 40 parks. Blue Spring State Park has a 72°F (22°C) spring, and is home to endangered manatees. It features camping, hiking, and canoeing. Speaking of the gentle giants, locally-run "manatee encounters" offer the chance for small groups to actually swim with them in crystal-clear springs.

Florida Eco-Safaris in St. Cloud is an assembly of nature preserves and the Crescent J Cattle ranch, which together makes up 4,700 acres (1,902 ha) of pristine Florida wilderness for trail rides and outdoor camping. The **Enchanted Forest Nature Sanctuary** on the East Coast winds through the ancient Atlantic Coastal Ridge and 393 acres (160 ha) of coastal hardwood forest.

Fun 2 Dive, Scuba & Snorkling Tours in Sanford offers Manatee snorkling trips and scuba diving where no experience is necessary. They also offer other tours, including eco-tours and wildlife photography tours.

FISHING

Florida's many lakes and rivers provide lots of opportunities for freshwater fishing, but it is most famous for its deep-sea sport fishing for species such as the marlin. The Daytona Beach area features some of the best ocean fishing found anywhere. Marlins are found in the Gulf Stream, while grouper and red snapper can be caught from the reefs. Two dozen private charter boats sail daily from the docks at Ponce Inlet. Fishing on Lake Tohopekaliga and

Snowy egrets keeping a lookout for prey in Merritt Island National Wildlife Refuge

A quiet day's fishing in the calm waters of a lake in Kissimmee

The Kissimmee chain of lakes means largemouth bass, and this area produces more bass over 10 lb (4.5 kg) than any other place in the world. Lakes in the Greater Orlando area also offer catfish and bream, and Merritt Island, to the east, is known for sea trout, snook, and tarpon.

HUNTING

About an hour's drive from Orlando, the Ocala National Forest *(see p118)* is the place for hunters, with whitetail deer and wild turkey in season. Seasonal hunting is also permitted in the wildlife management area in Osceola County at the **Triple N Wildlife Ranch**. There's quail, rabbit, raccoon, wild hog and coyote here, as well as large game, including deer.

LICENSING & SEASONS

A separate fishing license is required to fish on Florida lakes and rivers, or in saltwater. Proof of a successfully completed hunter safety course is required before a license to hunt with a firearm or bow is issued. From May to September it is possible to hunt alligators and applicants are selected through a random drawing. December to January is licensed duck season. Antlered deer and wild hog season is November to January, as is wild turkey. The season for quail, turkey, and squirrel is November to March. Saltwater fish season is virtually year-round.

DIRECTORY

BIKING, BIKE TRAILS, NATURE WALKS & PARKS

Blue Spring State Park
2100 W French Ave,
Orange City, FL 32763.
Tel (386) 775-3663.
www.floridastateparks.org

City of Orlando Parks Department
www.cityoforlando.
net/public_works/parks

Florida Trails
www.
floridaconservation.org
www.traillink.com

Florida Triathlon Events Sommer Sports, Inc.
838 W Desoto St,
Clermont,
FL 34711.
Tel (352) 394-1320.
www.sommersports.
com/home

Kelly Park
Kelly Park Dr,
Apopka, FL 32712.
Tel (407) 889-4179.

Wekiwa Springs State Park
1800 Wekiva Circle,
Apopka, FL 32712.
Tel (407) 884-2008.
www.floridastateparks.org

HORSEBACK RIDING

Horse World Riding Stables
3705 Poinciana Blvd,
Kissimmee, FL 34758.
Tel (407) 847-4343.
www.
horseworldstables.com

Westgate River Ranch
3600 River Ranch Blvd,
Lake Wales,
FL 33867.
Tel (866) 927-2624.
www.
westgateriverranch.com

HANG- & PARA-GLIDING

Central Florida Flyers
705 E Marks St,
Orlando, FL 32803.
Tel (407) 894-5715.
www.
centralfloridaflyers.com

Freefall Adventures, Florida
400 W Airport Dr,
Sebastian, FL 32958.
Tel (772) 388-0550.
www.ffadventures.com

Quest Air Soaring Center
6548 Groveland
Airport Rd,
Groveland, FL 34736.
Tel (352) 429-0213.
www.questairforce.com

Seminole-Lake Gliderport
Clermont, FL 34712.
Tel (352) 394-5450.
www.soarfl.com/
main.htm

ECOTOURISM

Enchanted Forest Sanctuary
444 Columbia Blvd,
Titusville, FL 32780.
Tel (321) 264-5192.

Florida Eco-Safaris
4755 N Kenansville Rd,
St. Cloud, FL 34773.
Tel (866) 854-3837.
www.floridaeco-
safaris.com

Fun 2 Dive, Scuba & Snorkling Tours
503 S French Ave,
Sanford, FL 32771.
Tel (407) 322-9696.
www.fun2dive.com

FISHING & HUNTING

Florida Fishing Seasons
Tel (850) 245-2555.
www.
fishingfloridakeys.com/
fish_seasons.htm

Florida Game & Fresh Water Fish Commission
3900 Commonwealth
Blvd, Tallahassee,
FL 32399.
*Tel (850) 245-2555;
1-888-HUNT-FLORIDA
(486-8356);
1-888-FISH-FLORIDA
(347-4356).*
www.florida
conservation.org/ license

Triple N Wildlife Ranch
5600 Crabgrass Rd,
St. Cloud, FL 34773.
Tel (407) 498-0991.

SURVIVAL
GUIDE

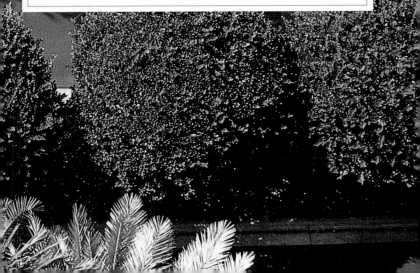

PRACTICAL INFORMATION

Theme parks, perennially gorgeous weather, and a location central to both Florida coasts brings 46 million people to the Orlando area every year, 26 times the number who live there. Not surprisingly, the main industry of Orlando is tourism. With four Disney theme parks, two at Universal, and two marine parks, the emphasis is on entertainment and creating the perfect family vacation. Mickey Mouse and other favorite characters attract children, while world-class museums, cultural events, and theaters appeal to parents. At peak tourist season, during the Thanksgiving, Christmas, and Easter holidays, airfare and

The State Seal of Florida

hotel prices run high, while late winter and early fall bring heavy discounts, shorter lines, and readily available rooms. But there is much more to Orlando than just the theme parks. Central Florida is ranked as one of the best ecotourism destinations in the world, with miles of freshwater lakes, the magnificent St. Johns River, and pristine wildlife sanctuaries spreading to the East Coast. The warm weather also promises a range of sporting activities, such as swimming, horseback riding, para-sailing, waterskiing, and golf. It is impossible to take in everything that Central Florida has to offer in one or even two weeks.

Orlando/Orange County Convention & Visitors Bureau

TOURIST INFORMATION

Some of the information booths at tourist and shopping areas in Orlando are really time-share dealers offering "half-price tickets" to theme parks in exchange for several bone-wearying hours of sales pitch. But there are genuinely helpful Orlando Tourist Center booths located downtown, on International Drive, and in many larger hotel lobbies.

Downtown's **Orlando City Hall** tourist office and the official Information Booth at Orlando International Airport are of particular help for brochures and discount coupons. Both these centers are open daily from 7am to 11pm. Concierge services are available at most hotels, and the customer service centers at the theme parks are an amiable information source. The Official Accommodations

Guide to Orlando, including a vacation planning kit, is available from the **Orlando/ Orange County Convention & Visitors Bureau**. Tourists can also call the **Florida State Tourism Board**'s toll-free number to order a visitor's guide to the state. The guest services at both Walt Disney World and Universal Studios are also extremely helpful. Interested callers can ask for vacation guides, which are mailed to them free of charge.

Both the daily **Orlando Sentinel** and the "alternative" **Orlando Weekly** newspapers publish calendar sections that apprise visitors of events in the area, which are duplicated on their websites. The *Sentinel* also hosts a new, hip online service called **Orlando**

CityBeat as a guide to trendy happenings in town. The monthly **Orlando Magazine** offers free advice on restaurants and cultural happenings. Free magazines, available at many coffee shops, bars, and restaurants, include *Industry*, *Watermark*, and *Axis*; these are a quick, easy way of keeping abreast of most events. Discount booklets, attraction guides, and hotel information pamphlets are easily available at popular chain restaurants such as Shoney's, Cracker Barrel, and IHOP.

ADMISSION CHARGES

Most museums, parks, and other attractions charge an admission fee. This can vary enormously, from $2 at

A hotel lobby in Orlando displaying tourist information brochures

◁ **Cabs waiting for passengers on an Orlando street**

A roadside tourist information center, Kissimmee

a small museum to over $65 for a day pass at a theme park.

A family outing at a theme park is hence an expensive proposition. The two Universal Orlando parks are $67.10 for adults ($55.40 for kids) per park, while SeaWorld charges $65.65 for an adult one-day pass and $52.95 for kids aged three to nine. Walt Disney World tickets for adults are $67.10 for a single day; kids are $55.40. Multi-day tickets are available at all parks and offer better value for money. At Disney they're called Park Hopper Tickets, allowing guests unlimited visits to all four Disney parks; the current price is $248.15 for four days ($210.90 for kids). Universal Studios offers a "4-Park FlexTicket" for unlimited entry at Universal Studios, SeaWorld, Islands of Adventure, and Wet 'n' Wild for 14 days; the rate is $202.30 per adult and $166.10 for kids. Special rates are offered throughout the year, or through the internet or ticket agencies, but they need to be bought in advance. There are "Florida Resident" rates and passes, in case you know a local. Note that all the rates mentioned include tax and are liable to change.

Many sights of interest offer discounts to children, card-carrying students, and senior citizens. The Orlando Museum of Art, for instance, charges $12 for adults, $10 for seniors and college students, and $5 for children aged seven to 18; there is no charge for children under six. Some institutions allow free admission on certain days or at particular times.

Reduce the admission price and buy budget meals in local restaurants by using coupons found in brochures available at tourist offices.

OPENING TIMES

Most of the attractions open daily. All the theme parks, for instance, are open 365 days in a year. Most of them open at 9am and close between 7pm and 11pm, depending on the season, with extended opening hours during the high season. State parks are usually open every day from sunrise to sunset, though the attached visitor centers may close earlier. Some sights close once a week, often on Mondays. Many, including the Orlando Science Center, Orlando Museum of Art, Mennello Museum of American Folk Art, and Morse Museum of American Art *(see p107 & p112)*, have extended hours on Friday and Saturday, and are open only in the afternoon on Sunday. Some sights close on major national holidays: typically New Year, Thanksgiving, and Christmas.

WHEN TO GO

Given its warm climate, Central Florida is a favorite winter destination for most North Americans. Late fall and early winter are very crowded in Orlando, especially at the parks. Naturally, the busy season is also when hotels and airlines are the most crowded and most expensive, so it is to your advantage to book as early as possible. If you're determined to join the crowded tourist season at Disney, planning vacations around the New Year at Magic Kingdom or the Epcot International Flower and Garden Festival in April can make the trip more worthwhile.

Plan your family vacation for mid-January–February and September–October to avoid crowds and the summer heat. If you're willing to brave some high temperatures, May is a relatively quiet month at the parks. Theme parks often have off-season multi-day deals, and hotels offer discounted rates.

Visitors strolling along a street near Disney's Broadwalk Resort

Children touching a rock from Mars at the Space Center *(see pp124–7)*

TRAVELING WITH CHILDREN

The reason most children come to Orlando is for the theme parks. However, some rides may be unsuitable for smaller children. Ask the park attendant for a description of the ride. Many so-called "thrill rides" are extremely scary for children, even ones that look safe at first view. New, technologically advanced rides that include 3-D, fog, and motion simulation, such as Men in Black – Alien Attack *(see p92)* and the Amazing Adventures of Spider-Man *(see p96)*, can be a little frightening for young kids. Never put a crying child on a ride; every attraction has a rest area off to one side of the doors, and if the child gets too distressed there are medical stations nearby. Also scout out the "lost child" area, and rely on park personnel if your child wanders off.

The glare of Florida's sun can be damaging to young eyes, so remember to take sunglasses as well as sunblock and hats. Small wagons and strollers, even multiple seat strollers, can be rented from Visitor Services just inside the gates at the Disney, Universal, and SeaWorld parks. It's worth remembering that Walt Disney World Resort guests are offered an "Extra Magic Hour" entry into the parks, one hour prior to the regularly scheduled park opening hours on specific dates. This helps families with small children avoid the massive early morning crowds.

Because of Orlando's dependence on tourists, most restaurants and hotels are child-friendly with special seats and menus as well as fun activities. Don't forget what may sound like a joke these days: the "early bird specials." Yes, they do exist. Some family-friendly restaurants in and around Orlando offer the punctual guest heavy discounts for arriving for breakfast before 8am or between 4 and 6pm for dinner.

Theme parks, museums, and other attractions generally have special rates for children between the ages of three and 18, while some allow free admission for those under three. One of the best child-friendly attractions is Kennedy Space Center *(see pp124–7)*, open every day of the year except December 25.

If you're driving, remember that Florida law requires all occupants of vehicles who are six years of age or older to wear seat belts, and you can receive a ticket for seat belt violations alone. Children up to six years old must be secured in a crash-tested child restraint seat. Car rental agencies will have the right seats available.

SENIOR CITIZENS

Florida has always attracted senior citizens for recreation or permanent settlement. Hotels, car rental agencies, airlines, and many shopping venues offer seniors special discount rates, and it never hurts to ask for a discount anyway. The giant discount malls on International Drive make a point of slashing their already low prices for senior shoppers. Members of the **American Association of Retired Persons (AARP)** are offered many area discounts, including sports and cultural events, and the **National Council of Senior Citizens**, also known as Senior Service America *(see p191)*, can provide hotel and car rental discounts. Amtrak, Greyhound, and the LYNX bus system *(see p196)* have special rates for travelers aged 50 and over. The average theme park guest walks

A senior citizen enjoying a round at Magnolia Golf Club *(see p176)*

Water fun for all at the Grand Floridian Resort & Spa, Orlando (see p140)

between 5 and 7 miles (8–11 km) a day, so it is important to know that standard and motorized wheelchair rentals are available from Visitor Services just inside the gates of all the theme parks.

TRAVELERS WITH DISABILITIES

Always be sure to make hotel management aware of any potentially serious health problems. Walt Disney World in particular has its own medical staff and facilities to deal with any emergency. Always carry a list of medications. All of the resorts and the restaurants at the theme parks have rooms that are wheelchair-accessible. Concierge services at major hotels can assist in getting handicapped parking

Wheelchair access sign

placards for cars. At Universal, wheelchairs are available for rental at $7 per day and Electric Convenience Vehicles are available for rental at $35 per day. It is recommended that you call up at least 24 hours in advance to make a reservation. Universal Orlando puts great store in the "queue experience" as an important part of riding an attraction, and guests in wheelchairs are asked to join the line and wait in queue along with everyone else.

Disney has a limited number of wheelchairs available at the Guest Services Desk, at the entrances to Magic Kingdom, Epcot, Animal Kingdom, and Disney-MGM Studios. Magic Kingdom and Epcot also have motorized wheelchairs.

Disney offers a "Guidebook for Guests with Disabilities," and you can get hold of a copy by calling the main information number.

Sign language interpreting services are also available at Universal Studios Florida and Islands of Adventure. There is no extra charge for anyone wanting this service.

COMMUNICATIONS

Online sources of Orlando information abound, from the websites of the **Orlando Sentinel** and **Orlando Weekly** newspapers, to city guides run by **CitySearch, icFlorida, Digital City Orlando, and MSN.** These not only give overviews of happenings and restaurants, but also offer bulletin board comments from local residents. The major television stations also have Internet calendars. There is a branch of business supply giant, Kinkos, or one of the major office supply stores – OfficeMax, Office Depot, and Staples – on practically every street corner, making fax and copying services readily available.

With the new push toward making wireless Internet more available, there has been a mushrooming of access points in local Starbucks and Borders book-store locations. Most major hotel chains, as well as the Orlando International Airport, also offer convenient Internet access. Downtown Orlando itself is a free Internet access zone. This includes the entire Lake Eola Park area.

Newspaper vending machines lined up in a row on a sidewalk in Orlando

Police officers on patrol, Florida-style

PERSONAL SECURITY

Most cities in the region, like elsewhere in the world, have "no-go" areas that should be avoided. The staff at the local tourist office or in your hotel should be able to advise. Note that downtown areas are generally unlike city centers elsewhere; they are first and foremost buisness districts, which are dead at night and often unsafe.

As beautiful as "The City Beautiful" may look, it also has the potential for less than secure situations. Certain areas of Orlando, such as the Orange Blossom Trail and areas surrounding the downtown main strip of Orange Avenue, should be avoided after dark, and even brightly lit sections of town shouldn't be navigated alone. If in doubt, take a taxi rather than walk. The downtown LYNX bus terminal is not a place to hang around in. Be aware of who is around you in the sprawling parking garages at the theme parks, and keep an eye on your belongings while enjoying the "party strips" of Downtown Disney's Pleasure Island as well as Universal CityWalk.

Carry as little money as possible when you go out. If you are attacked, hand your wallet over immediately; do not try to resist.

The major tourist centers of Central Florida are well policed. Given the region's eagerness to both attract and protect tourists, police officers are friendly and helpful to visitors. Orlando City police are visible in most high-traffic areas; the Mounted Police unit can be seen patroling downtown neighborhoods daily. The theme parks are fanatical about security and visitor service; Disney, for example, has its own fire and police departments and health personnel.

Even if you have only a slim chance of retrieving stolen property, you should report all lost or stolen items to the police. Most credit card companies have toll-free numbers for reporting a loss, as do **Thomas Cook** and **American Express** for lost traveler's checks.

A postcard from the "Sunshine State"

SAFETY FOR DRIVERS

Certain areas of Orlando are better avoided, and keeping alert to highway signs is a must. The well-traveled routes of major highways and main streets are the safest, but even the prominent thoroughfares can suddenly become illogical. The Florida State Police Department has a cellphone emergency 911 service in operation. The Automobile Association of America (*see p197*) places "Good Samaritan" vehicles on the highways to intercept emergencies of various kinds.

Keep some basic rules in mind while driving around the region. Local drivers change lanes frequently on expressways, so stick to the right and be alert near exits. Speed limits are rigorously enforced, and fines can be as much as $150. Avoid taking short cuts in urban areas. Stick to the main highways if possible. If you need to refer to a map in a city, don't stop until you are in a well-lit or busy area. Avoid sleeping in the car off the highway, although some rest areas on expressways have security patrols. Seat belts are mandatory for all under Florida law. The **Orlando City Hall** website lists road closures.

NATURAL HAZARDS

The major cause of vacation injury in Orlando is the heat. Standing in long lines under the dazzling Florida sun can mean sunburn, rashes, heatstroke, and heat exhaustion. Bring hats, sunglasses, lots of bottled water, and a high SPF waterproof sunscreen – reapply this often, especially at water parks. Plan park visits early in the day or after 5pm.

The natural beauty of Florida can be dangerous. Orlando is riddled with over 1,000 lakes, and chances are the larger ones might contain alligators. There are also several venomous snakes native to Florida. Don't forget to carry insect repellent for mosquitoes and summer gnats.

Florida's beaches are usually well-supervised by lifeguards, but do keep a close eye on young children. Riptides can be dangerous in some places.

A county sheriff, in the regulation dark uniform, and his patrol car

DIRECTORY

TOURIST INFORMATION

Florida State Tourism Board
Tel (888) 735-2872.
www.flausa.com

Kissimmee/St. Cloud Convention & Visitors Bureau
Tel (407) 847-5000.
www.floridakiss.com

Orlando/Orange County Convention & Visitors Bureau
Tel (407) 363-5872.
www.orlandoinfo.com

ONLINE INFORMATION

CitySearch
http://orlando.citysearch.com/

Digital City Orlando
www.digitalcity.com/orlando

icFlorida
www.wftv.com/icflorida

MSN City Guide
http://local.msn.com/Orlando

Orlando CityBeat
www.orlandocitybeat.com

Orlando City Hall
Tel (407) 246-2121.
www.cityoforlando.net

Orlando Downtown Wireless District
www.cityaccess.pureconnection.net

MAGAZINES & NEWSPAPERS

El Sentinel (Spanish language edition)
www.orlandosentinel.com/elsentinel

La Prensa
Tel (407) 767-0070.
www.laprensaorlando.com

Orlando Business Journal
Tel (407) 649-8470.
www.bizjournals.com/orlando

Orlando Leisure Magazine
Tel (407) 647-5557.
www.orlandomagazine.com

Orlando Magazine
Tel (407) 767-8338.
www.orlandomagazine.com

Orlando Sentinel
Tel (407) 420-5000.
www.orlandosentinel.com

Orlando Weekly
Tel (407) 377-0400.
www.orlandoweekly.com

The Wall Street Journal, Orlando office
Tel (407) 857-2600.

WHERE Orlando
Tel (407) 767-8338.
www.where-orlando.com

TV & RADIO

ABC: WFTV-Channel 9
Tel (407) 841-9000.

CBS: WKMG-Channel 6
Tel (407) 291-6000.

Fox: WOFL-Channel 35
Tel (407) 644-3535.

NBC: WESH-Channel 2
Tel (407) 645-2222.

PBS: WMFE-Channel 24
Tel (407) 273-2300.

UPN: WRBW-Channel 65
Tel (407) 248-6500.

WB: WKCF-Channel 18
Tel (407) 645-1818.

WJRR (101.1 FM)
Rock/Alternative
Tel (407) 916-1011.

WLOQ (103.1 FM)
Smooth Jazz
Tel (407) 647-5557.

WMFE (90.7 FM)
Public radio/Classical
Tel (407) 273-2300.

WOMX (105.1 FM)
Adult contemporary
Tel (407) 919-1000.

WTKS (104.1 FM)
Talk radio
Tel (407) 916-7800.

WWKA (92.3 FM)
Country
Tel (407) 298-9292.

OTHER NUMBERS

American Association of Retired Persons
Tel (888) 687-2277.
www.aarp.org

Mobility International
Tel (541) 343-1284.

National Council of Senior Citizens; Senior Service America
Tel (301) 578-8800.

Orlando Weather
www.orlandoweather.com

Seniors First
Tel (407) 292-0177.
www.seniorsfirstinc.com

EMERGENCY NUMBERS

All Emergencies
Tel 911 for police, fire, or ambulance.

Centra Care
Walk-in medical care.
Tel (407) 239-7777.

Moneygram
Tel (800) 926-9400.

Orlando Police Information Desk
Tel (407) 246-2470.
www.cityoforlando.net

Poison Control
Tel (800) 222-1222.

LOST CREDIT CARDS & TRAVELERS' CHECKS

American Express
Tel (888) 412-6945 (cards);
(800) 221-7282 (checks).
www.home.americanexpress.com

Diners Club
Tel (800) 234-6377.
www.dinersclub.com

Discover
Tel (800) 347-2683.
www.discovercard.com

MasterCard
Tel (800) 622-7747.
www.mastercard.com

Thomas Cook
Tel (800) 223-7373 (checks).

VISA
Tel (800) 847-2911.
www.visa.com

TRAVEL INFORMATION

More than 46 million visitors flock to the warmth and recreation of Central Florida each year, making it one of the most sought-after tourist destinations in the world. Orlando International is Florida's busiest airport, welcoming millions of visitors every year; and many more arrive by train and bus. The network of interstate highways

An American Airlines passenger jet

that converge in Orland carry almost 200,00 cars a day throug downtown. Amtrak offe daily service from poin North and West, with sleepe cars, and even has room for the fami car. Once there, almost all roads lead the theme parks, with a celebrated pub lic transit system taking some of the bur den off the very busy highways.

The brightly illuminated terminal of Orlando International Airport

ARRIVING BY AIR

Orlando's local airports are served by virtually all US domestic carriers and a wide selection of international airlines, including Orlando Native people-mover Airtrans, Aerolineas Argentinas, United Airlines and the British favorite Virgin Atlantic. A recent $1.2 billion expansion has made **Orlando International Airport** the third largest airport in the US, and the recent addition of discount carriers such as **Spirit Airlines, Song, JetBlue**, and United's new "low fare" service called **Ted**, is creating a flurry of cheaper flights to this vacation hub.

    Orlando-Sanford International Airport is undergoing a construction spurt of its own. This airport offers access from East Coast carriers such as Pan Am, Southeast, TransMeridian, and Vacation Express. **Daytona Beach International Airport** brings in daily flights from Atlanta on **Delta**,

Cleveland and Newark on Continental, and flights from the Bahamas on Vintage Airlines prop planes.

AIR FARES

Travel costs to the world's most popular vacation site depend very much on the season. Unfortunately for the vacationer, prime holiday time in Orlando is when fares are at the highest. The difference between late winter (February and March) airfares, when tourist traffic is low, and the

height of busy season (November and December) can more than double the price per ticket. The best deal can be found on midweek flights. Inexpensive fares can usually be found on the onlir travel websites, but they are geared toward larger carriers and do not include the more popular discount airlines such as JetBlue and **Southwest**. It is better to check online with these airlines directly, as they often have "cyberdeals" only available on the Internet. It can also be an advantage not to plan ahead, with some airlines offering last-minute specials on unsold seats.

AIRPORTS

One of the country's top airports for overall customer convenience, Orlando International Airpor boasts state-of-the-art services. Fast intra-airport ransportation via monorail and moving walkways leads to shuttle buses, taxis, and public transportation to Downtown Orlando and the parks. Mutilingual tourist information centers by the

A taxi outside the Orlando International Airport

The shopping area at Orlando International Airport

security checkpoints are open from 7am to 11pm. The airport can also offer an evening's rest, with the Hyatt Regency Hotel and its 446 rooms right in the main concourse. Banks of rental car agencies are located on the baggage levels in both terminals and taxi and bus-stands are outside Level 1. Also to be added to the attractions at the airport are shopping and dining, with stores from Disney, Universal and SeaWorld right in the terminal. Much quieter than the main Orlando airport, the Orlando-Sanford International is about 30 minutes from Downtown Orlando. It is a major hub for charter flights from Britain and Canada, and is increasingly being used by smaller carriers such as Southeast and Pan Am as a low-pressure alternative.

Only ten years old, Daytona Beach International Airport offers direct flights from various East Coast cities to the world's most famous beach *(see p116)*.

Highway Patrol insignia

GETTING TO TOWN

The LYNX bus system *(see p196)* runs from Level 1 of the A side of the Main Terminal, departing every 30 minutes from 5:30am to 11:30pm. Travel time to Downtown Orlando is approximately 40 minutes, and to International Drive 60 minutes, at a cost of $1.25 for either destination. Make sure you have exact fare; the transfers to connecting buses are free. Many hotels have their own courtesy buses, but there are also shuttle buses *(see p196)*: the **Mears Transportation Group** *(see p197)* serves most destinations in the area. Shuttle vans, accommodating up to nine people, have posted rates running $14 to $16 per person for trips downtown or to Disney. Taxis *(see pp197)* from Orlando International to hotels and theme parks are available at both terminals A and B, just outside baggage claim on Level 1. To avoid costly metered fares, look for a yellow Mears cab for posted flat rate fares to downtown and Walt Disney World; they accept credit cards. Ground transportation at Orlando-Sanford International is conveniently found right outside the terminal.

DIRECTORY

AIRLINE NUMBERS

American Airlines
Tel (800) 433-7300.
www.aa.com

Delta Airlines
Tel (800) 221-1212.
www.delta.com

JetBlue
Tel (800) 538-2583.
www.jetblue.com

Song
Tel (800) 359-7664.
www.flysong.com

Southwest Airlines
Tel (800) 435-9792.
www.southwest.com

Spirit Airlines
Tel (800) 772-7117.
www.spiritair.com

Ted (United Airlines)
Tel (800) 225-5833.
www.flyted.com

US Airways
Tel (800) 428-4322.
www.usair ways.com

TRAVEL SITES

www.expedia.com
www.travelocity.com
www.orbitz.com
www.priceline.com

AIRPORTS

Daytona Beach International Airport
Tel (386) 248-8069.
www.flydaytonafirst.com

Orlando International Airport
Tel (407) 825-2352.
www.orlandoairports.net

Orlando-Sanford International Airport
Tel (407) 585-4000.
www.
orlandosanfordairport.com

GETTING TO TOWN

Mears Transportation Group
Tel (407) 423-5566.

The People Mover monorail at Orlando International Airport

Getting Around

Just about a century ago, Central Florida was mostly dirt roads surrounded by orange groves. The present-day convergence of highways, parkways, and six-lane thoroughfares makes Orlando an automotive heaven. Several major roads run through, across, or near downtown, and almost all roads lead to the theme parks. Walt Disney World and Universal Orlando resorts have their own exits on Interstate 4 and the Central Florida Greeneway. Local streets leading to the parks are lined with restaurants and shopping malls.

You can get by without a car in Orlando, but life is much easier with one. If you don't bring your own, car rental rates are among the lowest in the US, and gas is relatively inexpensive. In addition, Floridians are generally courteous and considerate drivers.

Interstate Highway 4

City parking restrictions

Speed limit (in mph)

Rest area, indicated off an interstate

RULES OF THE ROAD

On a two-way street or highway, all drivers moving in either direction must halt for a stopped school bus. At intersections with traffic lights, you may turn right on red if the way is clear and there is no sign prohibiting the turn. Left turns on red from a one-way street into a one-way street are also allowed. Passing is allowed on both sides on any multi-lane road, including interstate highways.

According to Florida law, wearing seat belts while traveling in vehicles is compulsory for all *(see p188)*. Driving under the influence is treated very seriously, so don't drink even one beer. Violators can be fined hundreds of dollars

or even be imprisoned for a short period of time.

Most road signs are clear and self-explanatory. If you are caught disregarding instructions, you might be fined. The speed limits in Florida are as follows:

• 55–70 mph (90–105 km/h) on highways.
• 20–30 mph (32–48 km/h) in residential areas.
• 15 mph (24 km/h) near schools.

Speed limits can vary every few miles, so keep a sharp eye out for the signs. On an interstate you can be fined for driving slower than 40 mph (64 km/h). The speed limits are rigorously enforced by the Florida Highway Patrol, whose representatives issue tickets on the spot. A fine can set you back as much as $150.

Overhead signs at the junction of two routes

HIGHWAYS & TOLLS

Metropolitan Orlando is the crossroads of Florida's busy highway system, where the north–south Florida's Turnpike meets east-west Interstate 4. The Bee Line Expressway (State Road 528), which runs east-west, the Central Florida Greeneway (State Road 417) running

An aerial view of Orlando, showing busy, merging highways

outh and east into Walt Disney World, and East-West Expressway (State Road 408) connecting Downtown Orlando to I-4, are toll roads. Tolls range between 50 cents and $1.50 per station. Toll roads also operate on an electronic system called SunPass; transmitters can be purchased locally. Florida toll booths do not take bills larger than a $20.

NAVIGATING

The main thoroughfare in Orlando is Interstate 4. Heavily trafficked, it connects all the theme parks and outlet shopping areas in the west with downtown and the bedroom communities to the east. During the morning and the evening rush hours, the highways slow to a virtual standstill, the worst being I-4 through downtown and the area around Walt Disney World, so time your trips accordingly. Be aware that the exit numbers on I-4 were changed in 2003, so older maps and directions will surely be incorrect.

Because of the expense, the toll roads are the least traveled, and while I-4 can sometimes become a parking lot during odd hours, roads such as State Roads 417 and 408 can appear blissfully empty.

Much has been done to improve roads heading west from downtown, and roads such as John Young Parkway can sometimes offer a slower but surer route to the theme parks. The Bee Line is the fastest way from Orlando International Airport to Universal Orlando and

Mears Taxicab dispatch fleet, which includes cars for rent

SeaWorld, while the Central Florida Greeneway leads directly west to Disney.

Visitors staying at any one of the massive hotels on International Drive will soon discover Sand Lake Road, which leads to the parks as well as to several enormous shopping malls.

CAR RENTAL

To the chagrin of locals, rental car companies offer the best deals to out-of-towners, sometimes as low at $10 a day. Multi-day packages for weekend rentals are usually the best deals, and arranging those deals before you leave home can often mean substantial savings. Check your existing car insurance for rental before you agree to sign the contract. While a Collision Damage Waiver (CDW) is expensive, it sometimes covers damage to the vehicle that insurance will not, even if it was not your fault. Companies differ in their policies concerning gas; some charge for what you use while others will ask that you fill the car before you return it. The major companies *(see p197)* either have rental kiosks right in the airports – Orlando International's are right next to baggage

Logo of the Hertz car rental company

claim; Orlando-Sanford's rentals are right outside the terminal – or a short and free shuttle bus ride away. There are also several agencies in Orlando.

BIKE RENTAL

Orlando is ideal for moving around on a bicycle with its 200 miles (322 km) of bike trails. The Disney resort hotels – Caribbean Beach Resort, Grand Floridian, and others – offer rentals on Disney property, while **David's World Cycle** rents mountain and road bikes.

If you prefer the motorized variety, **American V Twin Motorcycles** rents Harley Davidson motorcycles. **West Orange Trail Bikes & Blades Co.** in Winter Garden offers not only bicycles but also in-line skates. Large groups of 20 or more can schedule guided bicycle tours.

The dreaded rush hour in Orlando

Bike riders on a trail in Walt Disney World® Resort

An Amtrak train moving along a track at the Auto Train yard, Sanford

TRAINS

With a much-discussed light rail system still in the planning stage, rail travel through Central Florida means **Amtrak**. From an Art Deco-inspired station in the heart of the city, Amtrak offers a limited schedule of local travel, including stops in Downtown Orlando, Winter Park, Kissimmee, and points south to Miami. Fares run from $6 for a short hop to Winter Park, to around $30 to Miami, one way. Auto Train is very popular as it provides transport for family and vehicle from Washington, DC to Sanford. But do check for height restrictions on SUVs.

Of course, Amtrak connects across America and into Canada too, with Orlando being one of the more popular destinations. But cross-country rail travel is both time-consuming and expensive when compared to airlines. The 24-hour trip from New York can cost twice the comparable plane flight. A four-day trip from Los Angeles by rail will cost more than $1,100 per person, but that includes the comfort of a bedroom and meals.

LONG-DISTANCE BUSES

Whether you are traveling from other parts of the country or within Florida, Greyhound buses offer the cheapest way to get around. Some services are "express," with few stops en route, while others serve a greater number of destinations. A few routes have "flag stops," where a bus may stop to deposit or collect passengers in places without a bus station. Pay the driver directly, or, if you want to reserve in advance, go to the nearest Greyhound depot. Passes provide unlimited travel for set periods of time – from between four and 60 days – but are useful only if you have a very full itinerary.

PUBLIC TRANSPORT IN CITIES

The award-winning **LYNX** bus system, with more than 40 routes and 4,000 stops through three counties, makes getting around Central Florida inexpensive and easy. The brightly decorated buses fan out from the central station north to Lake Mary, east to Winter Park and Orlando International Airport, and south to Walt Disney World and Universal Orlando. The theme park routes in particular are probably the easiest way to the parks if you're staying downtown, with scheduled service from 7am to after 10pm. Look for the signs with pink paw prints denoting LYNX

Orlando's LYNX bus logo

bus stops. Standard, one-way fare throughout the system is only $1.25, and passes are available for unlimited travel. A Single-Day pass is $3, seven days of travel will cost $10, and a month-long pass is $36. Long-term passes can be purchased at Albertsons Supermarkets or online at the LYNX website, with Single-Day passes available from the driver of any LYNX bus.

Downtown visitors have the no-cost advantage of the free LYMMO service, which runs along its own traffic lane every five minutes between 6am and 10pm (midnight on Friday and Saturday). The service connects the Church Street entertainment area to the TD Waterhouse Sports Center, with stops including the Regional History Center and the Orange County Courthouse.

SHUTTLE BUSES

Most major hotels offer free shuttle buses from the airports to the various resorts. Once you have arrived at your destination, the same hotels usually have van transportation

A hotel shuttle bus advertising the Orlando FlexTicket pass

o Disney, Universal Orlando, and SeaWorld. If not, **Mears Transportation** *(see also p193)* offers shuttle vans to various attractions in the area.

Shuttles from the **Daytona Shuttle Service** can make a trip to the East Coast beaches easy, offering a 60-minute ride to the sand flats of Daytona Beach, fishing on the Atlantic Ocean, and the sights of the Kennedy Space Center. Round trip shuttle fare is approximately $50 (children 2–12, around $15 each way).

TAXIS

The most readily available taxis are at stands at the Orlando International and Orlando-Sanford airports, taxi-only lanes at most larger hotels, and those circling the theme parks, particularly at the main entrances to the various parks and at Universal CityWalk and Downtown Disney's Pleasure Island nightlife entertainment areas. Those operated by **Mears Taxi Dispatch**, with their bright orange paint, and Yellow Cab, are metered and thought to be the most

An I-Ride Trolley for the I Drive area

trustworthy – avoid hiring one of the many "gypsy" cabs, which may end up costing several times what the fare is worth. Reserving a taxi from the airport or by cell phone will give the option of paying by credit card.

Street sign of the I-Ride trolley service

OTHER MODES OF TRANSPORT

One of Orlando's most popular tourist centers, International Drive provides special transportation for visitors in the form of old-fashioned buses, called the **I-Ride Trolleys**. Trolleys run from the Major Boulevard area and Prime Factory Outlet shops to SeaWorld, with 83 stops in between; the frequency is 20–30 minutes year-round, seven days a week, from 8am to 10:30pm. Multi-day passes are available. Another old-fashioned way to see the Orlando area is by the **Winter Park Scenic Boat Tour**, on Lake Osceola. Tour boats depart on the hour from 10am to 4pm daily. The 12-mile (19-km) narrated cruise via three lakes and two canals is the only way to see the true beauty of the park. An even older form of transportation is provided by **Why Walk Pedicab** and **Orlando Pedicab**. Both operate several free human-powered jitneys around downtown.

DIRECTORY

BREAKDOWNS

American Automobile Association (AAA)
Tel (407) 444-7000.
www.aaa.com

AAA General Breakdown Assistance
Tel (800) 222-4357.
NOTE: Rental companies provide 24-hour roadside assistance.

CAR RENTAL

Alamo® Rent a Car
Tel (800) 327-9633.
www.alamo.com

Avis Rent a Car
Tel (800) 831-2847.

Budget® Rent a Car
Tel (800) 527-0700.
www.budget.com

Dollar® Rent a Car
Tel (800) 423-4704.
www.dollar.com

Enterprise
Tel (800) 736-8222.

Hertz
Tel (800) 654-3131.

BIKE RENTAL

American V Twin Motorcycles
Tel (407) 903-0058.
www.amvtwin.com

David's World Cycle
Tel (407) 422-2458.
www.davidsworld.com

West Orange Trail Bikes & Blades Co.
Tel (407) 877-0600.

TRAINS

Amtrak
Tel (800) 525-2550.
www.amtrak.com

BUSES

Daytona-Orlando Transit (DOTS)
Tel (800) 231-1965;
(386) 257-5411.

Daytona Shuttle Service
Tel (800) 882-1127.

LYNX Buses
Tel (407) 841-5969.
www.golynx.com

Mears Transportation Group
Tel (407) 423-5566.

Orlando Hospitality
Tel (407) 363-4642.

TAXI RENTAL

Mears Taxicab Dispatch
Tel (407) 422-2222.

OTHER MODES OF TRANSPORT

I-Ride Trolley
Tel (407) 248-9590.
www.iridetrolley.com

Orlando Pedicab
Tel (321) 217-2233.

Why Walk Pedicab
Tel (407) 740-8294.
http://store.
bicyclerevolution.com/
whywalkpedicab.html

Winter Park Scenic Boat Tour
Tel (407) 644-4056

General Index

Acknowledgments

Main Contributor

Phyllis & Arvin Steinberg live in Florida. Phyllis writes about travel for US newspapers, magazines, and websites. She is also a food columnist for 24 newspapers in Florida and cruise editor for a popular travel website. Arvin writes travel articles for US newspapers, magazines, and websites, and is sports editor of a widely read travel website.

Joseph Hayes is a freelance writer for newspapers and magazines around the world, specializing in food, travel, and music. He is also an accomplished playwright, with productions in several countries.

Charles Martin is a Florida-based journalist and radio broadcaster who writes columns and articles on Florida events for numerous local, national, and international lifestyle magazines.

Factchecker
Kia Bocko

Proof Reader
Bhavna Seth Ranjan

Indexer
Shreya Arora

Photography
Dave King, Magnus Rew, Stephen Whitehorn, Linda Whitwam

Illustrations
Arun Pottirayil, Julian Baker

DK London
Publisher
Douglas Amrine

Publishing Managers
Jane Ewart, Fay Franklin

Editorial & Design
Brigitte Arora, Tessa Bindloss, Jane Edmonds, Esther Labi, Mary Ormandy, Mani Ramaswamy

Senior Cartographic Editor
Casper Morris

Senior DTP Designer
Jason Little

DK Picture Library
Hayley Smith, Romaine Werblow, Gemma Woodward

Production Controller
Shane Higgins

Special Assistance
Many thanks for the invaluable help of the following individuals: Kelly Rote, Central Florida Visitors & Convention Bureau; Susan Mclain, Daytona Beach Convention & Visitors Bureau; Georgia Turner, Georgia Turner Group; Dave A. Wegman, Greater Orlando Aviation Authority; Danielle Courtenay, Julie Doyle, Julie A. Fernandez, Orlando/Orange County Convention & Visitors Bureau; Lita O'Neill, Polk County Natural Resources Division; Jacquelyn Wilson, SeaWorld Orlando & Discovery Cove; Susan L. Storey, NBC Universal, Orlando; Jason L. Lasecki, Walt Disney World Resort; Sandra Sciarrino, Wet 'n Wild; Ian Williams.

Photography Permissions
Dorling Kindersley would like to thank the following for their assistance and kind permission to photograph at their establishments: Albin Polasek Museum & Sculpture Gardens, Audobon National Center for Birds of Prey, Buena Vista Watersports, Falcon's Fire Golf Club, Hard Rock Café Live, Holy Land Experience.

Placement Key – t=top; tl=top left; tlc=top left center; tc=top center; trc=top right center; tr=top right; cla=center left above; ca=center above; cra=center right above; cl=center left; c=center; cr=center right; clb=center left below; cb=center below; crb=center right below; bl=bottom left; b=bottom; bc=bottom center; bcl=bottom center left; br=bottom right; d=detail.

The publishers would like to thank the following individuals, companies, and picture libraries for their kind permission to reproduce their photographs:

ALAMY: Mark J. Barrett 117cla, Randa Bishop 107bl, Bernie Epstein 8cl; ANTIQUE & CLASSIC BOAT SOCIETY: 25tl.

CENTRAL FLORIDA FAIR: 24 tc; CENTRAL FLORIDA VISITORS & CONVENTION BUREAU: 20tr; CORBIS: 21bcr, 129 (inset), 170tc; Archivo Iconografico, S.A 13b; James L. Amos 182b, Tony Arruza 20bl, 103b, 117cra; Yann Arthus-Bertrand 194b; Bettmann 192tc; Gary Braash 21crb; Duomo 116tr; Raymond Gehman 28-29, 102; Martin Harvey 21tr; Lake County Museum 7(inset), 114tl, 185 (inset), 190c; David Muench 21cla, Marc Muench 117bl; James Randkley 12; Phil Schermeister 17b, 21cr; George Teidmann/ Newsport 27b,179bl; Partrick Ward 24cla; Nick Wheeler 130cl; RAIMUND CRAMM: 123cla; MARTY CSERCSEVETIS: 156bc; CYPRESS GARDENS: 121tr.

© DISNEY: 1c, 2–3, 3 (inset), 5tl, 10cl, 15t, 18tr, 18cla, 18clb, 18br, 30, 31b, 32tr, 32clb, 32bcr, 33tl, "The Twilight Zone™ is a registered trademark of CBS, Inc. and is used pursuant to a license from CBS, Inc." 33cra, *La Nouba* by Cirque du Soleil ® 33bl, 34bl, 36tr, 36br, 37tr, 37br, 38tr, 38bl, 39br, 40tl, 40br, 41tl, 42cla, 43tl, 44b, 46bl, 47tr, 48-49, 50tl, 50br, 51tl, 52tl, 52b, 53tl, 54bl, 55tl, "The

Twilight Zone™ is a registered trademark of CBS, Inc. and is used pursuant to a license from CBS, Inc." 56, 58-59, "TM & (c) 2003 The Jim Henson Company. JIM HENSON'S mark & logo, BEAR IN THE BIG BLUE HOUSE mark & logo, characters and elements are trademarks of The Jim Henson Company. All Rights Reserved. From the television series Bear in the Big Blue House created by Mitchell Kriegman" 60tl, 61b, 62tl, 62b, 64cl, "It's Tough to be a Bug!" based upon the Disney/Pixar film "A Bug's Life" © Disney/Pixar 64br, 65tl, 65br, 66tr, 66b, 67tr, 68-69, 70tr, 70cl, 70bl, 71tr, 71bl, 72tr, 72cla, 72bl, 73tr, 73cl, 74cl, 74br, 75tl, *La Nouba* by Cirque du Soleil ® 75c, © LEGO 75br, 130bc, 131tr, 131b, 134tr, "Woody" from the Disney/Pixar film "Toy Story" ©Disney 134cl, 134br, 136cl, 147br, 161tl, 164–5, 170cl, 171tl, 171b, 174-75, 177tc, 178br, 187b, 188br, 189tl, 195br.

ENZIAN THEATER/FLORIDA FILM FESTIVAL: 15c, 24crb, 166tc, 166bc; FALCON'S FIRE GOLF CLUB: 8br; FLORIDA DEPARTMENT OF ENVIRONMENTAL PROTECTION DIVISION OF RECREATION & PARKS: 115b; FLORIDA MALL: 157tl, 158cl; FLORIDA STATE ARCHIVE: 17c; FRANK LANE PICTURE LIBRARY: © David Hosking 180tr.

GENESIS SPACE PHOTO LIBRARY: 20tl, 20c, 20clb, 126bl, 126bc, 126br, 126bc; SEAN GILLIAM: 196t; GREATER ORLANDO AVIATION AUTHORITY: 132tl, 160b, 192cl, 193tl.

HARD ROCK CAFÉ: 130tc, 131tl; ©HEIDI TARGEE: 110crb.

INDEX STOCK PHOTOGRAPHY. INC., New York: 123cra; INSTITUTE OF SYSTEMIC BOTANY, UNIVERSITY OF SOUTH FLORIDA: Guy Anglin 21clb

KENNEDY SPACE CENTER – VISITORS CENTER, Cape Canaveral: 23c, 124tr, 125cr, 125ca, 126tr, 188tl; KISSIMMEE ST-CLOUD CONVENTION & VISITORS' BUREAU/Doug Dukane: 180b, 183tl.

MAD COW THEATRE: 109tl; MARINE SCIENCE CENTER, PONCE INLET: 21tl; MARY EVANS PICTURE LIBRARY: 29(inset); FRED MAWER: 124clb; MEARS TRANSPORTATION GROUP: 195tr.

©NASA: 15br, 22tr, 23tr; NICKOLODEON FAMILY SUITES BY HOLIDAY INN: 135tl.

ORANGE BLOSSOM BALLOONS: 172 tl; ORLANDO & ORANGE COUNTY CONVENTION & VISITORS BUREAU: 14ca, 27tl, 106br, 108tl, 109br, 112br, 158tr, 158b, 159tc, 160cl, 162cl, 162br, 163tr, 166cl, 167tl, 167b, 168br, 176tc, 178tr, 178cl, 179tc, 180tr, 180cl, 181tl, 182tl, 186cl, 197tc; ORLANDO TOURISM BUREAU: 136bl; ORONOZ, Madrid: 13tc.

PHOTOLIBRARY: PLANET EARTH PICTURES: 123cra. LA QUINTA: 132cb.

REUTERS: Charles W. Luzier 176cl; RITZ CARLTON ORLANDO GRAND LAKES: 133bl; MARIAN RYAN: 20cl, 20cr.

© SEAWORLD ORLANDO: 4br, 6-7, 9br ,14bl, 19br, 26tl, 78, 79b, 80bl, 83cb, 84ca, 84bl, 85tl, 86cl, 87tl, 87br; SILVER SPURS RODEO: 179c; STARWOOD: 133tl; ARVIN STEINBERG: 20cb, 20bcr, 21bcl; PHYLLIS STEINBERG: 116c.

THE MENNELLO MUSEUM OF AMERICAN FOLK ART: *Bird*, Paul Marco 107tr.

© 2006 UNIVERSAL ORLANDO. ALL RIGHTS RESERVED: 4tr, 9tl, 19tr, 81tr, 88c, 88b, 89cla, 89cb, 89br, 90tl, 90b, 91tl, 91br, 92tl, 92b, 93tr, 94-95, 96tl, 96cl, 96br, 97tl, 97br, 98tl, 98bl, 99br, 135br, 146br, 168tl.

VILLAS OF GRAND CYPRESS: 16bl.

WET 'N WILD ORLANDO: 19cr, 25br, 81br, 100tr, 100cla, 100clb, 100bl, 101tl, 101cra, 101crb, 101b, 101bl.©ZORA NEALE HURSTON NATIONAL MUSEUM OF FINE ARTS: *Festival Girl*, Jane Turner 106cl.

Front endpaper: © DISNEY: cla; SEAWORLD ORLANDO: tc; CORBIS: Raymond Gehman br.

JACKET
Front: ©DISNEY: clb, main. Back: © DISNEY: cla; DK IMAGES: Linda Whitwam clb; SEAWORLD ORLANDO 26 Busch Entertainment Corporation bl; © 2006 UNIVERSAL ORLANDO. ALL RIGHTS RESERVED: tl. Spine: © DISNEY: t; DK IMAGES: Stephen Whitehorn b.

All other images © Dorling Kindersley. See www.DKimages.com for further information.